AF566902

Travellers guide to East Africa

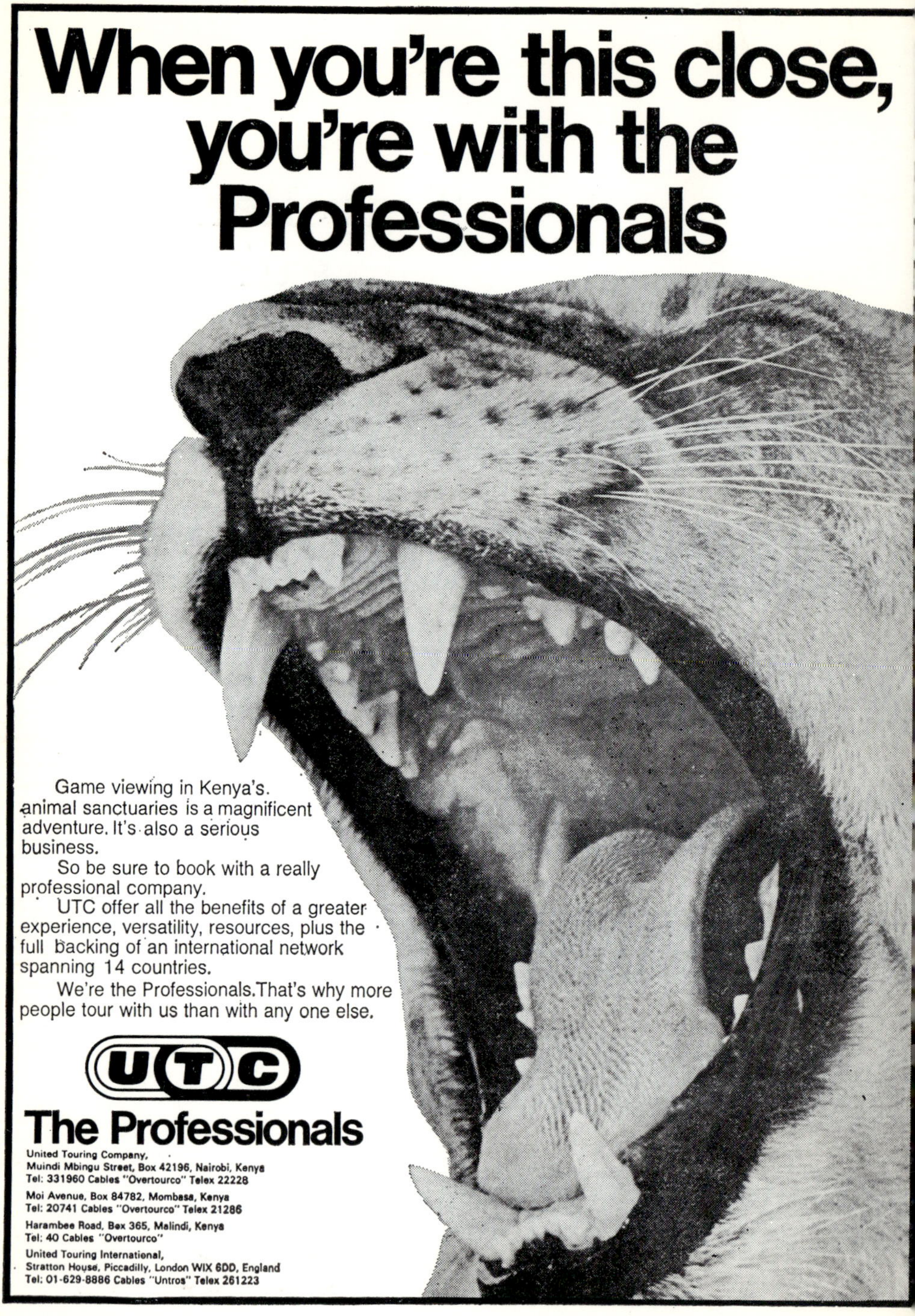

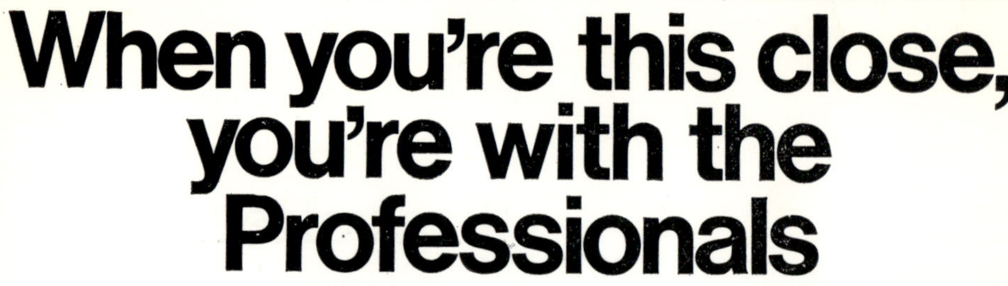

When you're this close, you're with the Professionals
Game viewing in Kenya's. animal sanctuaries is a magnificent adventure. It's also a serious business.
So be sure to book with a really professional company.
UTC offer all the benefits of a greater experience, versatility, resources, plus the full backing of an international network spanning 14 countries.
We're the Professionals. That's why more people tour with us than with any one else.
UTC
The Professionals
United Touring Company,
Muindi Mbingu Street, Box 42196, Nairobi, Kenya
Tel: 331960 Cables "Overtourco" Telex 22228
Moi Avenue, Box 84782, Mombasa, Kenya
Tel: 20741 Cables "Overtourco" Telex 21286
Harambee Road, Box 365, Malindi, Kenya
Tel: 40 Cables "Overtourco"
United Touring International,
Stratton House, Piccadilly, London WIX 6DD, England
Tel: 01-629-8886 Cables "Untros" Telex 261223

Travellers guide to East Africa

A concise guide to the wildlife and tourist facilities of Kenya, Tanzania, Uganda Zambia and Zanzibar

Nairobi - Tamarind Restaurant
seafood

HASTINGS HOUSE PUBLISHERS
NEW YORK

The publishers gratefully acknowledge the help of the Ministries of Information and Tourism, of Kenya, Tanzania, Uganda and Zambia and of Uganda Hotels Ltd in compiling this book. Prices and details quoted were correct at the time of publication but the publishers can obviously accept no responsibility for subsequent changes in them.

Contributors to the text include Richard Beeston, Richard Cox, Charles Harrison and Clive Woodcock. Revised by Richard Cox. Maps by Tom Stalker Miller MSIA.

First published 1966
Revised editions 1968
1970
1972
1980

DRAWINGS BY RENA FENNESSY
Cover: Elephant in Amboseli National Park, Kenya, with Mt Kilimanjaro in background. EAA photo.

Distributed by Geographia Ltd, 93 St Peter's Street, St Albans, Hertfordshire, England

American distribution by Hastings House Publishers, New York

Published by Thornton Cox Ltd, 84/86 Baker Street, London W1

Printed by The Anchor Press Ltd, Tiptree, Essex, England

© Thornton Cox Ltd 1980

ISBN 0 902726 33 1

Hippo below Kabalega Falls, Uganda

Contents

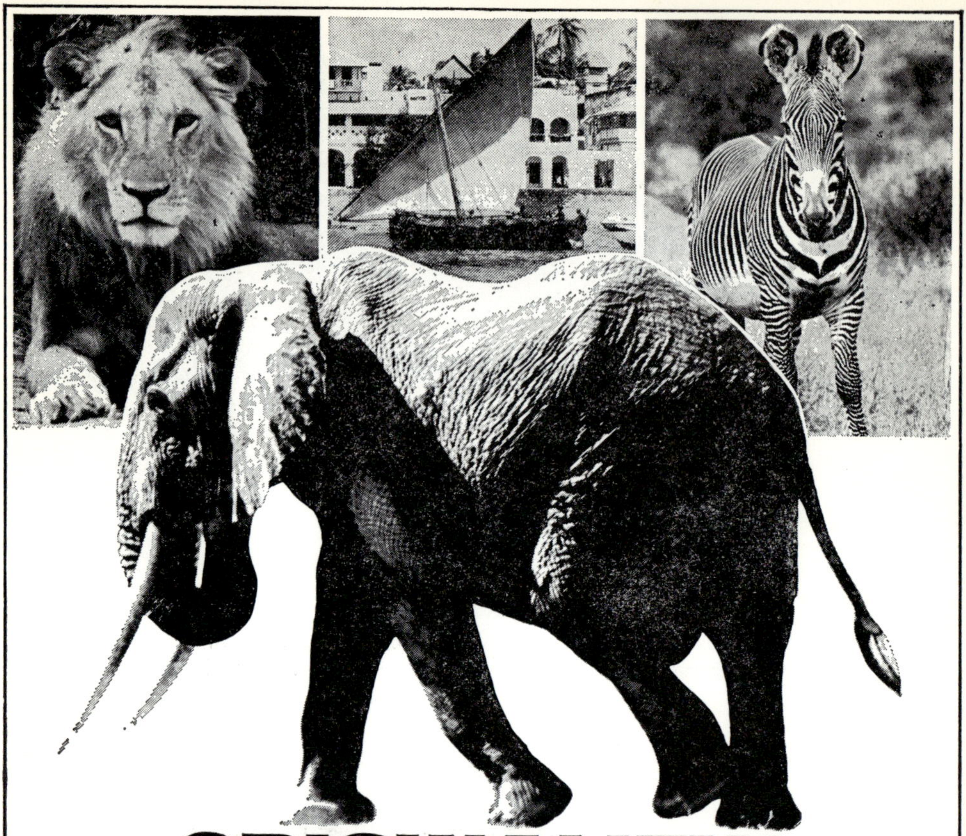

ORIGINALITY!

All our safaris are planned keeping in mind the needs of the individual visitor...

We extend this type of service to larger groups

We plan original safaris, new methods of travel and even create facilities where there are none!

We offer,

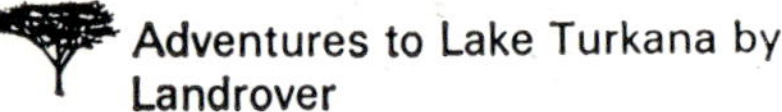

- Adventures to Lake Turkana by Landrover

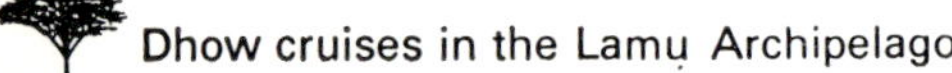

- Dhow cruises in the Lamu Archipelago
- Deep sea fishing in the Indian Ocean and a chance to catch the giant perch at Lake Turkana

- Camel safaris with porters and tents
- Safaris to all the National Parks and Reserves in Kenya

P.O. Box 42475, Nairobi Kenya
Telex 22025 - Acacia : Telephone 25641/25941
Also at Mombasa, Malindi and Lamu

Foreword

AN INTRODUCTION TO THE FINEST OF THE FEW GREAT WILDLIFE AREAS LEFT IN THE WORLD

Lions, elephants, rhinos, basilisks and unicorns all dwelt in East Africa, according to the medieval historians, who intermingled fact and legend. The Queen of Sheba was an ancestress of the Ethiopian emperors. King Solomon's mines, which supplied the Queen's mythical wealth, were said to lie in its snowcapped Mountains of the Moon. From somewhere deep in the interior sprang the mysterious River Nile, flowing down through the Sudan to give life to the civilisations of ancient Egypt. There were giants and pygmies and fantastically rich African potentates. East Africa was an altogether wondrous land.

Today it still is. Granted no unicorn has yet appeared on hunters' trophy lists or photographers' film—at least not to our knowledge. Neither has anyone we have heard of come face to face with a basilisk whilst on safari and been instantly turned to stone, which is just as well, considering the subsequent problems there could be with insurance claims. But all the other creatures that have excited and perplexed travellers since Ptolemy the Great compiled his famous map of Africa in the second century AD are there now. Twice a year the plains of the Serengeti, that seem as wide as an ocean, are dark with the migrating herds of many thousands of zebra and wildebeeste. Giraffe and gazelle are as familiar a sight as cattle. Zambia's Luangwa valley has been aptly described as "The kingdom of the elephant". Lions lie under the thorn trees in the National Park ten minutes' drive from the centre of Kenya's capital city, Nairobi. Hippopotami crowd the river below the famous Kabalega Falls in Uganda. The profusion of birds throughout East Africa is quite as breathtaking as its landscape.

At the other end of the scale are quintessentially elusive animals, like the bongo, a forest antelope, or the sitatunga. Never claim that you have seen all there is to see in this continent.

Fittingly, the backdrop of East Africa's scenery is of epic proportions and remarkable variety. It is bounded to the east by the Indian Ocean, where the dhows of Arabia ply down to Zanzibar, Dar es Salaam and beyond, and the coral lagoons and big game fishing rival the Bahamas. To the west it reaches inland 800 miles to the second deepest lake in the world, Lake Tanganyika, and includes Lake Victoria, the second largest. To the north lie the highlands of Ethiopia, a 3,000-year-old State with ancient castles and rock-hewn churches.

Striking down through the centre of this area goes the Rift, the great valley of Africa, part of a geological fault in the earth's surface that runs from Russia to Rhodesia, and cuts the channel of the Red Sea on the way. In Kenya the Rift is 50 miles across in places and two thousand feet deep. Its bed is pitted with extinct volcanoes, while not far from it rise the two highest peaks in the African continent, Kenya and Kilimanjaro, both volcanic, both permanently topped with snow. Either of these may have been the original Mountains of the Moon. Now the name and the legends attach to a third snowcapped range, the Ruwenzori range in Uganda, near the border of Zaire. Ice and frost are no rarity in other continents, but here they are made dramatic, and even frightening, by the incongruity of their existence above the vast, hot plains below.

It hardly needs saying that this is a land for the traveller to rejoice in. Indeed it has given the world its word for journey—*safari*. In the early years of this century, when Teddy Roosevelt started the great American sporting connection with East Africa, to go on safari was quite an undertaking. Roosevelt himself, on his post-Presidential safari, set off from Nairobi's Norfolk Hotel with a hundred African porters, all in blue sweaters, and an entourage of professional hunters. They carried everything they would need for several months in the bush, from gifts to ammunition.

Now hunting cars with four-wheel drive have made the porter obsolete, and East Africa possesses an ever-improving network of communications, with excellent hotels and safari lodges. But the fascination of the wildlife and the glory of the landscape haven't changed, nor has the outdoor living that inspired Hemingway's novels. The history and the legend are still here too, mixed up with the present-day life of the African peoples and the development of new nations. The remains of the Arab Sultanates, the ruined cities of Gedi and Kilwa, the narrow alleys and brass-studded doors of Zanzibar, are counterpointed by new hospitals, schools, churches and highways. There is also awareness of the need to conserve the game. President Nyerere's Arusha Manifesto of 1961 stated "Wildlife is an integral part of our resources and of our future livelihood and wellbeing." Unhappily this sentiment has been shared, but not backed up, in other countries. Although instituting improvements, like charting the great annual migrations of game, the authorities failed to stop massive depredations by poachers. The effects of this were at last realised in the late 1970s and in Kenya, for example, both hunting and the sale of game trophies are banned. Heavy fines face poachers. Even so, the preservation of the natural heritage has needed outside help, most notably from the World Wildlife Fund, which has given generous assistance to the game departments concerned and to the development of Parks and Reserves.

ANY SAFARI TO SUIT YOUR TASTE

Across Africa Safaris

STANDARD STREET, P.O. BOX 49420 NAIROBI. TEL: 332744.
HILTON BRANCH, NAIROBI TEL: 332744/29577

rent a car

SELF DRIVE • CHAUFFEUR DRIVEN

NAIROBI BRUCE HOUSE TEL: 23013/332744 TELEX 22501
MOMBASA P. O. BOX 82139 TEL: 21951 / 311453 TELEX 21108

The Ark • THE ABERDARE COUNTRY CLUB

Kenya's ship of the forest
Aberdare National Park
Reservations: **ACROSS AFRICA SAFARIS LTD.**
Tel: NAIROBI 26760

AERO INTERNATIONAL

FOR ALL YOUR TRAVEL REQUIREMENTS
Tel: 333023 - 333049 - 336488
BRUCE HOUSE, KAUNDA ST. BOX 49420, NAIROBI.

OUR GOOD SERVICE
IS OUR BEST ADVERTISEMENT

General Information

How to get to East Africa

Airlines

All the countries described except Zanzibar, which is part of the United Republic of Tanzania, run their own national airlines, namely Kenya Airways, Air Tanzania, Uganda Airlines and Zambia Airways. All run domestic and regional flights. At the time of writing Air Tanzania and Uganda Airlines did not run inter-continental flights. No scheduled services whatever link Kenya and Tanzania.

International carriers operating are too numerous to detail. Over 21 serve Kenya, including Aeroflot, Alitalia, British Airways, El Al Israel Airlines, Air France, KLM, Lufthansa, Olympic Airways, Pan American, Sabena, Scandinavian Airlines System, Swissair and Trans World Airlines. Tanzania and Uganda are served by most of these too. Zambia has Zambia Airways direct flights to Europe, plus Aeroflot, British Caledonian and UTA. Among the few which link East and West Africa are Ethiopian Airlines, Pan American, UTA and Air Zaire.

The international airports are Jomo Kenyatta (Nairobi), Port Reitz (Mombasa), Dar es Salaam, Kilimanjaro (Arusha, Tanzania), Entebbe and Lusaka.

Fares

It is not possible to quote fares sensibly. 90 day excursion fares from Britain run as low as £250 sterling on scheduled services of Air Kenya and British Airways, which is less than half the standard return fare. Charter flights have been hit by local regulations restricting the sale of tickets in local East African currencies. Overall it is wise to consult a travel agent. Remember that internal travel can be much cheaper if added on as additional sectors to an international ticket.

All four countries are liable to make possession of a return ticket a condition of entry for visitors.

Note that local currencies are not accepted for purchases on board aircraft and often not in airport duty free shops.

Package holidays

Many travel agencies in Britain, Germany, Scandinavia and the United States offer inclusive holidays in East Africa. In Britain, these include Thomas Cook & Son, Hickie Borman Grant & Co, Nilestar, Flamingo, Swan-Hellenic, Kuoni Challis & Benson, Lunn-Poly, Houlder Brothers, Ingham's and Lord Brothers, all in London; in the United States, Lindblad Travel and Orbitair in New York, Intrav in St Louis, and Percival Tours in Los Angeles; and in West Germany, Touropa/Scharnowreisen in Hannover, and N-U-R Neckermann in Frankfurt.

Shipping

In recent years virtually all passenger traffic has ceased. Even cargo ships rarely take passengers, and their schedules are anyway extremely unreliable.

Local Air Charters

There are more than 250 airstrips serving all parts of East Africa, including Game Parks and Reserves. Air charter companies include Air Kenya, Safari Air Services, at Nairobi's lesser airport, Wilson; Air Kenya, Amphibians Ltd and Mombasa Air Services at Port Reitz airport, Mombasa; Malindi Air Services at Malindi airport; Tanzanair and Flight Service International at both Dar es Salaam and Arusha; Uganda Airlines charters at Entebbe. Additionally the Aero Club of East Africa operates from Wilson airport, Nairobi and accepts qualified private pilots for membership, as well as giving training.

Aero Club

Zambia

All private flying was suspended in Zambia late in 1978 and at the time of writing this ban was still in force.

Although the Tanzania–Kenya frontier is closed, charter flights are sometimes admitted by the Tanzanian authorities.

Altitude and Climate

Being on the Equator most of East Africa has no summer or winter and the days vary little in length. Sunrise is between 6 and 6.30 am and sunset between 6.30 pm (1830) and 7 pm (1900). The sun rises and sets much faster than in temperate latitudes.

The climate is warm throughout the year, varying according to the altitude above sea level of the place you are at. At the coast daytime temperatures average between 75°F and 85°F (24°C and 29°C) with an average humidity of 75%. If there is no wind it can feel decidedly sticky, though at night it can be cool enough to wear a light pullover. Inland the humidity declines as you go higher up, and the nights become appreciably cooler. At 5,000 ft the average daytime temperatures are only slightly less than the coast's, but at night they fall to around 50°F (10°C). On the Ethiopian plateau it can be very chilly. In the mountains the temperature drops to freezing point.

The sun is often hotter than it feels and you can all too easily get sunburnt, or find yourself suffering from heat exhaustion. In this climate your body needs more liquid than it does in temperate latitudes, which means drinking more, though not necessarily more alcohol! It is sensible to take water with you when driving a long distance. Finally, the sunlight is strong and you need good-quality sunglasses to protect your eyes.

Rain usually comes down in short downpours, after which the sun comes out again. Broadly speaking the long rains come to Kenya, Uganda and Northern Tanzania in April/May and the short rains in November and early December. Central and Southern Tanzania and Zambia have intermittent rain from mid-December to May. However, in recent years the rainy seasons have been disobligingly erratic, so do not blame us if you find it raining at some other time. In Ethiopia the rains are from mid-February to April and mid-June to September.

Currency and Foreign Exchange

Kenya, Tanzania and Uganda each issue their own shillings as the basic unit. The shilling is a silver coloured round coin, divided into 100 cents. Lesser coins of ten and five cents are made of brassy yellow metal. Notes come in denominations of Shs. 5/–, Shs. 10/–, Shs. 20/– and Shs. 100/–. Theoretically these currencies are at par, but since the amounts one is allowed to take out are limited to Shs. 100/– in Kenya and Shs. 40/– in Tanzania, this question hardly arises. Nor do their international exchange ratios stay constant. The Kenya shilling is the strongest currency and at the time of writing was at Shs. 15/80 to the £ sterling, Shs. 7/62 to the US $ and Shs. 3/98 to the DM. Large amounts are commonly expressed in pounds, with one £ making 20 shillings.

Zambia

The Zambian Kwacha is divided into 100 ngwee. There are ngwee coins up to 50n and Kwacha notes. At the time of writing Kw 1.60 equalled £1 sterling or US $ 2.00.

Currency Regulations

All the countries have strict currency regulations, requiring a customs declaration to be completed on arrival. This form must be filled in and stamped by any hotel or bank which changes your money. It is then handed in to the customs on departure, though not always checked. Inevitably there is a currency black market in all four countries and tourists are frequently accosted by touts on the streets. Quite apart from such men being adept at cheating by handing over the "currency" in an envelope containing only ordinary paper, there are severe penalties if you are caught infringing the currency regulations and your passport will be impounded until after trial. Unspent foreign currency can, of course, be taken out.

Customs Duties

Visitors are allowed to bring in duty free all bona fide personal effects, provided they are declared on arrival and the proposed stay is not over six months. This includes cameras, binoculars, portable typewriters; one pint of spirits or perfumes; 50 cigars, or 200 cigarettes or ½ lb tobacco.

On certain articles a customs deposit can be demanded which is refunded on departure from East Africa. Motor vehicles covered by a triptique or carnet will be allowed duty free for the period of validity of the document.

Items that the customs tend to pounce on include transistor radios and tape recorders, though if they are demonstrably personal property they are normally let through. Gifts or anything intended for sale or exchange are dutiable. Guns and ammunition must be declared, and need a firearms certificate from the police which safari organisers can obtain for you in advance.

Almost anything that is posted to you while you are in East Africa will have duty levied on it, usually at 30% of the estimated value, while some items like perfume attract 100% duty. Even personal clothing has to be visibly used to escape duty if it comes by post. It is preferable to send one's belongings by air freight.

The main restriction when you leave is on taking out hides, skins and ivory. Anything made from game animals, from zebra-decorated sandals to a whole mounted leopard skin, must have a Game Department Certificate, which shops should provide for you at the time of purchase. This is to prevent the sale and export of illegally trapped animal skins.

Diplomatic Representation — See Useful Facts sections.

Dress and Cosmetics

Comfortable clothes matter a lot, as in all tropical climates. For women a woolly is essential and a light woollen suit useful. At the coast during the day light cottons and linens are the thing, preferably washable, and slacks and shirts for safaris. Sandals can be bought in East Asia. Swimsuits and beachwear are useful. So are one pair of flattish shoes, and a raincoat, preferably a lightweight one. Sunglasses and a sunhat (obtainable locally) are all but vital.

For men a lightweight suit is useful in the cities. Bring plenty of shirts —incidentally in our experience synthetic fabrics can become very sticky and there is no substitute for cotton if you want to stay cool. A pair of washable trousers will be useful and so will both long- and short-sleeved sweaters.

East African hotels and clubs are not excessively formal and a dinner jacket is rarely needed. White tuxedos are less often worn than black ones. In general a dark light- to medium-weight lounge suit for a man, and a silk dress for a woman, will be enough for formal occasions, even if you are at a gathering when the African leaders are in national dress. This latter incidentally is both dignified and colourful. Tanzania's is reminiscent of the Roman toga.

Anyone going on safari will need neutral-coloured clothes so as not to alert animals to their presence. Jungle green or khaki bush shirts, trousers and skirts can be made locally, or bought off the peg. You will look right in them and they will be cheaper both in tailoring charges and air freight than any similar clothes you bring with you.

Quite a number of internationally known beauty preparations are sold in the cities. Sun lotions and moisturising creams are vital in this climate, though they are expensive. Equally razor blades, shaving soaps etc are available. Most hotels now have plug sockets for electric razors in their bathrooms. The electricity supply in East Africa is 240 volts AC.

Driving

You drive on the left and you can use a current licence from your home country for up to 90 days. All the countries have speed limits: 88 kph (55 mph) in Tanzania and Uganda, 100 kph (62 mph) in Kenya. Distances are measured in kilometres.

Etiquette

In general the welcome you get in Africa is refreshing, and Africans will often stop to talk to the foreign visitor. They are relaxed and informal people. It's fair to say, however, that they are sensitive on several points, notably religion, colonialism and photography.

All four countries have Moslem minorities. Their mosques can be visited but it is best to ask the guardian of the mosque if you may venture inside. Before going in you must remove your shoes and please be fully dressed in all other respects.

Whilst politics do not impinge on the visitor at all, do remember that these countries have only recently become independent of British rule and dislike rude remarks about their newly won freedom. The old habit of addressing servants and waiters as "boy" has gone for ever. Some restaurants and hotels give their staff lapel name badges. In Tanzania one officially approved word for calling for service is *Rafiki*—the Swahili for "friend". Otherwise call out "Steward" or "Waiter". Using occasional Swahili words (see page 16) will pay dividends in terms of service, even if you only learn *Jambo* and *Asante sana*. Some Africans, especially Moslems, do not like being photographed. It is often believed that by taking a picture of a man you gain control over his soul. The East African governments have mounted a publicity campaign to explain to ordinary Africans that tourists and their cameras should be welcomed. If there is obvious hostility then be sensible and put your camera away, or ask the person concerned for his agreement. This may lead to a demand for money, in which case a shilling is usually enough.

Photographs

Never, under any circumstances, photograph government buildings, military camps and vehicles, or airports. Kenya is otherwise liberal towards photographers. In Tanzania, Uganda and Zambia, however, it is unwise to use a camera anywhere outside the Game Parks. The editor of this book was arrested twice while revising it.

Gratuities

Sometimes these are added to hotel and restaurant bills. Otherwise about 10% of the bill is fair, or 15% if you have had especially good service. Two shillings is normal for a luggage porter and five shillings for the room servant after one or two nights, depending on how helpful he has been. In Zambia tipping is officially illegal, though it continues.

Health

You must have valid international certificates of vaccination against smallpox and inoculation against yellow fever. Cholera and typhoid injections are desirable; equally it is wise to take anti-malarial pills, such as Nivaquin or Paludrine, even though many areas are not malarial. There are chemists' shops throughout East Africa, experienced doctors practise in most towns and there are excellent hospitals in the cities. Tap water is drinkable almost everywhere. When it is not, hotels leave a Thermos flask of cold drinking water in your room.

Do not swim in the inland lakes and rivers unless you are told it is safe, since they are often infested with bilharzia (a disease carried by water snails). Beware of over-exposure to the sun, which can definitely be injurious.

Language

English is spoken widely and is the accepted language in the cities, hotels, restaurants etc. However, as well as numerous tribal languages, East Africa has its own lingua franca, called Swahili. This is the official language of Tanzania and has its origin at the coast. Although you can manage perfectly well without knowing any Swahili, the following words and phrases will be useful. Swahili Grammars are available in East African bookshops.

Hello—Jambo
How are you?—Habari
Goodbye—Kwaheri
Please—Tafadhali
Thank you—Asante
Thank you very much—Asante sana
Today—Leo
Tomorrow—Kesho
Lion—Simba
Quickly—Upesi
Slowly—Polepole
Food—Chakula
Tea—Chai
Coffee—Kahawa

Beer—English understood, or Tembo (lit: elephant) in Kenya
Argument, problem—Shauri
Hot—Moto
Cold—Baridi
One—Moja
Two—Mbili
Three—Tatu
Four—Ine
Five—Tano
Six—Sita
Seven—Saba
Eight—Nane
Nine—Tisa
Ten—Kumi

Where is the nearest garage?	Wapi garage karibu zaidi?
Is the road ahead passable?	Naweza pita njia mbele?
Where is the nearest police station?	Wapi stesheni polisi karibu?
Where is the nearest telephone?	Wapi simu karibu?
Where does this road lead to?	Njia hii inakwenda wapi?
Do you know anyone who speaks English?	Unajua mtu anayesem kiingereza?

I want a room for one night with a bath	Nataka nyumba na bafu pamoja kwa siku moja
What time is it?	Saa ngapi?
Where is the nearest doctor?	Wapi dokitari karibu?
Where is the nearest hospital?	Wapi hospitali karibu?
Where is the German/French/ Danish/English/Swedish/ American Consulate?	Wapi Consul ya Gerumani/ Faranza/Denmark/ Ingereza/ Sueden/Marekani?
Please direct me to a good hotel	Wapi hoteli mzuri
How much?	Pesa ngapi?
What time will food be ready?	Chakula tayari saa ngapi?
I want a cold beer	Nataka tembo baridi.

Pronunciation is important but easy. Every letter must be sounded. The consonant "G" is always hard like the G in "got"; "CH" and "SH" have the same sounds as in English. There are no diphthongs; vowels are pronounced as shown below.

a is like the a in "father"
e is like the a in "say"
i is like the e in "be"
o is like the o in "hoe"
u is like the oo in "too"

Photography

The sunlight here is intense and you should allow a faster exposure than you would in Europe. The DIN, ASA and Weston meter settings recommended by film manufacturers are now for the minimum exposure, not the average, and so are just about right for East African conditions. However, where there is a lot of refracted light, as on the dazzling white sands of the coast or some of the open plains, you will need a still shorter exposure. A lens hood is invaluable, while an ultraviolet filter cuts down the effects of glare.

Photographing game you are obviously unlikely to get close enough to take a meter reading off the animal itself, which will need a greater exposure than the landscape it is in. A good way to check is by taking a reading off a dull-coloured piece of clothing, remembering to take a reading in shade if the animal you are about to photograph is lying in the shade. When using a telephoto lens, especially one you have not used before, it is wise to open the aperture an extra half stop.

Photographing Africans, whose dark skins reflect very little light, you need to open the aperture by at least one stop (e.g. f8 to f5.6).

Or of course you can halve the shutter speed (e.g. from 1/250th down to 1/125th sec).

Finally, be careful where you use a camera outside the Game Parks—see under Etiquette above.

Posts and Telegraphs

There are no house-to-house deliveries of mail, so all postal addresses are Post Office box numbers. In Kenya, Tanzania and Uganda internal letters cost 50 cts. Overseas airletter forms cost Shs. 1/–. Airmail letters cost Shs. 2/– for every 10 grammes weight to Europe. Postcards cost Shs. 1/30 airmail to Europe.

A local telephone call costs Shs. 1/–. Trunk call charges vary with distance. Subscriber trunk dialling has recently been introduced between the major East African cities and towns but is overloaded. International calls can be booked. The telephone system is efficient, but there is a dearth of public callboxes.

Sports

Golf, tennis, fishing, climbing, polo, racing, football and cricket are all widely available. The skin diving at the coast, called goggling locally, is superb and there is surfing, water-skiing and sailing.

Time

East African time is three hours ahead of GMT. Thus at midday (1200) in East Africa it is 10 am (1000) in London (British Standard Time) and Rome, 4 am (0400) in New York, 1 am (0100) in San Francisco, 7 pm (1900) in Sydney and 2 pm (1400) in New Delhi. Zambia is 2 hours ahead of GMT.

East Africa's Wildlife

Here are thirty-five of the animals you are most likely to see on safari

Swahili names are given in italics

If you want to know more visit the wildlife exhibitions in East Africa's museums and try the Bibliography at the end of this section. Two handy guides are the *Shell Guide to East African Birds* and the *Shell Guide to Wildlife*, from which we are grateful for permission to reproduce some of these drawings by Rena Fennessy.

The **African Elephant**, *Ndovu* or *Tembo*, is larger than the Indian, particularly its ears. A bull weighs up to six tons and stands 12 feet at the shoulder. The heaviest recorded single tusk, from Tanzania, reached 228 lb. Elephant are intelligent, live in herds and are vegetarians. They inhabit both the bush and the mountain forests. Their life span is about 60 years.

The **Hippopotamus**, *Kiboko*, whose name is Latin for "river horse", is really of the pig family. Hippos congregate in "schools" and spend most of the day submerged in water up to their nostrils. They come ashore to feed on grass at night. A grown hippo weighs two and a half tons, yet can outrun a man. Male hippos fight each other to the death.

The **African** or **Black Buffalo**, *Nyati* or *Mbogo*, has been forced to live in the forests and thick bush by encroaching civilisation, despite its basic food being grass. Buffalo stay in herds, and though shy are one of the most dangerous Big Game animals. A grown bull will weigh 1,500 lb and the span of its horns may be 50 inches.

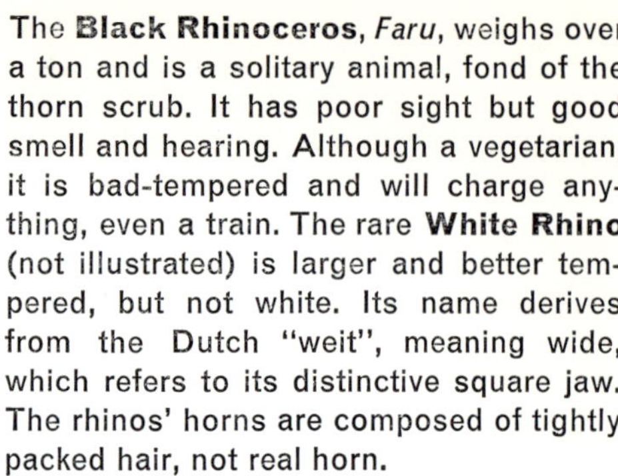

The **Black Rhinoceros**, *Faru*, weighs over a ton and is a solitary animal, fond of the thorn scrub. It has poor sight but good smell and hearing. Although a vegetarian, it is bad-tempered and will charge anything, even a train. The rare **White Rhino** (not illustrated) is larger and better tempered, but not white. Its name derives from the Dutch "weit", meaning wide, which refers to its distinctive square jaw. The rhinos' horns are composed of tightly packed hair, not real horn.

The **Giraffe**, *Twiga*, the tallest mammal, grows to 18 feet and weighs half a ton. It browses on leaves, especially acacia, likes open country and is inoffensive. Its small horns are covered in skin and soft hair. The **Reticulated Giraffe** is so called because its markings are square, within a network of whitish lines, instead of star-shaped.

The **Common Zebra**, *Punda Milia*, is found in open country over most of East Africa, always managing to look sleek and well fed. Zebra move in herds, often with giraffe, eland and other animals. They feed on grass, leaves and, if necessary, shrubs. A male zebra stands five feet high at the shoulder and weighs 700 lb. The rarer **Grevy's Zebra** is taller, has larger ears and narrower stripes.

The **Lion**, *Simba*, is found in open country throughout East Africa. A full-grown male weighs 400–500 lb. The lioness has no mane. "Prides", or families, of lion doze in the shade during the day and hunt at dusk, springing on the backs of the zebra, buffalo, wildebeeste or whatever they have stalked. They kill only when hungry, once in three or four days.

The **Leopard**, *Chui*, hunts by night, is wary, and extremely dangerous when wounded or cornered. It makes its lair in cliffs, or among rocks in thick bush. Its favourite food is baboon, though if hungry it will eat rodents and even insects. A grown male weighs under 150 lb. and measures about seven and a half feet from nose to tail.

The **Serval Cat**, *Mondo*, is short-tailed, long-legged and spotted, with large ears. It looks like a cross between a small leopard and a lynx. It hunts at night, feeding on birds and small mammals. The serval exists in many part of East Africa, particularly liking places that are marshy or near water.

The **Cheetah**, *Duma*, looks like a leopard, but with longer legs and smaller head. Also its spots are isolated, not grouped in a pattern. It hunts by day and is the fastest mammal in the world—it has been timed at 60 mph. Cheetahs stand three feet at the shoulder and are about seven feet long. They are easily tamed and have been raced against greyhounds in Europe.

The **Wart Hog**, *Ngiri*, is named after the warts on its grotesque head. It lives on the plains in families, or "sounders", and breeds in holes. During the day it crops grass, or digs for roots with its tusks, while kneeling on its forelegs. It is related to the Giant Forest Hog, largest of the African pigs, which weighs over 300 lb.

The **Spotted Hyena**, *Fisi*, is a night-time scavenger. Though its jaws can crush bones it is a coward and only attacks weak or aged animals. Its colour is yellowish and it weighs about 150 lb. Hyenas have a characteristic, unpleasant howl and they "laugh" when lions are around. There is a striped species in North-east Uganda.

The **Baboon**, *Nyani Mkubwa*, is a large dog-faced monkey seen in many parts of East Africa. It lives on the ground, usually moving in troops under the leadership of a big old male, and goes into the trees to sleep at night. Baboons will eat practically anything, animal or vegetable. The babies ride on their mothers' backs.

The **Patas Monkey**, *Kima*, roams in troops of ten or twelve, like the baboons. It normally stays on the ground, using low trees or anthills as observation points. Its habitat is the dry savannah of North-west Kenya and Tanzania, and Northern Uganda. In colour it is reddish, with white underparts and white sidewhiskers on its face.

The **Lesser Bush Baby**, *Komba*, is a nocturnal relative of the monkeys, and lives mainly in acacia bush. Driving at night you often see its large eyes winking at you out of the darkness. It is very active, climbing and making tremendous leaps in search of insects and fruit. During the day it sleeps, whole families cuddling together in hollow tree trunks.

Grant's Gazelle, *Swala Granti*, likes dry open grassland or even desert. It has graceful lyre-shaped horns, which both sexes carry, and is pale buff in colour, with a white rump and underside and a chestnut streak down the centre of the face. The male stands about 32 inches high at the shoulder. Gazelles are a species of antelope, with slender legs.

Thomson's Gazelle, *Swala Tomi*, known as the "Tommy", is more reddish in colour than the Grant's Gazelle which otherwise it is like, and has a distinctive black band running along its flank. It also has a habit of twitching its small tail. The Tommy lives in large herds on the plains.

The **Gerenuk**, or Walter's Gazelle, *Swala Twiga*, has a delicately incongruous long neck and a giraffe-like head. It is a dark rufous colour, paler on the flanks, and with white bands over its eyes. It stands 36 to 41 inches high at the shoulder and weighs about 100 lb. Only the males have horns. Gerenuk wander in small groups, browsing on leaves in acacia thorn country.

The **Dikdik**, *Dikidiki* or *Suguya*, stands only 15 inches high and weighs 12 lb. It lives in the driest thorn scrub and is usually seen in pairs. In colour it is grey or grizzled brown, has a shaggy coat and a distinctively long nose. The **Klipspringer** is in many ways similar, but larger, standing about 21 inches high at the shoulder.

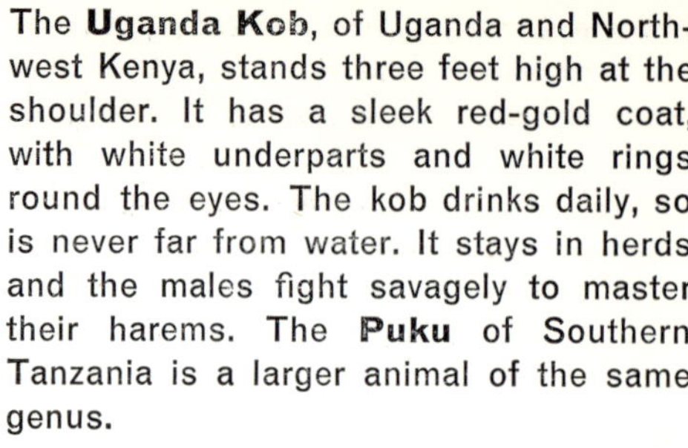

The **Uganda Kob**, of Uganda and North-west Kenya, stands three feet high at the shoulder. It has a sleek red-gold coat, with white underparts and white rings round the eyes. The kob drinks daily, so is never far from water. It stays in herds and the males fight savagely to master their harems. The **Puku** of Southern Tanzania is a larger animal of the same genus.

The **Impala**, *Swala Pala*, is a timid, medium-sized antelope, famous for leaping in the air when alarmed—it can jump 30 feet and rise 10 feet above the ground. Impala move in large herds. They have smooth chestnut-coloured coats and tufts of black hair on the hind legs above the hooves. Only the males carry horns. Found in acacia bush and scrub country.

The **Common Waterbuck**, *Kuro*, is a large antelope found in Eastern Kenya and Tanzania, usually near water. A bull may lead a herd of up to 30 cows, who have no horns. Their coats are shaggy, greyish brown, and with a white ring on the rump. The **Defassa Waterbuck**, of Uganda, has a round white patch instead of a ring.

The **Sable Antelope**, *Palahala* or *Mbarapi*, is a splendid animal, standing nearly five feet high, almost black, and bearing great scimitar-shaped horns. It is white on the underparts, rump, and face. In East Africa it is only found in a few coastal areas of Tanzania, and near Mombasa, and likes lightly wooded country. It stays in small herds.

The **Oryx**, *Choroa*, one of the most handsome, powerful and fierce antelopes, is found in varying species from Ethiopia to the Kalahari. It is reddish brown in colour, with black and white face markings. The female grows longer horns than the male —up to 40 inches. Oryx stand four feet high at the shoulder and weigh up to 450 lb. They move in small herds. Amboseli and Tsavo are good places to look for them.

The **Greater Kudu**, *Kandala Mkubwa*, likes rocky and mountainous bush. A male stands five feet high at the shoulder and weighs about 600 lb. The female has no horns. Kudus' bodies are a lavender grey colour, with white stripes. The **Lesser Kudu**, *Kandala Ndogo*, is rather smaller and has no fringe of hair running down its throat. It lives in thick bush and scrub.

Coke's Hartebeest, usually known as the *Kongoni*, is widely distributed in East Africa. It stays in large herds, grazing, while one animal acts as sentinel. When surprised it snorts, stamps a foreleg and gallops away. Its colour is light fawn, and its bracket-shaped horns and steeply sloping hindquarters make it easily recognisable.

The **Wildebeest** or **Gnu**, *Nyumbu*, seen in vast herds migrating across the Serengeti Plains every year, is one of the commonest antelopes in open country all over East Africa. It has a dark grey body, a white beard, a shaggy mane, and a clumsy gait. Its horns look slightly like a buffalo's. It stands about five feet high at the shoulder.

The **Eland**, *Pofu* or *Mbunja*, the largest of the antelopes, congregates in large herds, often alongside zebra and giraffe. They are found in open country over most of East Africa. Both sexes carry heavy twisted horns. A full-grown bull weights over 1,050 lb and stands six feet high at the shoulder. Their colour is greyish brown, with light stripes.

The **Ostrich**, one of the sights of Africa, cannot fly but has a kick than can kill a man and can run at 45 mph. Fully grown, it can be eight feet high. It lays eggs in clutches of 14 or more. You often see it on the plains among herds of animals. True to stories it does sometimes hide its head on the ground when approached.

Forest Animals

The **Bongo**, same name in Swahili, is the largest of the forest antelopes, though smaller than an eland. It stands four feet high at the shoulder and both sexes carry horns. In colour it is a bright reddish chestnut, with vertical white stripes. Bongo live only in the mountain forests, are very shy and seldom seen.

The **Bushbuck**, *Mbawala* or *Pongo*, is a beautifully marked small animal, with a white underside to its tail. It prefers forest thickets to open country, is shy, and lives in families, not herds. A male stands three feet high at the shoulder and weighs about 100 lb. The **Sitatinga,** *Nzohe*, is a swamp-dwelling variant of the same species.

The **Colobus Monkey**, *Mbega*, is jet black in colour, with a magnificent white mantle round its back, a white face and a white-tipped bushy tail. It lives in highland forests, like the Aberdares of Kenya, eats leaves and very rarely descends from the trees.

Sykes Monkey, *Kima*, often called the Blue Monkey, is dark blue-grey in colour, with black forelimbs, hands, feet, crown of head and tip of tail, It eats fruit and greenery, and inhabits forests near water. It is known for its friendliness. Variants of the species are called Silver and Golden Monkeys, from their colouring.

The **Chimpanzee**, *Sokwe Mtu*, the most intelligent of the apes, inhabits the forests of Southern Uganda and Western Tanzania. Chimpanzees are smaller and more active than gorillas, and are wonderful acrobats. They live in family parties of twelve or more, chatter noisily and are vegetarians, though they take occasional birds' eggs.

The **Mountain Gorilla**, *Sokwe*, is the largest of the apes, sharing with man the lack of a tail. A few groups inhabit the forests of South-west Uganda. They live off wild celery and bamboo shoots, move on all fours and sleep in nests. A male weighs about 420 lb. Despite their great strength gorillas are peaceful by nature.

Birds

More and more bird lovers are coming to East Africa, which shelters over a thousand species. Some are ugly like the vulture and the marabou stork; some are tiny and brilliantly coloured like the bee-eaters and sunbirds; some are predatory like the hawks that circle constantly above you. The go-away bird insults you and the rainbird warns you of storms. The profusion of birds is almost bewildering.

Butterflies

Equally there are myriads of tropical butterflies in the woods and forests.

Bibliography

Among well-known reference books are: *Birds of Eastern and North Eastern Africa* by Praed and Grant (Longman, Green); *The Conservation of Wildlife and Natural Habitats in Central and East Africa* by Sir Julian Huxley (UNESCO Paris 1961); *A Field Guide to the National Parks of East Africa, A Field Guide to the Birds of East and Central Africa*, and *A Field Guide to the Butterflies of Africa*, all by John G. Williams (Collins).

For general reading on animals there are Joy Adamson's books about the lioness Elsa, *Born Free* and *Living Free* (Collins); Alan Moorehead's *No Room In The Ark* (Cassell); Professor Grzimek's classic *Serengeti Shall Not Die*; and *The Enormous Zoo* by Colin Willock (Longman. Green).

Hunting and Photographic Safaris

Dozens of books have been written about big game hunting in East Africa, from the memoirs of the legendary hunters like Karamoja Bell and F. C. Selous (after whom the Selous Reserve in Tanzania is named) through to Hemingway's *Green Hills of Africa.* All carry the same message—the fascination of animals and the bush. They've given a magic to the word "safari" which is simply Swahili for "journey".

However the opportunities for hunting have declined drastically in recent years. It is totally banned in Kenya; in Tanzania it is permitted, especially in the southern parts of the country, but there are few if any white professional hunters; whether hunting will continue to be permitted in Uganda is uncertain; only in Zambia is anything like the old style safari possible—and interestingly there has been a revival of the foot safari, with African porters. Bird shooting is still more easily obtainable.

Inevitably the emphasis has turned to photographic safaris, often run by former professional hunters. At their best—and most expensive—these take you to little known parts, and when yet set up camp for the night your amenities include personal servants, spring mattresses, refrigeration, hot baths, luxurious tents and a two-way radio link with the outside world. You will find the firms offering these listed in the text on each country. Not surprisingly many firms now offer a mix between the camping safari and the package tour, and there are short specialised safaris by canoe, on camels in Kenya's northern province, on foot in Zambia's Luangwa valley, and up the great Kenya and Kilimanjaro mountains.

Zambia Airways connections Lusaka-East Africa.

Lusaka–Nairobi	**Nairobi–Lusaka**
Sunday Flight No. QZ600. Aircraft type Boeing 737. Depart Lusaka 10.25, arrive Nairobi 14.00.	**Sunday** Flight No. QZ601. Aircraft type Boeing 737. Depart Nairobi 15.20, arrive Lusaka 17.00.
Tuesday Flight No. QZ614. Aircraft type Boeing 737. Depart Lusaka 09.00, arrive Nairobi 12.35.	**Tuesday** Flight No. QZ615. Aircraft type Boeing 737. Depart Nairobi 16.10, arrive Lusaka 17.50.
Friday Flight No. QZ710. Aircraft type Boeing 707. Depart Lusaka 10.30, arrive Nairobi 14.00.	**Friday** Flight No. QZ711. Aircraft type Boeing 707. Depart Nairobi 16.00, arrive Lusaka 17.35.
Lusaka–Dar es Salaam	**Dar es Salaam–Lusaka**
Saturday Flight No. QZ628. Aircraft type Boeing 737. Depart Lusaka 10.10, arrive Dar es Salaam 13.30.	**Saturday** Flight No. QZ629. Aircraft type Boeing 737. Depart Dar es Salaam 14.30, arrive Lusaka 15.50.

Lusaka Farmers House, Cairo Road. Telephone: 52211.
Nairobi Nairobi Hilton. Telephone: 27722.
Dar es Salaam IPS Building, Askari Square. Telephone: 29071.

airkenya

TAKE A FLYING SAFARI

Beechcraft Super King Air

SEE THE MOST IN THE LEAST TIME

The lazy calm of LAMU's Arab harbour — fabulous game areas like the MASAI MARA, AMBOSELI and the TSAVO NATIONAL PARK — the famous elephants by MARSABIT MOUNTAIN'S crater lakes — the jade green sea of LAKE TURKANA far in Kenya's north.

YOU can see sights that take days to reach by road in fast, twin engined comfort by air, flown by professional pilots and at rates competitive with car hire.

CHOOSE THE PLANE TO MEET YOUR PERSONAL SAFARI NEEDS

AIR KENYA'S large fleet includes:
Big twin engine Beechcraft King Airs, Piper Navajos and Cessna 402s, carrying 7 to 14 passengers.
Twin engine Beech Barons and Cessna 310s for parties up to five.
Single engine Bonanzas and Cessnas for three to five people.
Rates from Shs. 2/- per passenger mile.

AIR KENYA LIMITED, WILSON AIRPORT
P.O. BOX 30357 NAIROBI KENYA
TELEPHONE DAY & NIGHT 501601/2/3/4
CABLES: AIR KENYA
TELEX: 22939 AIR KENYA

AIRCHARTER — AIRFREIGHT — AIRCRAFT SALES & SERVICE

Treetops – the hotel in a tree

Kenya

• NYALI BEACH HOTEL • SAMBURU LODGE • TREETOPS • SINDBAD HOTEL •

OUTSPAN • TREETOPS • KEEKOROK LODGE • TREETOPS • SAMBURU LODGE • TREETOPS • OUTSPAN

OUTSPAN • TREETOPS • KEEKOROK LODGE • TREETOPS • SAMBURU LODGE • TREETOPS • OUTSPAN

Six of the best!

Block Hotels run the finest and most famous game lodges and coast hotels in the whole of Africa and enjoy an unrivalled reputation for cuisine and service.

Keekorok

Keekorok Lodge -the perfect base for safaris to the famous Masai Mara Game Reserve, Kenya's Serengeti noted for its large population of lions and vast herds of plains game. In addition to the comfortable private bathrooms and a well-stocked bar guests can enjoy the truly unique experience of floating over the plains in one of Keekorok's hot air balloons.

Nyali Beach

Kenya's sun-kissed Coast is great for a holiday — staying at the Nyali Beach, makes it even better. All bedrooms are air conditioned, have radio, mini bars and are sea facing. There is a 40 metre fresh water swimming pool and entertainment is planned nightly through the week. Famous for its cuisine the hotel also has a coffee shop, a la carte Restaurant and snack bar by the pool. There are conference and banqueting facilities for up to 250.

Outspan

The Outspan Hotel, an English Country Hotel in the heart of Africa is the base for expeditions to the unique Treetops and the nearby Mount Kenya National Park and Aberdares National Park. Recreational facilities include golf, tennis, squash, swimming and fishing. The Outspan Hotel is also the perfect venue for conferences.

Samburu

Samburu Lodge situated on the banks of the Uaso Nyiro River offers luxury cottages and rooms facing the river where elephants, Grevy's zebra and Reticulated Giraffe come to drink. Crocodiles can be seen at close quarters from the riverside bar and Leopard regularly appear on the floodlit bank across the river.

Sindbad

The Sindbad Hotel is situated on Kenya's Indian Ocean Coast near the quaint and historic town of Malindi. Built in Arabic style, the Sindbad has all the facilities of a romantic, luxury beach hotel. The world famous Tsavo National Park, which contains some of the largest herds of Elephant and plains game is within easy reach. There is a weekly entertainment programme and for the sporting type, all water sports, plus golf and horse riding are available.

Treetops

Situated high in the Aberdare Forest, Treetops is Kenya's world-famous game lookout—the hotel-in-the-trees. Treetops is an adventure and is particularly noted for the large number of elephant and rhino regularly seen. From 40 feet high the visitor will watch a never-ending procession of animals as they come to the waterhole. Like any luxury hotel Treetops has its own bar, dining room, lounge and comfortable bedrooms.

For further details and reservation please contact Block Hotels Central Reservations Office P.O. Box 40075, Nairobi, Kenya.
Telephone: 22860/22869/331635 Cables: Snuggest Telex: 22146

• NYALI BEACH HOTEL • SAMBURU LODGE • TREETOPS • SINDBAD HOTEL •

The Country

Kenya is a land of kaleidoscopic contrasts. Much of its recorded history centres on the coast. Ptolemy, the great geographer, wrote in the second century AD about Mombasa under the name of Tonike, and the long white coral beaches, verged with palm trees, were familiar to Indians, Arabs and Portuguese, as well as later travellers. But now most visitors' first impression is of the utterly different scenery outside Nairobi, of the sweeping Athi Plains and game straying among the thorn bushes of the Nairobi National Park. North-west of the capital different again, with upland farms reminding one of a sunlit England, while higher still the thick rain forest of Mount Kenya and the Aberdares are as mysterious as perpetual snow on the Equator is paradoxical. Finally, the arid semi-desert of the north, bordering on Ethiopia and Somalia, seems in yet another world. Kenya fires the imagination of everyone who goes there. It is not surprising that in a few years since Independence it has become internationally recognised as one of the most magnificent and exciting holiday areas anywhere.

Geographically the country covers 582,647 sq km (225,000 sq miles) and lies across the Equator. Its Indian Ocean coastline is 608 km (380 miles) long, while its centre is cut by the Great Rift Valley, running north to south and containing a variety of lakes. The largest river is the Tana, which flows in a wide curve eastwards from the slopes of Mt Kenya (17,058 ft) to the Indian Ocean. The climate is described in the General Information section.

Kenya's People

Kenya is home to Arabs, Asians and Europeans as well as more than 48 main African tribes. Some, like the Masai, are famous as warriors. Others, like the El Molo up at Lake Turkana (Rudolf) or the Waliangulu elephant hunters near Tsavo Park, are few in number, shy and still backward. The largest are the Kikuyu (2.8 million), whose homelands are between Nairobi and Nyeri; the Luo (1.9 million) of the Kisumu area on Lake Victoria and the Kamba, centred on Machakos and Kitui. President Daniel arap Moi comes from the small Kalenjin tribe of western Kenya. The total population is nearly 14 million. A century ago there was great rivalry between the tribes, but today everything is concentrated on collaboration and Kenya's motto is *Harambee*, which means "Let's all pull together".

Traditional dancing

Nonetheless traditional dances and costumes are cherished as part of the country's cultural heritage. They are brimful of vitality too, and the Chuka drummers, for instance, have drawn crowds to overseas performances in London and elsewhere. Broadly there are two ways of getting to see traditional dancing. First if there is a celebration on, such as Independence Day (December 12), there are likely to be public performances. Secondly, if you are on a tour, you may find an exhibition arranged at some point, for instance at Bomas of Kenya in Langata or Mayer's ranch near Kijabe in the Rift valley. Many hotels have performances—indeed the fierce dancer wielding a spear may be the same man who earlier carried your suitcase to

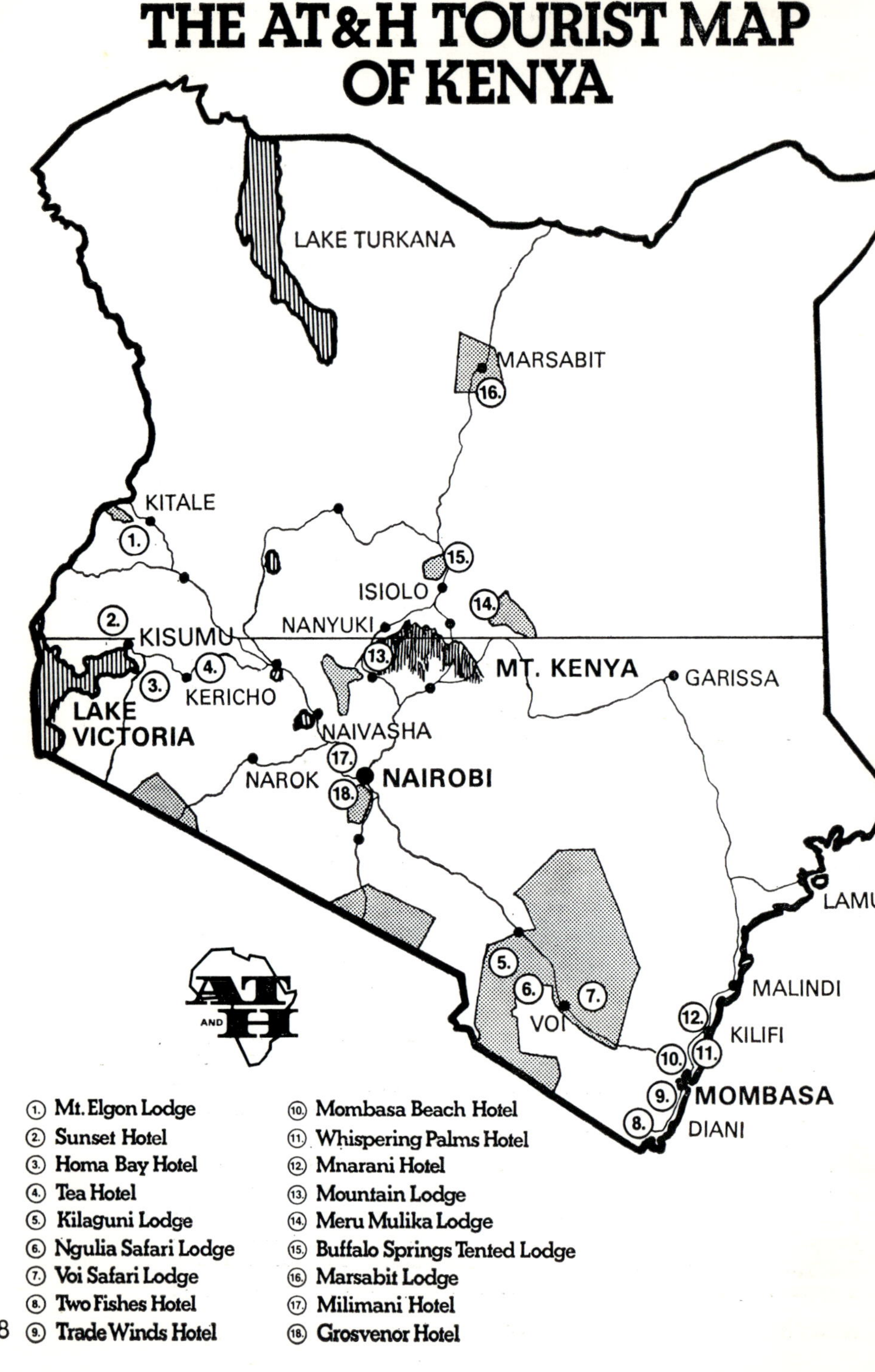
THE AT&H TOURIST MAP OF KENYA
LAKE TURKANA
MARSABIT
16.
KITALE
1.
15.
ISIOLO
14.
2.
NANYUKI
KISUMU
4.
13.
MT. KENYA
GARISSA
3.
KERICHO
LAKE VICTORIA
NAIVASHA
17.
NAIROBI
NAROK
18.
LAMU
5.
6.
7.
VOI
MALINDI
12.
KILIFI
10.
11.
9.
MOMBASA
8.
DIANI
AT AND H
1. Mt. Elgon Lodge
2. Sunset Hotel
3. Homa Bay Hotel
4. Tea Hotel
5. Kilaguni Lodge
6. Ngulia Safari Lodge
7. Voi Safari Lodge
8. Two Fishes Hotel
9. Trade Winds Hotel
10. Mombasa Beach Hotel
11. Whispering Palms Hotel
12. Mnarani Hotel
13. Mountain Lodge
14. Meru Mulika Lodge
15. Buffalo Springs Tented Lodge
16. Marsabit Lodge
17. Milimani Hotel
18. Grosvenor Hotel

your room! One word of warning here. If you happen accidentally upon a local *ngoma*, which is Swahili for a dance or celebration, make sure to ask if you may stay and watch, especially before taking photographs. These are private affairs.

Asians

When the British colonised and developed East Africa they introduced both Asian and European minorities. The Asians came mostly to work on the railway, then branched into trade. Since independence many have left and there are now about 80,000 of them, mainly in the cities, and you will notice their mosques, temples and bazaars, the Sikhs' turbans, and the women's brightly coloured saris.

Europeans

The European settler have progressively been replaced by African farmers. However, their influence remains evident both socially and in business. Down at the coast there is a sizeable Arab community.

Independence day was on December 12, 1963, and a year later Kenya became a Republic in the Commonwealth, under the Presidency of Mzee Jomo Kenyatta (*Mzee* is a honorific title, roughly translatable as "wise old man"). He died in 1978 and his successor is the Hon. Daniel arap Moi. The National Assembly sits in Nairobi. Administratively Kenya is divided into seven provinces—The Coast, Rift Valley, Central, Nyanza, Western, Eastern and North-Eastern.

A glance at the map of Kenya shows that *Nairobi* is at the centre of a spider's web of communications. *North* road and rail lead along the eastern side of the Aberdare range, up to Nyeri, Mount Kenya and the sudden, dramatic escarpment beyond which lies the vast semi-desert expanse of the Northern Frontier, Lake Turkana and Ethiopia. To the *north-west*, road and rail run past Lakes Naivasha and Nakuru in the Rift Valley and then west over the Mau Summit to Lake Victoria and Uganda, *South-east* road and rail march side by side to Mombasa and the coast via the Tsavo Park, while directly *south* is the road through Masailand to Arusha in Tanzania. For convenience we will divide Kenya into the areas to which these major routes lead, but dealing first with the National Parks and Game Reserves and with the capital city itself.

Hotels and Game Lodges

In recent years Kenya's tourist facilities have been transformed with many new hotels and lodges being built and standards improving dramatically. In consequence we now only mention a selection of hotels. For a complete list consult the classified Hotel Directory, available through Kenya Tourist Offices abroad.

Prices

In fact the classification is somewhat arbitrary, but does help and in most cases we give it, limiting ourselves to grades (or classes) A, B and C. At the time of writing the approximate price ranges in the high season were:

Grade A hotels Nairobi: around Shs. 500/– per night double, inclusive of taxes, but without breakfast.

Grade A lodges or country hotels: Shs. 730/– to Shs. 800/– double full board. Coast hotels about Shs. 100/– cheaper.

Grade B hotels Nairobi: around Shs. 350/– double per night including taxes but without breakfast.

Grade B lodges or country hotels: around Shs. 400/– double full board. Coast hotels similar.

Grade C hotels Nairobi: around Shs. 220/– double per night with breakfast. Country and coast hotels cheaper.

It is impossible to recommend most of the Grade D establishments. However there are very cheap places to stay and for students or young people the YMCAs and YWCAs offer terrific value.

In the low season of April to mid-July most coast hotels and game lodges offer reductions of up to 50%, and there are special terms for local residents.

National Parks and Reserves

These are the two kinds of area in which game is protected and facilities are maintained for visitors to see and enjoy it. All have roads and most have airstrips. Except for the Mountain Parks, which may be inaccessible in wet weather, and are open throughout the year. Entrance fees are Shs. 20/– per adult—Shs. 20/– per car or light aircraft except where otherwise stated. Season tickets are available to Kenya residents. The gates are open approximately from dawn to dusk and regulations include a ban on travel at night—you must then be either out of the Park or at a game lodge. You can only move about by vehicle and the speed limit is 20 mph—which is commonsense because you see nothing if you hurry. Nor may you leave the vehicle except at clearly indicated places—again commonsense because big game, though often used to cars, are still dangerous. Indeed, they are less shy of cars than of human beings. There are no restrictions on amateur photography, but professional work requires a licence. The Parks are run by the Wildlife Conservation and Management Department of the Ministry of Tourism and Wildlife. The Department's HQ is on the Langata road, near the entrance to the Nairobi National Park (postal address Box 40241, Nairobi, telephone 891601). Each Park has wardens and a staff of rangers. These rangers wear khaki uniforms and a Foreign Legion type of hat. National Reserves are run by local authorities on similar lines with game scouts, though (unlike the National Parks) the indigenous tribes continue to live in them. Forest Reserves are simply areas of planned afforestation.

Although the game lodges all have special booking agents, listed as they occur in the text, any travel agent can make your reservations.

Camping

Camping is allowed in most Parks.

The increasing awareness of the need to protect special habitats and flora as well as fauna—not to mention tropical fish and coral—has led to the establishment of many new Parks. A complete list is in the index, and all are mentioned in the text. Among the best known are:

AMBOSELI NATIONAL PARK

380 sq km (147 sq miles) of swamps and plains country inside a 3,260 sq km reserve all dominated by the snowcapped peak of Kilimanjaro. About 3,500 ft above sea level. See page 60.

MASAI MARA GAME RESERVE

1,813 sq km (700 sq miles) round the Mara River in S.W. Kenya. Mostly 5,000 ft up. One of the best parts of Kenya in which to see plains game. See pages 55–56.

MERU NATIONAL PARK

Some 60 miles N.E. of Mount Kenya, 1,000 to 3,400 ft up, 870 sq km. (336 sq miles). Noted for Grevy's zebra and reticulated giraffe. See page 50.

MOUNT KENYA NATIONAL PARK

717 sq km (277 sq miles) round the upper slopes of snowtopped Mount Kenya, starting at 11,000 ft. Big game in the forests. Climbers' huts for mountaineers. See pages 49–50.

NAIROBI NATIONAL PARK

Unique in being only five miles from the city centre. 114 sq km (44 sq miles). Lions are the speciality. Open all year round. See page 44.

LAKE NAKURU NATIONAL PARK

A bird sanctuary on Lake Nakuru, 100 miles from Nairobi in the Rift Valley. Thousands of flamingoes make the water seem pink from a distance. Altitude 5,765 ft. See page 57.

SAMBURU GAME RESERVE

Near Isiolo in the north, 3,000 ft above sea level and therefore hot. Only 101 sq km (39 sq miles) of fairly dense bush but wildlife congregates at the river, where the main lodge is. See page 52.

TSAVO NATIONAL PARK

20,780 sq km (8,024 sq miles) of bush and occasional hills on the plains east of Kilimanjaro. Mostly 2,000–4,000 ft up. Divided into two sections, East and West, by the Nairobi–Mombasa road. Noted for great herds of elephant. See pages 61–63.

Poaching

Finally, a word about poaching. The value of ivory and the Oriental belief that powdered rhino horn is an aphrodisiac, not to mention Western furriers' demands for leopard and other skins, coupled with a local desire for free meat result in the Game Wardens fighting a constant battle to safeguard Kenya's wildlife from poaching by traps, poisoned arrows and other means. Indeed rhino are an endangered species. This is why hunting is banned as is the sale of ivory and game trophies. It is illegal to export any game product without a licence—which extends to the elephant hair bracelets offered for sale by street vendors (these are often plastic imitations anyway). The East African Wildlife Society, Box 20110, Nairobi, exists to help preserve wildlife and welcomes new members. It has an office in the Hilton hotel.

Safaris and Transport

Air

Kenya Airways runs scheduled services to Kisumu, Malindi, Mombasa and other towns. A number of air charter firms offer fast, twin-engine services which are unbeatable for long distances and inaccessible places, such as Lake Turkana. Mile for mile it can be cheaper than driving, and of course distances are direct. At Nairobi's smaller Wilson airport, ten minutes' drive from town, there are Africair (Box 45646), Air Kenya (Box 30357), CMC Aviation (Box 30135), and Caspair (Box 30103). At Mombasa's Port Reitz airport there are Amphibians Ltd (Box 80607) and Mombasa Air Services (Box 99222). Also on the coast at Malindi are Malindi Air Services (Box 146). Air charter rates run around Shs. 2/– per passenger mile.

Trains

Kenya Railways main routes are Nairobi to Mombasa, which runs overnight, and Nairobi–Kisumu, going on to Kampala in Uganda. The former is good value. First class sleepers, with two berths, cost Shs. 138/– per person one way, bedding is Shs. 15/– and there is a good restaurant car. But the service going up-country is necessarily slow, due to the hills.

Car Hire

This is available in all main towns. Typical self-drive charges for a small Datsun or Ford Consul are around Shs. 400/– a week plus Shs. 1/30 a kilometre. All hotels arrange car hire. Unless you have an American Express card or Diners card you will have to put down a deposit, normally Shs. 1,000/–.

Buses

Taxis

The Kenya Bus Company serves the whole country and very cheaply, but buses are liable to be very crowded. A better alternative are the long distance taxis which ply between towns, and on which seats can be booked. Ordinary taxis, however, are expensive.

Safaris

Nairobi is the centre for individually tailored safaris. The best known firms are Ker, Downey and Selby Safaris Ltd (Box 41822, Nairobi), Abercrombie and Kent Ltd (Box 20224, Nairobi) and a smaller firm, Trans African Guides (Box 49538). These firms are able to offer complete staff, tentage, vehicles etc. Costs are high.

Tours

A multitude of tour operators offer safaris visiting game lodges rather than camping. Among the best are United Touring Company (Head office Box 42196, Nairobi) with many branches; Archers Tours (Box 40097, Nairobi), African Tours and Hotels, a large concern managing hotels and lodges (Head office Box 30471, Nairobi), Flamingo Tours (Box 44899, Nairobi), Nilestar Tours (Box 42291, Nairobi), and Thorn Tree Safaris (Box 42475, Nairobi).

If you want to do your own thing, then Safari Camp Services (Box 44801, Nairobi) will hire you four-wheel drive vehicles and camping equipment. For several people, this is the cheapest way.

The firms mentioned above can cater to such special interests as ornithology, botany, pre-history, fishing, mountaineering and so on.

Nairobi

This is a surprising city, especially to anyone whose ideas of Africa revolve around tropical jungle. Nairobi's semi-skyscrapers soar white and dazzling as a mirage out of the surrounding Athi Plains. Its avenues are adorned with statues and lined with great stretches of riotously coloured bougainvillaea. The suburbs, occasionally visited by the lions who lived here before, are alive with hibiscus, oleanders and glorious blue flowering jacaranda trees.

Climate

The pleasant climate has had a lot to do with Nairobi's booming success. Being 5,500 ft up the nights are cool, while during the day the sun is warm, but the humidity is low. The temperature rarely exceeds 27°C (80°F.).

Nairobi lies 139 km (87 miles) south of the Equator and 480 km (300 miles) west of the Indian Ocean; it has a population of about 750,000. Like New York, the city centre is constantly renewing itself. Side by side you can see all the stages of its hustling growth since it was a railway construction camp, a pioneers' town. In 1902 the famous wildlife authority, Colonel Meinertzhagen, recorded in his diary—"The only shop is a small tin hut which sells everything . . . The only hotel here is a wood and tin shanty. It stands in the only 'street'." Today the main streets are still wide enough to turn a wagon and team of oxen. You can still find a few shops that are more like shanties. But many hotels are now well up to international standards and there is a bloom of exciting modern architecture, like some of the Government buildings, the extension to the City Hall, the fine new buildings of the University and the Kenyatta Conference Centre tower.

Places of worship

The Roman Catholic cathedral, completed in 1963, is also of strikingly modern design. It is built on the site of an earlier church which was the first stone building in Nairobi, and three of the bells from the old church now hang in the 200-foot campanile. The Protestant cathedral in Kenyatta Avenue is an older stone building set in an attractive garden. The Jamia mosque off Banda Street, has an arresting silver dome. There is a Jewish synagogue on University Way.

Shopping

The main shopping streets are Kenyatta Avenue, intersecting Kimathi Street by the New Stanley Hotel, Moi Avenue (formerly Government Road), Standard Street, Kaunda Street, Mama Ngina Street and Tom Mboya Street. Within the central area, in walking distance of the New Stanley, you will find photographic goods, cosmetics, clothing and

Information

the invariably helpful Information Bureau (telephone 23285).

Welcome to Nairobi Hilton

Almost as soon as you've checked in at the magnificent Hilton in the centre of Nairobi you can begin viewing game.

The Nairobi National Park is only minutes from the hotel and as you enter the park you will find the animal orphanage, which is a kind of hospital for sick animals and a home for neglected wildlife.

After viewing wild animals, it is a short ride back to the welcoming comfort of the Nairobi Hilton. The circular tower-block

construction of the hotel ensures that all rooms have panoramic views, and there is a heated pool and health club offering sauna and massage.

The Amboseli Grill Room offers superb cuisine in an East African setting, with music and dancing. The Tsavo Restaurant features local and international specialities. Easy relaxation is found in the Ivory Bar and at the Watamu Pool Terrace where long cool drinks and light snacks are served.

From the Nairobi Hilton, you might like to venture into big game country and visit the Hilton's two exciting game lodges.

Welcome to Taita Hills Lodge

Two hundred miles from Nairobi, at the gateway to Tsavo National Park, is the Taita Hills Lodge, known as a 'base lodge' – a departure point for excursions and safaris into the surrounding region – it lies amid game-filled virgin bush which offers some of Kenya's most exciting animal viewing.

At Taita Hills you will find the height of luxury in the heart of the bush. Spacious bedrooms with baths, one of East Africa's finest dining rooms complete with decorations inspired by the area's early explorers, a circular lounge with its three-storey-high open fireplace... play tennis, go camel trekking or simply laze by the pool with a 'sundowner' – East African for cocktail.

Nearby you can see traditional African dancing in an African village and buy locally made handicrafts. But Taita Hills is mainly for legendary excursions, and one trip that has to be made is the six miles to Salt Lick Lodge. Here, after a candle-lit dinner, you will want to stay up most of the night to see the wildlife.

Welcome to Salt Lick Lodge

Hilton's famous Salt Lick is like nothing you have ever experienced. In the style of an African village, it is a complex of towers roofed in typical African thatch, perched on stilts and connected by bridge-like walkways. Its name is taken from the natural salt lick which lies in front of it, and where the neighbourhood's game come to wallow, lick the salt and be viewed by guests at the lodge.

During the day and especially at night, when the lick is floodlit, you can see a wonderful variety of animals. From the terrace, the cocktail lounge and even the restaurant which provides delicious cuisine, you can look down on elephant, buffalo, lion and other species.

The bedrooms are the most comfortable of any game-viewing lodge in the East African bush.

As well as excursions, safaris and game runs where you can see zebra, impala and giraffe, Salt Lick also affords thrilling game viewing from a special ground-level bunker reached by a tunnel from the lodge. Here, behind a safety window, you may photograph the animals and achieve a wonderful record of the most exciting adventure of your life!

Reservations: Nairobi Hilton Hotel Tel. 334000 Salt Lick and Taita Hills Lodges Tel. 334000 Or Mombasa Tel. 20741/312734.

NAIROBI HILTON & LODGES

Specialities include camping gear from Low and Bonar and safari clothes from Colpro; jewellery, including rubies, tsavorite (a type of green garnet found near Tsavo National Park) and tanzanite (a sapphire-like blue stone from Tanzania). Amber beads from Somalia can be a good buy, too, but make sure they do not have seams—if they do they are plastic! Rowland Ward engrave goblets with wild-life scenes.

Curios are available in countless places. These include carved wooden animals and people, baskets, daggers and spears, and beadwork. Try the stalls at the City Market on Muindi Mbingu Street And always bargain. Prices are what you make them.

Also near the City Market are Asian shops selling silk saris and silverwork.

If you fancy the hurly-burly of African markets, go down River Road or take a taxi to the colourful Kariokor market just away from the downtown area.

Something different from curios are genuine tribal crafts, of which African Heritage in Kenyatta Street and Studio Arts 68 in Standard Street have excellent collections. These, like first edition books on Africana, are likely to be expensive, if they are old.

Galleries

Gallery Watatu in Standard Street stocks paintings, sculpture, prints and batiks, while the East African Wildlife Society at the Hilton has prints, drawings, beadwork and books, and Kumbu Kumbu, also in the Hilton, has sculptures.

Hairdressing

Schoutens, in the New Stanley Arcade, are a good ladies' and men's hairdressers. Another men's barber is in the Six Eighty hotel, while there are ladies' salons at the Hilton, Intercontinental and Serena hotels.

Travel Agents

Of the many tour operators, a few are recommended in the Safaris and Transport section above. Reliable travel agents include Bunson Travel Ltd (Box 45456, telephone 21992) who also run AA Travel; J. W. Kearsley & Co. (Box 46660, telephone 20363) and Mitchell Cotts and Co (Box 30182, telephone 29201).

Taxis

Taxis are licensed by the City Council, but you should always agree the fare beforehand, irrespective of the meter.

Hotels

The first class, grade A, hotels near the city centre are the Hilton (Box 30624); the Intercontinental (Box 30667); the New Stanley (Box 30680), a famous international rendezvous; the equally renowned Norfolk (Box 40064) once a pioneers' hotel and now completely modernised with a countryfied atmosphere; the Nairobi Serena (Box 46302) bordering on the lawns of central park; and the Panafric (Box 30486) at the far end of Kenyatta Avenue from town. All except the New Stanley have swimming pools. Also central are the grade A Six Eighty hotel on Kenyatta Avenue and the grade B Ambassadeur on Moi Avenue.

Among the smaller good hotels with more moderate prices are the College Inn (Box 30471), in the city centre; Hotel Chiromo (Box

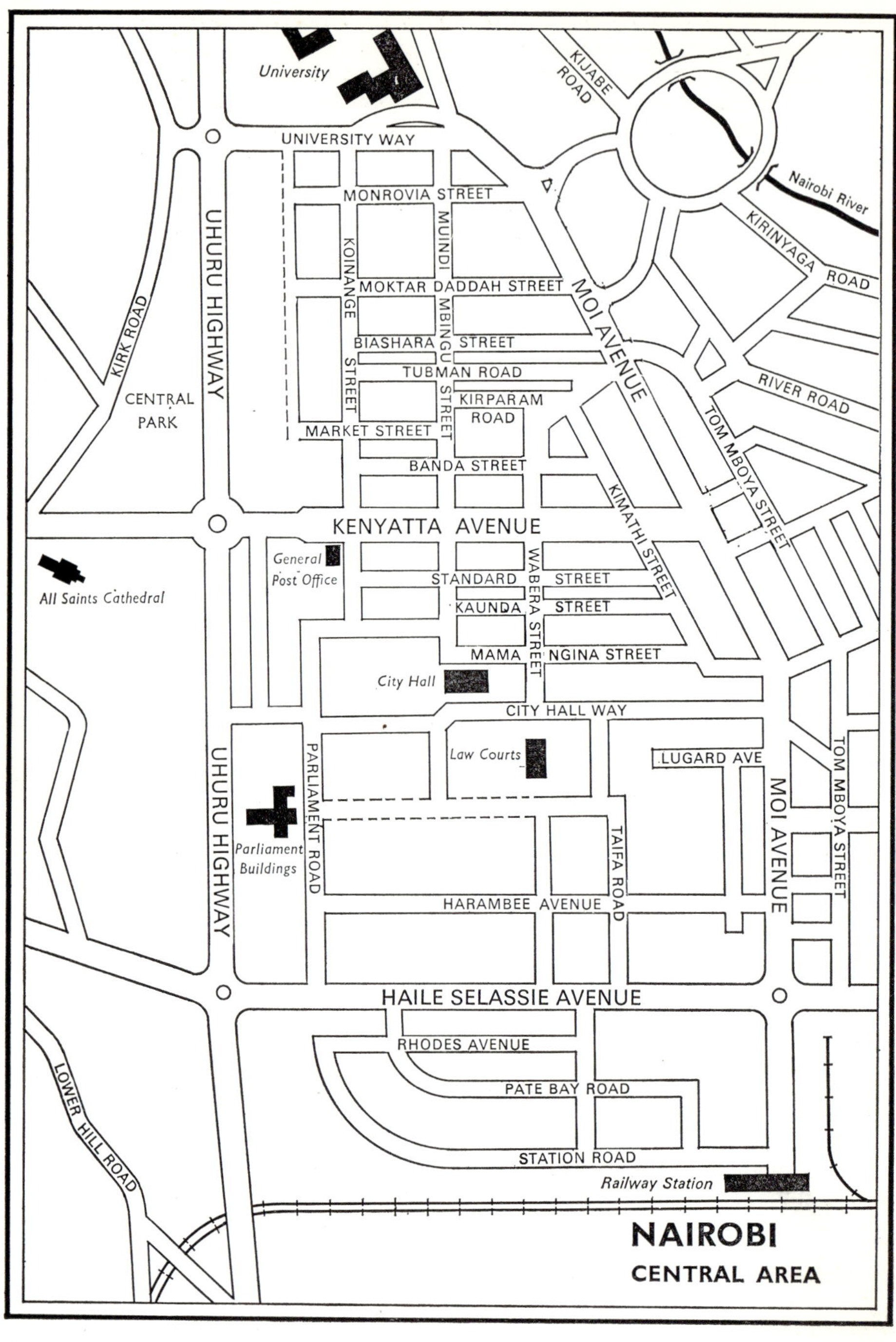

NAIROBI
CENTRAL AREA

44677) near the National Museum; the Fairview Hotel (Box 40824), and the Ainsworth (Box 40469). All these are graded C. Slightly further out are the Safari Park Hotel (Box 40288), seven miles from the centre on Murang'a Road with a swimming pool, tennis courts and riding; the Jacaranda (Box 14287), three miles out near the Westlands shopping centre and an excellent place for those driving round East Africa; and the new Utalii Hotel (Box 27067) four miles out along Murang'a Road. Eighteen miles from Nairobi, situated over Kingfisher Gorge and bordering Nairobi National Park, is Masai Lodge (Box 20130), an excellent place to stay away from the noise of the city, and a good place for a drink and a meal after a drive in the Park.

Apart from visitors, hardly anyone lives in central Nairobi, though everyone works there. They live in the suburbs, thus giving the city four rush-hours a day because they drive home for lunch. The bus services are crowded, so if you do stay at one of the many outlying hotels you will need either taxis or a self-drive car.

Restaurants

The New Stanley is the city's acknowledged social meeting place during the day. You can have coffee or a snack at the open air Thorn Tree café, or take a more formal meal in the restaurant upstairs. Rival open air cafés are the Lord Delamere at the Norfolk and the Watamu pool terrace at the Hilton.

For an evening out, Nairobi is blessed with a variety of diversions. For dining and dancing there are the Hilton and Panafric grillrooms, which have excellent food and sometimes a cabaret. Le Château at the top of the Intercontinental specialises in French food. The Bacchus Club on Standard Street, a new favourite with local residents, which usually has a cabaret has day membership available Monday to Thursday. Other places worth trying are Alan Bobbe's bistro, the Three Bells, Lavarini's for Italian food, the Pagoda and the Mandarin for Chinese dishes and the Maharaja for curries. Prices run between Shs. 35/– and Shs. 70/–, though the Bacchus and the hotel grillrooms would cost more.

Nightlife

Nairobi has two casinos offering blackjack, roulette, and so on: the International Casino near the Museum and Casino de Paradise, seven miles out at the Safari Park Hotel. They have dancing. Of more raucous local nightclubs the New Florida and the Chiromo can be recommended.

Theatre

The Donovan Maule Theatre Club is a delightfully designed small theatre with a resident company playing modern European and American dramas in repertory. Day membership, snacks and drinks are available. The National Theatre has productions and concerts at irregular intervals, while the French Cultural Centre organises special. film shows, concerts and talks. The World Wildlife Fund has regular showings of wildlife films there; details are posted in the lobbies of leading hotels. For cinemas see the local press.

Films

National Museum

The museum is well worth a visit for its exhibits of wildlife and tribal ornaments. It has the largest collection of African butterflies in the world and over 1,000 species of birds. Also of special interest is the display dealing with prehistoric man in Kenya. The museum carries out a great deal of research and is particularly known for its discoveries on early man begun by the late Dr Louis Leakey, of world fame.

Snake Park

Next door to the museum is an Aviary and the Snake Park which houses many species of snakes, with a fine collection of cobras, pythons and other rare varieties. There is also a crocodile pool and a tortoise pit. Incidentally, unless you actually tread on a snake, or corner it, you are most unlikely to be bitten. Snakes try to avoid meeting humans.

Arboretum

A mile or so away on Hospital Hill is the Arboretum, an 80-acre park of native and exotic trees, many spectacularly beautiful. City Park, two miles from town on the Limuru Road, has extensive gardens and includes some of the indigenous forest, long since cut down elsewhere in the vicinity. If you're observant, you might see a troupe of vervet monkeys feeding and grooming themselves.

Aquarium

The Aquarium on Mama Ngina Street has over 300 fish of 30 species, most of them from Kenya's coral coast. It's open daily except Sundays, and admission is Shs. 3/–.

Sport

Racing and polo have long been favourite Kenyan sports. There are regular meetings at Nairobi racecourse, in a perfect setting, close to the city. Hurdle and flat races are also run at the Limuru Country Club, 17 miles out. This club has a first-rate 18-hole golf course too, and offers temporary membership to visitors, as do the Sigona Golf Club the Muthaiga Golf Club (separate from Muthaiga Club), and the Royal Nairobi Golf Club. The Polo Club, where visitors are welcome, meets at Jamhuri Park on Wednesdays, Saturdays and Sundays, near where the Agricultural Society holds a tremendous five-day show every September. Parklands Sports Club (Box 40116, telephone Nairobi 55164) welcomes temporary members to its swimming pool, tennis and squash courts.

East African Safari

Finally, there is the toughest motor rally in the world, the East African Safari, held every Easter. The city goes crazy over the Safari, the streets are hung with flags and all else is forgotten.

Nairobi National Park

For the live entertainment that most people come to see, the 44-square-mile Nairobi National Park ranks first, and is so close to the city one could call it a suburb inhabited by animals. The main gate brings you into the wooded Langata corner, where you are quite likely to find lion strolling along the road. More often, though, they are lying up in the shade of a thorn tree, or among some rocks. The early evening is the time to see them, when they are waking up from their afternoon siesta. Other wildlife include zebra, kongoni, gazelle, wildebeeste, giraffe, impala, an occasional rhino, baboons, crocodile and hippos in the river pools, leopard, cheetah, hyena, eland, warthog and ostrich. Remember not to get out of your car except at the signposted picnic places, and that this is still at your own risk. The Park is open all the year. The Masai Lodge is close to the Park.

The National Parks Office and a delightfully laid out Wildlife Education Centre are by the main gate, as is an animal orphanage sponsored by the World Wildlife Fund. It accepts abandoned and sick animals from all over Kenya, rearing and later releasing those which are able to fend for themselves. The orphanage offers a unique opportunity to see young hippo, lion, antelope, monkeys and other species in spacious enclosures. The orphanage nursery allows children to watch and participate in their feeding.

Animal orphanage

Out in this direction are the Ngong hills, whose 8,000 ft humps are a local landmark and which are an excellent place for a picnic. The view from them across the Rift is superb, the air being so clear that you can often see a hundred miles or more, while zebra, giraffe, eland and buffaloes wander round their slopes. A road negotiable by cars in dry weather leads to one of the peaks.

Ngong hills

Karen, at the foot of the Ngong hills, is named after the Danish authoress Countess Karen von Blixen, who wrote a classic about her life here called *Out of Africa*. Her farmhouse is open to the public, thanks to the Danish Government, but it is appreciated if people telephone (Karen 2366) before visiting it.

Karen

North to Nyeri, Treetops, the Aberdares, Nyahururu (Thomson's) Falls, and Maralal

From Nairobi to Nyeri is all Kikuyuland, densely populated and so almost devoid of animal wildlife, though not of birds. The steep ridges that rise towards the Aberdares force the road to twist and climb, making the 155 km (96 miles), though all tarmac, a 2 to 2½ hour drive, while the train puffs along for seven hours and five minutes.

Near Kiambu and Thika there are coffee and sisal estates, easily visited by arrangement, but greater interest lies in the Kikuyu villages. A family may occupy three or more of the traditional round thatched huts, though increasingly they are being replaced by more modern rectangular houses. Both land and firewood are in short supply, which is why cattle graze on the road verges and you may see women pass by carrying loads of wood bought from traders, held up on their backs by a traditional leather thong passing round the forehead. Kikuyu women do much of the work on the family plots of land (*shambas* in Swahili), and some men have several wives. However, the Kikuyu are one of the most forward looking tribes in Africa and female emancipation is on the way.

The Kikuyu

The Blue Posts Hotel, by the Chania Falls near Thika, is a pleasant spot to stop for a drink and has a large swimming pool. To the east rises a great humped hill, Ol Doinyo Sapuk (7,041 ft) the name being Masai for "the mountain of the buffalo". A road, negotiable by cars in dry weather, leads to the top. The hill, a National Park, is the haunt of many birds, including the (African) harrier hawk, while the river above the Fourteen Falls at Thika, and the dense forest overhanging

Thika

it, shelter both birds and crocodiles. There is a lot of tall papyrus grass about too, like that from which the ancient Egyptians made paper. Elspeth Huxley wrote enchantingly about this neighbourhood in *The Flame Trees of Thika*. The town is nothing much—but the flame trees, which one sees elsewhere too, grow high and thick, with dark green foliage in which blossom dozens of reddish orange flowers, as vivid as shell-bursts.

Fort Hall

At Fort Hall there is a church decorated with remarkable Goya-like mural paintings by a Chagga artist called Elimo Njau. They show the life and crucifixion of an African Christ in a local landscape. Otherwise there is little more than Kikuyu villages and markets until you reach Nyeri, save that you may see the glaciered peak of Mount Kenya rising out of the clouds ahead of you. Traditionally to the Kikuyu it is the dwelling place of the god Ngai, and like Mount Olympus in Greece it is shy of revealing itself, except in the early morning and the evening. A lot of Kenya's Africans are animists, believing God resides in natural objects, like trees and hills. However about 25% are reckoned to be Christians.

Nyeri

Nyeri itself, 5,750 ft up, is a well-laid-out township, with a 9-hole golf course and many excellent trout streams. It has an airfield but no scheduled airline services. The best tourist shop is in the Outspan Hotel (Box 24, Nyeri, telephone 9), which is one of the best up-country hotels in East Africa, and stands half a mile from the centre of Nyeri in its own delightful grounds. It has very considerable facilities, including squash, tennis, trout fishing, swimming, car hire and riding. The hotel hires out all sporting equipment. Official fishing licences cost Shs. 5/– for 48 hours. Lord Baden Powell, founder of the Boy Scout movement, spent his last years at the Outspan—and very enjoyable they must have been.

Treetops

Trips to the world-famous game-viewing hotel, Treetops, start with lunch at the Outspan, after which a hunting car takes you up into the forest, bringing you back next morning for breakfast. The cost is Shs. 334/– per person, plus Shs. 20/– National Park entrance fee. This is the only way of going to Treetops, you cannot simply drive there yourself, even if you could find the track. Book through Treetops Booking Office (Box 40075, Nairobi) or any travel agent.

Treetops stands by a pool on a low spur of the Aberdare forest known as the Treetops salient. When it's raining in the bamboo higher up, which it often is because the rainfall is 80–100 inches a year, the game come down to drier ground in the salient and are attracted to Treetops itself by the adjacent salt licks and the pool. Buffalo, rhino, elephant, giant forest hog and antelope are common visitors. The Aberdare Park Warden says he has counted 500 elephant in the area at one time. They are kept off the farms below the forest by a ditch more than five miles long, six feet deep and six feet wide, the maintenance of which occupies at least forty men all the year.

The original hotel was literally in a tree, and the present Queen of England was staying there in 1952 when her father died and she acceded to the British throne. The present hotel is larger, built 40 feet high on stilts among the trees and has a dining-room, bar, bedrooms and verandahs, from which you get a grand circle view of the forest wildlife beneath, aided after dark by an artificial moon.

Aberdare National Park

The Park road from Nyeri to the Aberdare National Park (the highest game park in the world) and Naivasha climbs 4,000 ft in 22 km (14 miles); it is closed in wet weather. It passes first through Forest Reserve, mainly planted with fast-growing exotic trees like gums; then into the alpine bamboo, feathery-leaved but impenetrably dense, with occasional bars of sunlight slanting down through it like rays from the windows of a great cathedral. Not far past the Park gate you suddenly emerge on to open moorland, 10,000 feet above sea level. Up here you are allowed to leave your car and go up to 100 yards from the roads and rivers. There are two spectacular waterfalls, Karura dropping 894 feet in three stages, and Gura 791 feet, also in three stages. Especially near the water there are fantastic growth of moss and giant vegetation, peculiar to the East African mountains. Groundsel and lobelias, small plants in Europe, reach 15 feet high here. It is as though one had suddenly been transported to Brobdingnag, the giants' country of Gulliver's Travels. In good weather the Park road leads to superb views of the Rift as it descends on the other side of the Aberdares to the Kinangop Plateau and Naivasha. The road is partly tarmaced on the Naivasha side.

Game scouts

The wildlife in the Park is mostly shy like the bongo. There are elephant, buffalo, rhino, eland, waterbuck, reedbuck, colobus monkey, serval cats, mountain buzzard, crowned hawk eagle and Jackson's francolin. We ourselves saw a black leopard on one trip. There are a few lion and hyenas too. You may also come across patrols of game scouts, clad in khaki denim uniforms, and armed with rifles. Their job is checking on trespassers and poachers.

The Ark

Near the Park and the township of Mweiga is the Aberdare Country Club, where riding and fishing are available. The Club is the starting-point for trips to The Ark, an excellent game-viewing lodge high in the forests of the Aberdares, where animals you may see include leopard and the elusive bongo. The King and Queen of Sweden are among notables who have stayed there. A visit to The Ark starts with lunch at the Aberdare Country Club, followed by an 11-mile drive up the forest road in the company of a professional hunter. You have dinner and spend the night at the lodge, returning after breakfast the following morning. Charges, which include accommodation, food and transport, are from Shs. 780/– for a double room, plus the National Park entrance fee. Bookings for both the Aberdare Country Club and The Ark should be made through Across Africa Safaris, Box 49420, Nairobi.

Going north from Nyeri you can follow round the side of the Aberdares through Mweiga to Nyahururu (Thomson's Falls), Rumuruti and Maralal. The alternative is to go north past Naromoru to Nanyuki and Mt Kenya (see next section). Between Nyeri and Naromoru is the signpost to the excellent Mountain Lodge, 7,200 ft up and one of the best high-altitude bird watching spots. It also attracts large numbers of big game. You must arrive between 4.00 pm (1600) and 6.30 pm (1830). Cost of Shs. 500/- double for dinner, bed and breakfast. Bookings Box 30471, Nairobi. The lodge can also be reached from the Karatina–Nyeri road, if you are coming direct from Nairobi.

Mountain Lodge

The new tarmac road from Nyeri to Nyahururu, a distance of 115 km (74 miles) takes you across the glorious plains of Laikipia, ranching land dotted with umbrella thorns and spiritually akin to Texas. On the estates of up to 100,000 acres Santa Gertrudis is as much a household word as Hereford or Boran, these last being the African humped cattle with which imported stock are often crossed to combine yield with resistance to local conditions. Cattle have a tough life out here, what with tropical fevers and ticks, which they catch all too easily from the buffalo, buck, giraffe and other game that also wander over Laikipia. However there is no tsetse fly, so many farmers keep horses. Game ranching, incidentally, is becoming quite a business up here, for instance at the American owned Solio Ranch.

Nyahururu (Thomson's Falls)

Nyahururu, a township formerly called Thomson's Falls after the same explorer who gave the "Tommy" gazelle its name, has a hotel, the Thomson's Falls Lodge (Box 38, telephone 6) right by the waterfall and with gardens overlooking the dramatic gorge below it. The rooms are comfortable, if simple, and have private baths.

From Nyahururu a road leads down to Rumuruti, with an airstrip but no hotel. However 30 km (19 miles) north of the township is the small Colcheccio Club (Box 50, Rumuruti), a ranch style house with fine views towards Mt Kenya. The nearby river attracts many birds and game, including Grevy's zebra and reticulated giraffe. The club has tennis, riding, and a pool and charges Shs. 880/- double full board, inclusive of game drives.

Maralal

From Rumuruti, the road continues 112 km (70 miles) north to Maralal, near the Lorogi Plateau and the Karisia Hills, which used to be a favourite hunting area. The Maralal Safari Lodge (Grade C, bookings Box 30471, Nairobi) has simple but comfortable wooden bungalows and a waterhole where the area's plains game often come to drink. Cost is Shs. 300/- double, full board. There is a garage in Maralal and an airstrip a couple of miles out.

Losiolo Escarpment

About 24 km (15 miles) out of Maralal on the increasingly rough road to Lake Turkana (formerly Rudolf) you come upon one of the most spectacular views in Africa: the Losiolo escarpment, overlooking the Rift Valley and its volcanic moonscape. To find the escarpment, engage the services of a local guide at Maralal. The main road north from Maralal continues a bruising 304 km (190 miles) to Loiyangalani (see below). The journey by road should be undertaken only by well-equipped expeditions with four-wheel drive. Unbelievably, there is a weekly bus service from Nairobi, whose passengers camp at night-stops. See page 53.

Naro Moru, Nanyuki, Mount Kenya, Meru National Park

The excellent tarmac road from Nyeri to Nanyuki (51 km, 32 miles) passes the trading post of Naro Moru, once the centre of a European farming district, now farmed by Africans. Lying on the lower slopes of Mt Kenya, it is attractive country and many of the scenes in *Born Free*, the film of Joy Adamson's book about her tame lions, were shot around here. About half a mile from the main road is the comfortable Naro Moru River Lodge (Grade C, Box 18, Naro Moru, telephone 23). Set on the river, which is stocked with rainbow and brown trout, the lodge has pleasant cedar log cabins, each with its own bathroom. Cheaper self service chalets for two or more people are also available. As well as riding, walking, fishing and birdwatching (Jackson's Francolin and Lanner Falcon are among local species), the lodge offers foot safaris up Mt Kenya. These involve no rock climbing, though you need to be reasonably healthy. They last 2 to 4 days and cost from Shs. 625/– to Shs. 1,100/– per person. A one day trip is also possible. Clothing and equipment can be hired. See below for more about the climb itself.

Naro Moru

Mount Kenya and the Aberdares also have several fishing camps for the ardent trout fisherman, including Thiba, Thego, Kimakia and Kiandongoro. At these places you must bring your own food, bedding and equipment, but there are hot and cold water, beds and cooking equipment. Further information from the Fisheries Dept, Box 40241, Nairobi. Some trips to Mountain Lodge include a luncheon stop at Thego Fishing Camp.

Fishing

Nanyuki, a railhead and small town mainly dedicated to farming and safaris, is the real stepping-off point for the Northern Frontier and the place to climb Mount Kenya from. It lies 6,400 ft up at the foot of the mountain and smack on the Equator. In fact the Silverbeck Hotel there claims the Line runs across its bar floor, so that you can be in the northern hemisphere while your drinking companion is in the southern. A couple of miles out is the renowned Mt Kenya Safari Club (Grade A, bookings Box 54546, Nairobi). Calmly luxurious, it has its own golf, airstrip, bowls, swimming pool, sauna baths, riding, fishing, displays of traditional dancing—the lot in fact. Peacocks wander on the terrace and the 200 staff have looked after many of the world's famous people. Temporary membership is available.

Nanyuki

The Sportsman's Arms (full board, single Shs. 60/– a day) is the base for visiting the Secret Valley Lodge (Bookings Box 3, Nanyuki) a two storey treehouse run on the same lines as Treetops. It is in the Secret Valley, up in the bamboo forest on the slopes of Mount Kenya, and you are almost certain to see leopard there, as well as elephant, buffalo and rhino.

Secret Valley

Several safari organisers have their headquarters around Nanyuki, among them John Alexander (Box 20127, Nairobi); David and Anton

Allen (Box 174, Nanyuki); Julian McKeand (Box 35, Nanyuki), who does camel safaris in the Northern Frontier District; and photographic safari specialist Digby Tatham-Warter (Box 250, Nanyuki).

Climbing Mount Kenya

How much of a challenge you make of climbing Mount Kenya depends largely on you. By merely walking to the top hut you are getting higher than Mont Blanc in the Alps, and the trek up through the forest and across the moorland is rewarding, though not for anyone who gets short of breath at normal altitudes. There are the same animals as the Aberdares, plus some of the most lovely birds in Africa—malachite sunbirds, golden-winged sunbirds, yellow francolin and the Abyssinian long-eared owl, and the same curious "old man's beard" hanging ghostlike from the trees. In four days you can "conquer" the easiest peak, Lenana, 16,355 ft, and see the glaciers, lakes and giant vegetation of the mountain slopes.

The twin peaks of Batian (17,058 ft) and Nelion (17,022 ft) are a stiff test for experienced mountaineers. They are actually hard cores of rock exposed by erosion of the crater rim, for Mount Kenya, like Kilimanjaro, is an extinct volcano. More information can be had from the safari firms, or the National Parks or the Mountain Club of Kenya (Box 45741, Nairobi). The Mountain Club publishes the excellent *Guide Book to Mount Kenya and Kilimanjaro* with full details of climbing routes and sections on the geology, flora and fauna of the mountain. There are several huts, a tent camp and a self-help lodge available to climbers who cater for themselves (Lodge bookings to Naro Moru River Lodge, Box 18, Naro Moru.)

Meru

Embu

Round the eastern side of Mount Kenya lies the Meru and Embu country. The direct road from Nairobi to Embu forks off the Nairobi–Nyeri road at Sagana. Its 131 km (82 miles) are now all tarmac and there is an all-weather murram road from Embu to Meru, which although it may some day be tarmaced, remains one of the most tortuous stretches of the Safari Rally. At Embu there is a pleasant small hotel set in well kept gardens called the Izaak Walton Inn—named after the famous angler because of the fine trout fishing in the mountain streams here (Grade C, Box 1, Embu).

The Meru district is densely populated and mainly known for fishing, rare butterflies and Meru oak, one of Kenya's most beautiful indigenous woods. Plus, of course, the Meru National Park. There is a small museum in Meru town, with displays of traditional dress and ornaments.

Meru National Park

From Meru town to Meru National Park is 78 km (49 miles). The road, though dirt, can be negotiated by any kind of vehicle. Meru National Park's 821 square km contain an excellent system of roads and tracks, plus several airstrips. By the Meru National Park runs the Tana river, 440 miles long, which winds through the Northern Frontier down to the Indian Ocean near Lamu. Up here its banks attract wildlife like jam does flies and a motorboat is available for river exploration. There is plenty of game in the Reserve, including reticulated giraffe and Grevy's zebra, lion, leopard, black rhino, elephant, buck and a great variety of birds. A herd of white rhino, previously extinct in the area, was introduced here from South Africa; they are now breeding successfully and may be seen at their compound near park headquarters or else feeding in the vicinity, escorted by a ranger. The altitude of the Park varies from about 1,000 ft along the Tana to 3,400 ft in the Nyambeni foothills. West of Leopard's Rock there is a wilderness area with no roads, while the site of Elsa's camp, used by the Adamsons, is on the Ura river in the south of the Park.

Lodges

There are several kinds of accommodation available in or adjacent to the Park. The Meru Mulika Lodge (Grade A, bookings Box 30471, Nairobi) has comfortable rooms in rondavels, a water hole where game comes to drink and a swimming pool. A few miles away is Leopard Rock Safari Lodge, a self-service lodge with ten *bandas* (huts), each with private bathroom. The only thing you need take is your own food. Charges are Shs. 44/– per adult per night, and bookings can be made through AA Travel, Box 14982, Nairobi. There is a public campsite (Shs. 5/– per person per night) near park headquarters.

Kora Game Reserve

Adjacent to Meru National Park, on the south of the Tana River, is the newly established Kora Game Reserve, created largely through the effort of George Adamson, who still lives there, rehabilitating tame lions for release here. Kora is about 500 square miles of remote, dry bush country with game similar to that found in Meru National Park. There are tracks negotiable by ordinary cars, but no accommodation as yet. Camping is permitted.

The Northern Frontier, Marsabit, Lake Turkana

The vast semi-desert that stretches north of the Highlands and the Tana River to the frontiers of the Sudan, Ethiopia and Somalia is more than half of Kenya. Approaching it from Nanyuki you find yourself abruptly at the top of a 1,500 ft escarpment. Spreading away below is a reddish landscape out of which occasional mountains rise, hot, barren, save for scrub, and fiercely exciting. In it rivers mysteriously disappear, as the Uaso Nyiro does into the Lorian Swamp, or run for miles beneath the sand. Elephant are coated with red dust. The nomads herding their goats and camels and fat-tailed sheep to water holes remind one of Biblical scenes, though most of them are Moslems. Only well-organised safaris survive here and a number of safari firms now specialise in arranging them. Two are Ker, Downey and Selby (Box 41822, Nairobi) who have taken Britain's Prince Charles on safari, and Abercrombie and Kent (Box 20224, Nairobi) who have developed 8 to 10 day trek safaris by both hunting car and camel.

Indeed the north is one of Kenya's main tourist development areas, with a circuit taking in Meru, Samburu, Marsabit, Lake Turkana (Rudolf) and Maralal. The road from Isiolo to Marsabit is corrugated but passable in all but very wet weather, while Marsabit to Lake Turkana remains difficult if not impossible in ordinary cars. Thus as yet this magnificent country remains accessible only to people who are prepared to make special plans.

Sixty-four km (40 miles) north of Nanyuki on the main Isiolo road is the turnoff for Wilderness Trails (Bookings, Box 20139, Nairobi), a luxury tented camp on a ranch, part of which is a private reserve, with Grevy's zebra, greater kudu, reticulated giraffe, elephant and many birds. There is also a prehistoric site.

Samburu Game Reserve

Of course the main reserve round here is Samburu, north of Isiolo. It is countryside of fairly dense bush but equally thick with game. As well as elephant, buffalo, rhino, Grevy's zebra, and reticulated giraffe you can see leopard, cheetah, lesser kudu, eland, oryx, gerenuk, dikdik, impala, gazelle and waterbuck. Among the myriad birds are pygmy falcons, goshawks and sparrow weavers. The Samburu Lodge (Grade A, bookings Box 40075, Nairobi) built on the bank of the Uaso Nyiro river (pronounced Washo Nero) is as luxurious as any in Kenya, with a filtered swimming pool. At night leopards often come for bait hung in a tree across the river.

Isiolo and Shaba Game Reserves

A connecting causeway leads to the small Isiolo Game Reserve, where Buffalo Springs attract game, while close by is the new Shaba Game Reserve, still undeveloped. Both these have campsites.

The Samburu themselves are tall, handsome people, and their *moran* (warriors), decorated in red ochre, are every inch noblemen. The Samburu women adorn themselves superbly in coil upon coil of heavy bead necklaces.

Wajir

Tana River

The near desert north of Archer's Post, out of which rise such havens for game as the Matthews Range of hills and the Ndotos, is only sparsely populated by nomadic tribes like the Samburu and the Rendille. The trading posts are few and far between—which means the petrol stations are too! The towns can be counted on the fingers of one hand, and only Marsabit is really on a tourist circuit. Far over in the north east is Wajir, intriguing with its castellated and white-washed buildings, and once the home of an institution jokingly called the Wajir Yacht Club. Then there is Moyale on the Ethiopian border and Garissa down east on the Tana river. All have airstrips.

Garissa

Garissa, 380 km (236 miles) east of Nairobi on Kenya's greatest river, the Tana, is reached by road via Thika (roughly 5 hours). Only in 1976 was the first complete navigation of the Tana made. Lined by trees, it attracts myriad birds and many animals, not least hippo and crocodile. Way down on the river, near Hola, are two new reserves, the Arawale and the Tana River Primate Reserve (see Coast section below).

At the trading post of Garissa itself, a remarkable American missionary, Brother Mario, a one-time Detroit nightclub owner, began the Garissa Boys' Town for local Somali orphans. By irrigation they have made a fruit farm in the desert round the school and their Garissa melons are famous in Kenya.

Marsabit

Returning to the northern circuit, Marsabit, 277 km (172 miles) north of Isiolo, is completely different from the other northern outposts, not in the tin roofed *dukas* (local shops) of the town, but in their setting. Marsabit is a 5,593 ft volcanic mountain rising green and forested out of a black lava strewn semi-desert. The area is a National Park noted for its large tusked elephant, reticulated giraffe and leopard. In the early evening the game comes down to drink at the crater lakes. Ahmed, once the "king of elephants" is now dead—his replica stands at the National Museum in Nairobi. His successor, Abdul, is reckoned to have tusks weighing 150 lbs each. Marsabit Lodge (Grade B, bookings Box 30471, Nairobi) is by one of the craters. The township has an airstrip and is about 1½ hours' flying time from Nairobi.

Singing Wells

It is interesting to see now the tribes up here—Boran, Rendille and Gabra—adapt to the harsh environment. Camel trains are a common sight and it's worth having a guide take you to one of the "singing wells", the most colourful ones being at Sagante. The wells are deep so the Boran stand on scaffolds one above the other, chanting rhythmically while they pass up giraffe hide water buckets. Cows, goats and donkeys crowd around, anxious to drink.

Lake Turkana

Lake Turkana (formerly Rudolf) makes you feel you have walked into a *National Geographic Magazine* story. The lake itself, shimmering blue in the middle of a near desert, is savagely beautiful. Migrating wildfowl from Europe, cormorants, sacred ibis, egrets and other waterbirds flock along its shores, while pelicans fly ponderously above like flying boats on patrol. The lake is also curious. Three rivers flow into it, and none out. In fact 11 feet of water a year are taken off its 3,000 square miles by evaporation. Less explicable is why Nile perch grow to such a giant size here or indeed what geological upheaval separated the lake from the Nile aeons ago. The record perch is 375 pounds and there are also tiger fish and tilapia.

Loiyangalani Oasis

There is an oasis with an airstrip at Loiyangalani on the lake's eastern shore, where hot springs out of Mount Kulal run in a stream down to the lake.

The Oasis Lodge (Grade B, bookings Box 42475, Nairobi) is on the site of the fishing camp where Prince Philip and Gregory Peck have stayed. It is still possible to camp nearby. The adventurous can get here by road with Safari Camp Services' 7 day bus trip, coming up via Maralal. (Bookings, Bruce Travel, Box 40809, Nairobi) at Shs. 1,700/- return.

Close to the oasis live one of Africa's most curious tribes, the El Molo. They exist on fish, harpooned from log rafts, and the occasional hippo. They number around 100: as they did when Count Teleki discovered the lake in 1888, and are thought to be related to the Bushmen of the Kalahari Desert in southern Africa.

East Turkana National Park

Some 145 km (90 miles) north of Loiyangalani lies the new East Turkana National Park; 1,570 square km bordering the eastern shore of the lake. Besides a profusion of birds, there are herds of oryx, topi, waterbuck and other antelopes. The road from Loiyangalani to the park is still rough, although negotiable by four-wheel drive vehicles. Camping is possible with the permission of the warden whose office is at Alia Bay.

Koobi Fora

In the park at Koobi Fora is a site explored by Richard Leakey, director of Kenya's National Museum and the son of the late Dr Louis Leakey and Mary Leakey. The site has yielded important finds, including part of a skull about 2.8 million years old that may have belonged to the first known ancestors of modern man. The skull is known by its catalogue number, "1470". Visitors can see some of the other fossil finds in the area, including those of other hominids and of a three-toed horse.

Ferguson's Gulf

Across on the western side of the lake is a magnificent natural bird sanctuary at Ferguson's Gulf. You can stay comfortably at the Lake Rudolf Angling Lodge (Grade C, Box 509, Kitale), which provides facilities for fishing, while Eliye Springs (Grade C, Box 45, Nakuru) has slightly cheaper accommodation in bandas. There is an airstrip at Ferguson's Gulf, while by land it's a pioneering journey through Nakuru, Kitale and the government post of Lodwar, with its battlemented headquarters.

The Turkana

The Turkana themselves are as impressive as the Samburu or the Masai. Their men have their hair elaborately plaited and set with white feathers, like a coxcomb, while their necks are chokered with bead necklaces and their upper arms bound in rings of shining wire. They are nomads and almost worship their cattle. To them cattle are a man's intermediaries with his ancestors' souls, they are depended on for milk, for buying wives and for security in old age. One of the government's problems is persuading the Turkana to take them to market and exchange them for mere money.

West to the Great Rift Valley, the Masai Mara, Highlands and Lakes

Scenically one of the best ways to see the Rift and the Highlands is by railway. The line divides at Nakuru; one service then goes to Kisumu on Lake Victoria, the other through Eldoret to Kampala, the capital of Uganda. There are first-class coaches, sleepers, and restaurant cars, though inevitably it's slow, owing to the hills. But there remains much to be said for taking the train to Nakuru or Kisumu and hiring a car when you get there.

Limuru

The most pleasant road from Nairobi is not the main one, but the Limuru road which joins it a few miles short of the Rift. Both are tarmaced. Limuru itself, two thousand feet higher up than Nairobi, has a delightful country club and golf course. You can get an excellent meal at the Kentmere Club (telephone Kiambao 253), which has a delightful garden. Temporary membership, only necessary for one member of your party, is Shs. 10/–.

The Great Rift Valley

The first sight of the Great Rift Valley itself will remain with you for ever. Suddenly you come out of a thin belt of forest, round a corner and there, two thousand feet below you down a sheer escarpment, is the Rift, quite literally the greatest valley in the world. Its floor is tawny red in the drought, or a dusty green after the rains. Thirty miles away its further wall rises dark purple against the blue sky, a procession of clouds drifting across its peaks. Straight ahead stands the clear-cut cone of Longonot, 9,111 ft high, deep in whose crater wisps of steam eddy up from among the trees. Dozens of volcanoes erupted in the Rift, the greatest being Kilimanjaro; almost all are now extinct. The reason was that the valley is the result of two roughly parallel faults in the earth's surface between which, in an age before history, the land subsided and the earth's crust was weakened. The Rift stretches from Lake Baikal in Russia down through the Lebanon and the Red Sea to Rhodesia. In Kenya it hold Lakes Turkana, Baringo, Bogoria (Hannington), Nakuru, Elmenteita, Naivasha and Magadi. A western branch of the Rift forms Lake Tanganyika, and also Lakes Albert, Mobutu (Edward) and George.

Along the escarpment African boys sell a variety of souvenirs including attractive woven baskets though sometimes you have to fight off their attentions. At the bottom is a chapel built by the Italian prisoners of war who made this road in 1942–44. Just before Longonot, near Kijabe, a road turns to the left to Narok, the Loita plains and the Masai Mara Game Reserve. Near Kijabe, and signposted is Mayer's ranch, where you can see displays of Masai dancing every afternoon in a traditional *manyatta* (encampment). The great white space age aerial dish on the plains not far away transmits telephone calls by satellite to Europe and the United States, an extreme contrast to the life of the Masai, though it would be wrong to assume the Masai are backward. Many of their children now go to universities.

Masai Mara Game Reserve

The Narok road leads to the magnificent country round the Mara river, one of the most striking and unmolested areas in all Kenya, ranging from open plains to riverine forest and supporting a great variety of plains game and birds, including all the big five and roan antelope. Most years the great wildebeest migration from the Serengeti across the border in Tanzania reaches the Masai Mara around July or August (see page 90) and the "clowns of the wild" often remain until December. The Game Reserve itself covers about 1,813 sq km (700 sq miles) and because it is such an outstanding place for game viewing, now has several lodges and camps.

Lodges

Keekorok Lodge (Grade A, bookings Box 40075, Nairobi) is the oldest and most atmospheric, in an area where hunters used to bring their clients to shoot lion. It has a pool and airstrip. From here you can pursue the most spectacular way to see game, namely in a hot air balloon, but it is expensive. This can also be arranged from the newer Mara Serena in the western part of the Mara, near the dramatic Ololol escarpment and the Mara river. The Serena Lodge (Grade A, bookings Box 48690, Nairobi) is architecturally inspired by Masai huts and has a hippo viewing platform, while rick hyraxes run around below the verandah. Unbelievably these small creatures are not rodents but are related by bone structure to the elephant.

Camps

Among several tented camps in the Mara, the best known is

Governor's Camp (Box 48217, Nairobi). Justifiably expensive, it's on a site further north along the river, where colonial governors used to camp, on the edge of the Lorogoti plain. There is an airstrip nearby. Further west, just outside the Reserve on the Talek river, is Fig Tree camp (bookings through World Travel Bureau, Box 41178, Nairobi), while another luxury camp is Abercrombie and Kent's Kichwas Tembo (Box 20224, Nairobi) over in the east near the Narok road. Finally private camping is possible near the park gates, by application to the Warden.

Further west from the Mara the land slopes down to the shores of Lake Victoria, dealt with at the end of this section. Meanwhile we return to the main road up the Rift Valley to Naivasha and Nakuru.

Naivasha

Naivasha is a township famed for the magnificent yellow-barked acacia thorn trees that grow in the neighbourhood—nicknamed "fever trees" because it used to be believed the trees caused malaria. Actually, the trees grow along watercourses where mosquitoes can breed. The town is 85 km (55 miles) from Nairobi. The Bell Inn (Box 85) serves meals and snacks, while the newer Malaika Hotel (Box 149) situated on a hill overlooking the town and the lake, offers full-board accommodation for Shs. 225/– double. Round the south side of Lake Naivasha (6,187 feet above sea level) is the Lake Naivasha Hotel (Grade B, bookings Box 40075, Nairobi) where all rooms have a private bathroom, there is a swimming pool, and punts and motor-boats for fishing and bird-watching can be hired, along with fishing tackle. The management offers a bottle of Scotch for the biggest fish caught each month. Four miles further along the South Lake Road is the less expensive Safariland Club (Box 72), which offers similar facilities, and also has a camping site. Around the lake are a number of small marinas which also offer facilities for boating, fishing, camping, water-skiing and so on including Fisherman's Camp near Hippo Point.

Marinas

Crescent Island

From any of these places, you can arrange a trip to Crescent Island, a bird and wildlife sanctuary where over 350 bird species have been recorded and Thomson's gazelle, waterbuck, monkeys and other wildlife live. A stroll with a pair of binoculars makes a very pleasant few hours. The lake shore is fringed by papyrus swamps inhabited by Goliath heron, storks, and warblers and everywhere can be seen coot, purple gallinules and lily trotters.

Hell's Gate

About three miles beyond the Lake Naivasha Hotel, a poorly sign-posted track just next to the small power station goes to Hell's Gate Gorge, which is locally known as Njorowa. The cliffs are the breeding ground of cultures, Verreaux's eagles, augur buzzard and thousands of swifts. The star attraction, if it can be found, is the lammergeyer, a bearded vulture rare in East Africa. Gazelle and sometimes eland and buffalo graze in the open valley beyond the gorge. If you penetrate far enough down here you will find natural steam jets and great clefts in the earth full of red volcanic rock, a reminder of the thinness of the earth's crust in the Rift. Hell's Gate indeed! There is also a small crater lake south-west of the main lake.

East from Naivasha the road up to the Kinangop Plateau leads on to the Park Road over the Aberdares to Nyeri (see page 47). A board at the turn-off in Naivasha states whether this road is open.

Lake Elmenteita

At Gilgil a tarmac road branches off up the side of the valley to Nyahururu. Following the Nakuru road you pass Lake Elmenteita, a soda lake that is a nesting place for pelicans, greater flamingoes and sacred ibis. There are also many remains of early man near here. Gamble's Cave near Nakuru was occupied by Stone Age man from about 30,000 BC. Visitors must apply first to the Centre of Pre-history, telephone Nairobi 22648. There are other pre-historic sites at Hyrax Hill, just outside Nakuru, and at Kariandusi, near Gilgil.

Nakuru

Nakuru itself is the centre of a large farming area which holds an annual Agricultural Show in June. There are two hotels, the Stag's Head (Box 143), and the Midland (Box 908). Both are graded B. One good buy in the town is a locally made sheepskin jacket, made to measure if you want. But the great attraction is the Lake Nakuru National Park, with its fantastic agglomeration of lesser flamingoes. These are estimated to number between 1½ and 2 million and make the lake shore seem pink, while 389 species of other waterbirds have been recorded.

Lake Baringo

If you have time it is worth going on to Lake Baringo, dramatically set in a branch of the Rift, north of here. The Lake Baringo Lodge is on the western side. However the lake is way off the main road which continues to the Mau Summit, one branch then going to Kisumu, the other to the pleasant farming town of Eldoret.

Kitale

Mount Elgon National Park

Kitale, at the foot of Mount Elgon, is a pleasant township rather similar to Eldoret with one hotel, and is the stepping-off point for a visit to the Mount Elgon National Park 48 km (30 miles) away. This lies between 8,000 and 14,000 ft, being a strip of 65 square miles running up the side of the mountain, the 14,178 ft summit of which is in Uganda. The Park has herds of buffalo, elephant and eland, inhabiting the forests and moorland slopes, splendid bird life and caves filled with bats, into which you can climb if you've got the nerve.

Mount Elgon can be climbed; for information contact the Mountain Club of Kenya (Box 45741, Nairobi) or see Peter Robson's book *Mountains of Kenya*. A high-altitude day climb through the moorlands is possible. Mount Elgon Lodge is a converted farm house with beautiful views over the Charangani Hills. Charges are Shs. 385/- double, full board. (Bookings Box 30471, Nairobi.)

Saiwa Swamp National Park

The Pokot tribe, whose men wear conical ivory lip plugs and decorate their hair with ostrich feathers, inhabit the area north of Kitale. You should stop 16 miles north of Kitale at the Saiwa Swamp Park, a small tract of swampland created as a reserve for the sitatunga, a rare antelope with spiral horns and stripes on the flanks that stays up to its knees in water most of the time and feeds on swamp vegetation. The park has no entrance fee and no roads; you walk to the swamp and climb tree platforms for game viewing.

Beyond Saiwa lies the town of Kapenguria, north of which is the dramatic Kongelai escarpment, an excellent bird watching spot. The road then leads on to Lodwar and Lake Turkana (see above).

The main Nakuru to Kisumu road passes a hotel at Molo, the Highlands (Grade C, Box 142, Molo) just before the Eldoret turn-off. Golf, tennis, riding and trout fishing are available and the country is wonderful. There used to be a pack of foxhounds here, though they actually hunted buck.

Beyond Molo you toil up over the Mau Summit. In the Mau Forest live a few of the extremely shy Wanderobo tribe, diminutive honey-hunters, who dress in skins and are Kenya's oldest inhabitants.

Kericho

Over on the other side of the summit is Ceylon in Africa, Kenya's great tea estates, centred on Kericho. The Tea Hotel here (Grade A, Box 75) is one of the best up-country hotels in East Africa. Tennis, golf and trout fishing are available and visits to a tea estate can be arranged. Remember that you are 6,000 ft above sea level and that it is cool at night.

Nyanza

Kakamega Gold

From Kericho the road brings you down to the Nyanza area and Kisumu, Kenya's port on Lake Victoria. The area round the Kavirondo Gulf here has seen a lot of mining. In the 1930s Kakamega, north of Kisumu, enjoyed a real old-style gold rush. Prospectors poured in from the U.S.A., Canada and South Africa. It looked like another Yukon. Hotels and nightclubs sprang up. But the dream collapsed and today there are no hotels and the mines are flooded, not worth reopening, though there is still some gold in them. However, near Kakamega there is the only forest in Kenya that is West African in character. It was separated from the rest of the West African forest by the drying up of the climate and the resulting replacement of trees by grasslands. Kakamega Forest has many types of birds, butterflies, insects, trees and shrubs not found elsewhere in Kenya. There is an unfurnished do-it-yourself rest house which can be booked through The Forester, Box 88, Kakamega.

The Luo

The Luo, Kenya's second largest tribe, farm the fertile land around Lake Victoria, fish its abundant waters and are astute businessmen. You will be served their lake fish in many parts of Kenya.

Kisumu

Kisumu is a busy commercial centre, though with some tourist attractions. The New Kisumu Hotel (Box 1690) is graded C while the air-conditioned Sunset Hotel (Box 215) is newer and is on the southern edge of the town near Hippo Point, appropriately named, beyond which is the village of Dunga, where every morning at dawn scores of fishing canoes run out under sail. Canoe races are traditional events. Normal sailing is available, so is golf. As well as the railway and daily air services from Nairobi, the town used to be the starting point for steamer voyages around Lake Victoria, which may be resumed.

In the neighbourhood are three ornithological sites: a heronry, a sanctuary for ibis, and a pelicanry. The best season for the first two is April to June. The latter, 96 km (60 miles) south at Oyugis, is best seen August to March. Also south, near Homa Bay, is the Lambwe Valley National Park, 46 sq miles of grassland and bush known for two special antelopes: Jackson's hartebeest and roan antelope. There are interesting prehistoric remains in this area too, particularly on the islands in Lake Victoria, which can be reached from Homa Bay.

Lambwe Valley National Park

The Kamba, Masailand, Amboseli Reserve, Tsavo Park

All of the Mombasa road's 485 km (301 miles) are tarmac. From Nairobi it leads out south-east past the National Park and on to the Athi Plains. It then skirts Kitui passing close to Machakos District, where the Kamba of Wamunyu practise their traditional wood carving. These craftsmen work sitting on the ground, with legs outstretched, whittling the wood with a hoe-shaped blade called an *ngomo*. The Kamba are Kenya's largest tribe and are also noted for being fine soldiers, and for spectacular dancing, spiced with fantastic gyrating leaps in the air and double somersaults.

The Kamba

Masai warriors

Broadly speaking the Kamba live north of the Mombasa road, and the Masai south. Indeed Masailand stretches from Nairobi to Tanzania the frontier divides the tribe—and westward to the Mara river described in an earlier section. The Masai have a legendary warrior tradition. The young *moran*, or warrior, athletic, aquiline-featured, his hair braided and thickened with red ochre, looks like a figure off a classical Greek vase as he stands leaning on his spear. His traditional stories are folk epics of lion hunts and he grows up believing that they are told only at night because if you waste time telling stories during the day you will go blind. Like the Turkana *moran* he lives by and for his cattle. The traditional Masai food is blood mixed with milk and curdled, the blood itself being expertly taken from a vein in a cow's neck without injuring the beast. Most Masai still live nomadically, building their *manyattas* wherever there is grazing. A *manyatta* is a group of low huts made of dung and surrounded by a thorn fence, inside which the cattle are brought at night for protection. You see them everywhere in Masailand, often abandoned because the herdsmen have moved on to new pastures.

Olorgesaillie

Deep down their part of the Rift Valley, just north of Lake Magadi, the extraordinary soda lake that is a major mineral resource, is Olorgesaillie. Here the famous anthropologist Dr Leakey discovered a prehistoric living site of the Pleistocene period, about 400,000 years old. There is a field museum and a simple rest camp, where you have to bring your own food, bedding and crockery. Enquiries and bookings should be made to the Curator, the National Museum, Box 40658, Nairobi. Olorgesaillie is 64 km (40 miles) from Nairobi on the partly paved road out past the Ngong Hills to Magadi, in a truly primeval landscape. Curiously flamingoes, avocets and other birds like the lake's brackish water.

West of Magadi is the splendid scenery of the Nguruman escarpment, running from lowland plains to mountain forest, with fine views down the Rift and an abundance of wildlife: not a bad place to camp.

Amboseli National Park

The main road from Nairobi to Arusha runs pretty well parallel to the Rift, up on the plains with the snows of Kilimanjaro ever present in the distance. Kajaido, though giving its name to the district, is only an assembly of tin-roofed *dukas* (local shops). Then just before the Tanzanian frontier you come to the Amboseli National Park's Namanga gate, 165 km (103 miles) from Nairobi. The Namanga Hotel (Grade C, bookings Box 30471, Nairobi) is like a game lodge in character and has a swimming pool. The other entrance to the park is at Lemi Boti, reached by a rather rough road from Emali on the Nairobi–Mombasa road.

Before the 1,235 sq miles of the Amboseli Game Reserve had their most vital 146 sq miles designated as a National Park the Masai shared with central area the area with the game which they seldom kill for meat, being preoccupied with their cattle. But there was not pasture for both and under an agreement with the government the Masai moved out after a pipeline had been constructed to bring them water outside the park. In times of drought, however, they might return. Lake Amboseli, though blue on maps, is a dry bed of soda most of the year and even produces mirages like a desert. A road cuts across it. But the Loginya and other swamps remain wet, attracting large herds of elephant and buffalo who migrate to them during the dry season. Amboseli protects herds of kongoni, eland, oryx, wildebeeste, gazelle and zebra. Of the cat family there are caracal, cheetah, civet cat, leopard, lion and serval cat, though without a guide you may never find them. The rhino, formerly famous, have been all but poached to extinction.

The landscape is dominated by Mt Kilimanjaro, as the cover of this book shows, though the snowcapped summit is often in cloud and is most likely to be seen early or late in the day.

Accommodation

At Ol Tukai, where the park headquarters is located, are the Amboseli Lodge (Grade B, bookings Box 20211, Nairobi), with a waterhole attracting wildlife, and also the cheaper Amboseli Chalets. Thirdly there are self-service bandas, bookable through the Wildlife Conservation and Management Department. The most comfortable place is the Amboseli Serena Lodge (Grade A, bookings Box 48690, Nairobi). At night meat is tied to a post on the lawn and jackals, hyenas and the ferocious little honey badger come to feed.

East of Amboseli is Abercrombie and Kent's luxury tented Kilimanjaro Camp (Box 20224, Nairobi). Since this is outside the park, and the wildlife does not recognise the boundary, escorted game walks and nocturnal drives are possible here.

The Mombasa Road

We now return, metaphorically, to the route to the coast—the Mombasa road. Like other roads in East Africa it has mileage boards marked with abbreviations of place names—thus Msa stands for Mombasa and Nbi for Nairobi. The more relaxing way between the two cities is still by air or on the comfortable overnight train. But scenery and the Tsavo Park being on the ground, and only visible in daylight, the road route has great compensations, including hotels en route. Half way to the coast, is the Tsavo Inn (Grade B) at Mtito Andei, with its own swimming pool, opposite the main entrance to Tsavo National Park West. Indeed you can hear the lions roaring while you are safe in bed at night. Equally it makes a good lunch stop.

Mtito Andei

Thirty-nine km (24 miles) before Mtito Andei, at Kibwezi, there is a turn-off for a self service lodge, the Bushwhackers Camp, which is cheap. Bring your own food. You can aiso camp. Back on the main road is the refurbished Hunter's Lodge at Makindu (see map).

Tsavo Park

The Tsavo National Park is roughly kidney shaped and its 8,000 sq miles are bisected in the middle by the Mombasa road. For administrative convenience the part north-east of the road is called Tsavo East, with a headquarters near Voi and the part south-west of the road is Tsavo West, with Wardens' offices near Mtito Andei. Overall this famous National Park covers a vast section of the two hundred miles of thorn scrub, spiked with the bulbous trunks of baobab trees, that separate the tropical vegetation of the coast from the great central plateau of the African continent. It was the endless thorn scrub here that kept the peoples of the interior remote from western civilisation for so many centuries. Try walking through it as the early missionaries did and you will soon understand. It has various names—the Nyika, which means thorn country, the Nyiri Desert, the Taru Desert. Much of the year it is burnt dry and dusty by the sun. Then overnight the rains transform it. Convolvulus flowers burst out white and purple, grass seed germinates, the bushes are suddenly green. Explorers hated it for the very reason that makes it a major attraction today—the game. "Full of wild beasts, such as rhinoceros, buffaloes and elephants," the German missionary, Rebmann, noted in his diary on May 11, 1848. Indeed it is full, though overgrazing has depleted the vegetation in parts and the elephant population is now only an estimated 15,000 to 20,000. They are fairly accustomed to cars now, but if you meet one on the road drive cautiously.

Tsavo's lions are noted for their ferocity. J. H. Patterson's book, *The man Eaters of Tsavo*, describes how they obstructed the building of the railway in the 1900s by the simple expedient of eating the linesmen. Nowadays they seem to prefer the eland, kongoni, impala, klipspringer, kudu, reedbuck, waterbuck and Burchell's zebra which also inhabit the Park. Humans are apparently an acquired taste, like Pernod or sauerkraut.

Tsavo West

In Tsavo West, which is rather hillier, the volcanic area where the Mzima Springs and other waters rise attracts most species of game. The Springs, 40 km (25 miles) from Mtito Andei, form a series of clear pools. An observation tank in the top pool enables you to watch hippo and crocodile from underwater. Other major viewing places are at the Kangethwa dam, the Kilaguni waterhole and an artificial spring right in front of the Kilaguni Lodge verandah, where a sign reads "Animals are requested to be quiet whilst guests are drinking, and vice versa."

There are three lodges near Mzima Springs. Kilaguni Lodge (Grade B) is justifiably renowned. It has its own airstrip, swimming pool and reasonably priced Game Park tours. Bookings by African Tours and Hotels Ltd, Box 30471, Nairobi. East of the Springs is the Ngulia Safari Lodge built on the edge of the Ndawe escarpment with a magnificent view over vast plains. There is a swimming pool in the grounds, and an airstrip a short distance away. It is graded A, bookings as for Kilaguni. Nearby is Ngulia Safari Camp, on a site "haunted" by lions which leave no footprints, according to local legend. You must bring food and bedding. Kitani Lodge, west of Mzima Springs, is also self service, though bedding can be hired and there is a food shop. Both are cheap and you book through AA travel, Box 14982, Nairobi. There is also a campsite near the Chuyulu gate.

Chuyulu Hills

The Chuyulu hills to the north are one of the most recent volcanic ranges in the world. The road to Amboseli crosses a black lava flow from Shetani volcano which is only 250 years old, while a loop road offers an excursion into the hills themselves, up into forest 7,000 ft above sea level. Around the lava you may see klipspringers, antelopes whose hooves are adapted to bouncing around rocks.

As the map shows, Tsavo West stretches far down south of Mzima Springs into a part known as the Serengeti Plains, which are being increasingly opened up. The name is confusing. The plains are nothing to do with the great Serengeti National Park 200 miles away in Tanzania—just similar country. Mt Kilimanjaro rears up into the clouds here and there are lodges near the Voi–Moshi road, notably the Taita Hills and Salt Lick Lodges, both graded A and run by Hilton Hotels, Box 30624, Nairobi. At Salt Lick five hundred or so buffalo come to the floodlit waterhole most nights.

Along the road from Voi to Moshi is a meandering railroad line built by the British during World War I to bring supplies to the front against the Germans, who had colonised Tanganyika. The British chased the German commander, General Paul von Lettow-Vorbeck and his troops all the way through what are today Tanzania, Mozambique, Zambia and back into Tanzania without capturing them; they finally surrendered in 1918 on hearing of the Kaiser's capitulation in Europe. The story is well told in Charles Miller's *Battle for the Bundu*. The high ground north off the Tsavo river was one British defensive line against the initial German attack and astonishingly traces of the war are still to be found there, including empty whisky bottles!

Lake Jipe

Close to the Tanzania border, south of the road, is Lake Jipe, a paradise for water birds, among rarities being pygmy goose. There is a self service camp and a motorboat can be hired.

Lake Chala

Similarly close to the frontier, but north of the road and reached by a turn-off before Taveta, is the surprising Lake Chala, a circular crater lake full of crocodiles. You can descend by a footpath.

Taita Hills

Voi

The Taita Hills, near Voi, are steep and fertile, while the Taita people are friendly and it can be fun to explore their villages and markets. The hills are also the source of many kinds of semi-precious stones. Voi itself is only 1,800 ft up and appreciably hotter than Nairobi, though the nights are cool.

Tsavo East

Tsavo East is less hilly than Tsavo West, apart from the dramatic line of the Yatta Plateau escarpment which rises almost parallel to the Mombasa road. Beyond this escarpment, to the east, is a seemingly endless expanse of low lying semi-desert, spiked with thorn bushes, most of which you can only visit by special permission of the Park Warden. All roads north of the Galana river, which cuts across Tsavo East, are closed to the public. Lugard Falls and Crocodile Point on the river are worth a visit, though the best places to see animals are unquestionably Mudanda rock and Aruba. The former is a great hump of rusty coloured rock overlooking a huge waterhole making a natural amphitheatre. It is signed off the park road between the Manyani gate and the Voi gate and you can leave your car to climb up. The Voi Safari Lodge, along this road, is ingeniously set on the Worsessa look-out hill above the plain and a small waterhole. It is graded A, bookings to Box 30471, Nairobi. The Aruba dam, pretty well in the centre of this part of the park, is a successful man-made watering place for game. The self-help Aruba Lodge is run by the Ministry of Tourism. Finally, five km outside the Sala Gate on the Galana river, is the Crocodile Tented Camp, haunt of the reptiles. It is on the road to Malindi and is owned by the Eden Roc hotel (Box 350, Malindi).

Further up in Tsavo East on the bank of the Athi River, a tributary of the Galana, is the more exclusive Cottar's Camp. It's expensive, has the real feel of a safari camp, its own airstrip and runs its own hunting cars for game drives. We saw many elephant, rhino, buffalo, waterbuck, giraffe, warthog, various antelope—and no other cars—on our trip along the river banks. Bookings through AA Travel, Box 14982, Nairobi. You must have a pass or accommodation voucher before entering this part of the Park.

Remember you must be into your lodge by 7.00 pm (1900) which means being at the park gates considerably earlier. Also note that midday temperatures down here reach 90° to 100°F, which is too hot for both animals and sightseers—so early morning and early evening are the times for game viewing.

Galana Game Farm

Outside the eastern boundary of the Park is a highly imaginative $1\frac{1}{2}$ million acre game ranching scheme, largely American financed but run by Kenyans. Called the Galana Game Farm, it has a permanent lodge on the Galana river, and 9 private airstrips. Bookings through M. J. Prettejohn, Box 20139, Nairobi.

The Coast

The Kenya Coast is a series of long bays between coral headlands, punctuated by occasional river creeks. It is lined with waving palm trees, mangoes, casuarinas and gorgeously flowering hibiscus, oleander, frangipani and bougainvillaea. The beaches are great sweeps of white coral sand, while about half a mile out in the Indian Ocean runs a coral reef protecting almost the whole length of the shore from sharks, and creating a series of lagoons where the water is crystal clear and an enormous variety of tropical fish feed on the coral. The skin-diving—known locally as goggling—rivals the Caribbean's, and so does the big game fishing. It would make a superb backdrop to a James Bond story.

All down the coast lie the mouldering remains of the Arab Sultanates established here from about 900 AD onwards. Surprisingly their tenure only officially ended on Kenya's and Zanzibar's Independence, when the Sultan of Zanzibar, subsequently deposed, surrendered his legal right to the 10 miles wide "coastal strip". The British had recognised this claim throughout their rule of the two countries. The Arab colonisers exported ivory, Ethiopian gold, leopard skins and rhino horn from the interior, and also slaves, a practice that has left its mark on Arab–African relationships today, even though the slave trade was put down by the British in the 1870s. However, Arab culture has also imparted a well-mannered, unhurried aura to the coastal way of life. Indeed Arab intermarriage with the Giriama, Bajun and other African coastal tribes produced the Swahili people and their language, which has spread to become the lingua franca of all eastern Africa. Links with Arabia are maintained by the dhow fleets that ply down to Mombasa and Dar es Salaam on the north-east Monsoon, the Kaskasi, in January; and return to the Arabian Gulf and India in May on the south-east Monsoon, the Kuzi.

Swahili

Climate

The coast's climate is tropical. February and March are the warmest months (86°F mean maximum temperature) but really it's the relative humidity of 75% that one notices, so April and November, when the wind is slack, can seem the hottest. The cooler season from July to mid-December is when many local people think the coast climate is at its best. It's advisable to take anti-malarial pills: see also General Information. A useful local publication on the coast is Leslie Brown's *East African Coasts and Reefs*.

Mombasa

Kenya's second town, the largest port on this coast north of Durban, is strictly speaking an island, connected to the mainland by the Makupa Causeway. It's an island that has seen plenty of history. Almost certainly known to Phoenician sailors who circumnavigated

Opposite top: Rare albino zebra in a herd on a game ranch below Mt Kenya. Photo Richard Cox
Bottom: Lion. EAA photo

Africa in 500 BC, it is identifiable as the port named Tonike in a sailing guide to the Indian Ocean published in Alexandria in AD 80. The first European to land, Vasco da Gama, the famous Portuguese navigator, met with a hostile reception from the Arabs here in 1498 and sailed on to Malindi. The Portuguese occupation that followed was only routed by the Arabs in the eighteenth century, and the town remained a key possession of the Sultan of Muscat's Empire until in 1832 he transferred his court to Zanzibar. The opening of the railway in 1901 revived Mombasa as the Gateway to East Africa, and the train remains an excellent way of getting to Nairobi. You go overnight in a sleeper, well fed in the restaurant car, and saving a night's hotel bill. Alternatively Kenya Airways run flights each way every day and offer excursion fares.

The Old Town

The most fascinating part of Mombasa is the Old Town that lies between Makadara Road and the old harbour (see map). Its narrow streets are overshadowed by high houses with elaborately carved ornamental balconies. Itinerant Arabs sell coffee from traditional long-beaked copper pots. Oriental music drifts out from the shops of moneylenders, goldsmiths, tinsmiths, tailors, makers of sweetmeats and other traders, mostly Asian. Oriental mosques and temples, like the new Jain Temple, its pillars and domes as white as icing on a gargantuan wedding cake, jostle for space with bustling African markets and stalls. Everywhere there is hustle, life and a multitude of languages. Mombasa, in fact, has the same cosmopolitan feeling as Hong Kong, Singapore and other world ports. Both old and new parts deserve a visit.

Dhows

To find the old harbour go down Nkrumah Road, past the interesting old Treasury Square with its monuments, and past Fort Jesus. The street becomes Mbarak Hinawi Road and leads past alleyways to the tiny Government square and the Customs Landing Stage. Between January and March you can be shown round the dhows. For a few shillings a boatman will row you out to one. The *Nahoda*, the dhow captain, will usually welcome a visitor with coffee, black and bitter, from a tiny cup, and may well have fine carpets and Arab chests for sale among his cargo. Dhows and other boats sail up the coast to Lamu and with some discomfort you could take passage in one.

The shops around Government Square offer carpets, arab chests, brasswork and carvings. Nearby is Yusuf Jaffer's perfume shop, where exotically named scents line the walls. They are made without alcohol, which means they do not evaporate (and persist for weeks if you don't bathe!).

It's worth paying a few shillings for one of the Old Town's numerous self-appointed guides. Get him to show you the cliff west of Government Square, down through which a flight of steps leads to a cave with a well, where the slaving dhows used to take on water secretly.

Opposite top left: Malachite kingfisher. Photo John Karmali
Top right: Fish Eagle
Bottom: Flamingoes on Lake Nakuru. Photos Richard Cox

He should point out the pure Arabs in their beaded hats and embroidered cloth gowns; the Hindus; and the Swahili men who wear a long white robe, or more often a brightly printed length of cloth wrapped round the waist like a skirt and known as a kikoi, while the women wear kangas, wrapped round beneath the armpits and falling to mid-calf length. Kangas are brighter and gayer than kikois and are a real fashion bargain. They are cheap, infinitely varied and, like the useful straw sunhats made locally, you can get them all along the coast. Women of the Moslem faith modestly drape themselves from head to toe in an all-enveloping black garment called a buibui. Cynics, however, claim the buibui remains popular because it doesn't matter what the wearer has on underneath, or if she has done her hair.

Kikois
Kangas
Straw hats

Fort Jesus

At the north corner of the Old Town stands the Portuguese castle, Fort Jesus, weathered and immense. Its building began in 1593. A century later the Arabs took it in 1698 after a 24-month siege, though they lost it again. The Portuguese finally left in 1729. Today its guns still command the harbour, looking out beyond English Point, but the Fort itself houses a comprehensive museum dealing with the culture, architecture and history of the coast. Fort Jesus is open daily and a detailed booklet about it is on sale at the entrance. Among many interesting things there are two cycads, fern-like plants which have been in existence for 200 million years, and relics being salvaged from a Portuguese warship which sank near the fort.

Beneath the battlements a path leads along the shore where you can watch local fishermen casting their nets, and giant iguana lizards scuttling among the rocks. This path is one of the best places to photograph the Fort, which is not an easy subject.

Ivory Room

On Mvita road, near Treasury Square, is the Wildlife Conservation and Management Department's ivory room, where elephant tusks, rhino horns and other game trophies taken from poachers or dead animals are displayed. The room is open on weekdays.

Shopping
Information

The rest of Mombasa is a modern, thriving city, basing its prosperity on Kilindini Harbour. One of the main shopping streets is Moi Avenue, formerly Kilindini Road, leading to the port, past the famous arch of giant elephant tusks (metal not ivory!) close to which is the Information Bureau (Box 85072, telephone 25428). Round here and in Digo Road and Nyerere Avenue you can buy wood carvings, curios, brass-bound Arab chests of all sizes, Indian saris, sandals, straw hats and baskets. Teadin's and Kenrocks, both in Moi Avenue, are good for gemstones. Biashara street near the Municipal market (itself worth a look) selling African fabrics and also Moslem caps, called *kofias* in Swahili. A visit to the African market in Mwembe Tayari, off Jomo Kenyatta Avenue, is amusing. You can buy kikois, kangas, gay shirts of African design and beaded hats, not to mention all the necessary herbs and relics for witchdoctoring. Medicines and photographic goods can be bought from chemists in Moi Avenue. There are several good small shops for men's clothing, shoes and touris curios, and a Home Industries shop which displays locally made goods.

Hotels

The best and most modern hotel on Mombasa island is the Oceanic (Grade A, Box 90371), a mile from the centre with a swimming pool and dancing nightly in an air-conditioned restaurant. It provides free transport to its own beach at Bamburi. The other hotels in Mombasa mostly have air-conditioned bedrooms and are centrally situated, but none has a beach of its own. These include the Manor (Grade B, Box 84851) in Nyerere Avenue; the Hotel Splendid (Box 83686) on Msanifu Kombo Street and the Castle (Box 84231) in Moi Avenue, all moderately priced. Because there are no beaches on Mombasa island itself the various beach hotels on the mainland to the north and south of the island are possibly more popular for those who like swimming. These are multiplying so rapidly that it is only feasible to mention a few. In the high season from August to March it is essential to book well in advance. Much cheaper rates are available in the off season.

Nyali

The Nyali Beach Hotel, Grade A, Box 90581 (four miles across the Nyali Toll Bridge) is the best known of the beach hotels. It has open-air dancing and a bar beside a new swimming pool, as well as a bar on the beach. It runs its own buses to Mombasa and meets trains (as do most of the other hotels up and down the Kenya coast). Just north of Nyali Beach is a more expensive rival, the Mombasa Beach Hotel (Grade A, Box 90414), is on a low cliff overlooking the sea and has shops, a grillroom and a pool.

Sailing

Golf

Most hotels can arrange sailing and big game fishing. Otherwise a place to hire boats is the Bahari Club, near Nyali bridge (Box 90413, telephone 471316). There is a golf course near the Oceanic Hotel and another in Nyali. A new bridge across the creek is being opened in 1980.

Restaurants

Mombasa has few good restaurants. About the best, both for atmosphere and food, is the Tamarind on the Nyali side of the creek looking towards the old harbour. In the town the Mistral and the Capri have continental cuisine, for Chinese food try the Hongkong and for Italian the Bellavista. The Manor Hotel is reliable, while the grillrooms of the Oceanic, Nyali Beach and Mombasa Beach hotels have a nightclub atmosphere. The International Casino is in the Oceanic.

Nightlife

As to nightlife, it's a matter of taking the rough with the smooth. The beach hotels have bands or discos, though the New Florida in Mama Ngina Street is about the only nightclub *per se*. Or you could spend a sailor's night out at the Sunshine or the Casablanca.

Theatre

There is one theatre, the Little Theatre Club, on Mnazi Moja Road which provides a good evening's entertainment. Temporary membership is available. There are several cinemas.

Taxis

The yellow banded taxis are municipally licensed, however always negotiate the price beforehand. Fares in town should be Shs. 10/– to Shs. 15/– and to the Nyali area hotels around Shs. 35/–. To go further out, say south to Diana Beach would be Shs. 200/–.

Car Hire

Reliable car hire firms include United Touring Company, Archers,

African Roadways, Avenue Motors, Pollman's and Kenatco Transport. A favourite, and cheap, car to hire is the open mini-moke.

Tours

Local tours and game lodge bookings can be made through many agents. Bunson Travel Service Ltd (Box 84965) is deservedly well known, as are Mackenzie Dalgety Ltd (Box 90120), Etco Ltd (Box 90631) and Kearlines Ltd (Box 84675), all of them are in Moi Avenue. Thorn Tree Safaris (Box 81953) in Nkrumah Road have an enterprising variety of tours, including dhow trips around Lamu and the islands. The most popular game viewing tours are to the Tsavo National Park and to the Shimba Hills Reserve, both easily accessible. These are often done by air charter (for firms see Safaris section).

Hospitals

Mombasa has excellent hospitals, the one most used by Europeans being the privately run Katherine Bibby Hospital, close to the sea. Hotels can provide the names of doctors.

Consuls

The following countries maintain Consuls in the town—Austria, Belgium, Denmark, Finland, France, German Federal Republic, Great Britain, Greece, India, Italy, Netherlands, Norway, Sweden and Switzerland.

North of Mombasa, Kilifi, Malindi and Lamu

To reach Kilifi and Malindi you drive out over Nyali bridge, where the old Portuguese harbour light towers still stand, and turn left past Freretown. This was a Church Missionary Society settlement of freed slaves, whose descendants run their own District Council and keep up their old church. Mombasa was a great centre for missionary work and there is a handsome memorial to the German missionary Dr Krapf on English Point, who with Rebmann founded the first Christian Mission in East Africa at Rabai, west of Mombasa, in 1846.

Past the Nyali beaches and hotels, already mentioned, the road runs behind Shanzu and Bamburi beaches, a strip of coast which ends at Mtwapa creek 14 km (9 miles) north of Mombasa. Among many hotels devoted to package tours, two are the Whitesands (Grade B, Box 90173, Mombasa) and the smaller, less expensive Bamburi Beach (Grade C, Box 83966, Mombasa). Unlike some which are overhwelmingly Italian or German, these two keep a balance of nationalities and are popular with the English. Don's Inn at Shanzu is good for seafood.

Mtwapa creek is crossed by a toll bridge. Just on the other side are an aquarium and an excellent restaurant, Le Pichet. On the creek F. G. MacConnel and Co organise deep sea fishing, goggling and water skiing, as does the Mtwapa Marina Aqua Sports Centre.

Arab Ruins

Beyond Mtwapa creek there is a long stretch of sandy beaches up to Kilifi creek 57 km (36 miles) from Mombasa. Shortly after the bridge is the turn-off to Nyumba la Mtwana, meaning "the slave master's house", the ruins of a 15th century mosque, an Arab pillar tomb and other buildings. These are reminders of the many centuries during which the Omani Arabs dominated the coast and there are many such remains all the way up to Lamu. If you are interested, go to the Fort Jesus museum which has a large scale map, indicating them all, together with photographs. Equally the "Kenya Coast" map, published by the Survey of Kenya, marks them all but without descriptions. They can be overgrown and hard to find.

The beaches have various hotels and cottages to rent, while at Kanamai is a youth hostel and camping site run by the National Christian Council of Kenya.

Here you are in Giriama country and in the villages you will see Giriama women wearing short, white, flouncing skirts, fluffed out by vast bustles of coconut fibre. At Vipingo there are large sisal estates. Incidentally travel up to Malindi can be cheap, since there are several Peugeot taxi firms which operate like minibuses and charge very reasonably.

Kilifi

At Kilifi, 57 km (36 miles) from Mombasa, is the Mnarani Hotel (Grade B, Box 14, Kilifi), a big game fishing establishment with its own airstrip, jetty and facilities for water-skiing, sailing, goggling, scuba diving, and underwater photography, as well as fishing. The hotel is on the south side of Kilifi creek, which is safe for swimming and which offers one of the most spectacular birdlife sights in Africa. This is the evening flight of hundreds of carmine bee eaters, tiny but splendidly coloured birds who spend the day feeding inland, then return to a small mangrove island just before sunset to roost. You can hire a motorboat from the hotel to watch this and will see herons, egrets and many other waterbirds on the way.

Crossing Kilifi creek involves a free car ferry. Close to it is a serpentinum with hundreds of snakes. The main part of the village is on the north side, past which the tarmac road runs through to Malindi. Sixteen kilometres (10 miles) south of Malindi are the fascinating ruins of Gedi, an Arab colonial city of the 15th century, rescued from the jungle, excavated, and now preserved as an historical monument. The unique golden rumped elephant shrew lives among the ruins, whilst there is much birdlife in the nearby Jilore Forest Reserve.

Gedi

Watamu

By Gedi is the turn-off to the growing resort of Watamu, which has one of Kenya's few National Marine Parks, part of a National Reserve stretching from Mida Creek up to Malindi. You can swim or water-ski freely, but not collect any seashells. The goggling is superb, especially in the coral garden just inside the reef by Turtle Bay. For this, however, you must pay a park entrance fee of Shs. 20/–. Equipment, and glass-bottomed boats can be hired from Ocean Sports Ltd (Box 340, Malindi) whose shop and informal bar and restaurant are right on the beach. Theirs is some of the best food north of Mombasa, while their rooms, in thatched bandas, are excellent. The Seafarers Hotel (Box 274) is next door, while there are two massive package tour hotels in the vicinity, the Turtle Bay Hotel (Box 40503, Nairobi) and the Watamu Beach (Box 300, Malindi). As at Malindi, there are

Turtle Bay

frequent fishing competitions, boats and tackle can be hired and enthusiasts stand with binoculars on the shore identifying the fish recognition pennants that fishermen fly when they have landed a catch. These are yellow for shark, black for tunny, light blue for marlin green for bonito and white for kingfish or barracuda.

Mida Creek

Near Watamu, within the National Reserve, is Mida creek, one of the best places for bird and marine life on the entire coast. Carmine bee eaters roost here and in March/April and November/December hundreds of species of migrating shore birds pass through. Near the mouth of the creek are Tewa caves, partly underwater, where giant groupers (up to 800 lbs) and rock cod can be seen close to.

Malindi

Malindi, despite considerable recent expansion, is still a delightful small resort. It has almost everything one could want; a few Arab ruins, shops, an attractive old village with tall whitewashed houses and quiet shadowy streets leading to the sea, where there is a real beachcombing atmosphere. The bay runs in a wide sweep of sand beach on which a break in the reef lets the rollers in (but not the sharks) so you can surf ride. During November there are fishing contests as part of the annual Malindi Sea Festival, while in February, when the marlin and sailfish are running, the International Bill-fish Competition takes place, with participants from all over the world. For serious fishing Malindi has several firms—notably I. Rooken Smith's Malindi Sports Fishing. For goggling and marine life you want to visit Silversands—where there is also an aviary of exotic birds —or the Malindi Marine National Park. This is out to the south round Casuarina Point and, like Watamu, has magnificent coral gardens.

Marine National Park

Malindi has four good hotels, mainly tied to major German tour operators—there is even a German language newspaper. The most sophisticated hotel, with English connections, is the Sindbad (Box 30). Lawfords (Box 20) is a banda type of beach hotel, very relaxed with frequent beach barbecues. The other two are the Blue Marlin (Box 54) and the Eden Roc (Box 350). All have swimming pools and there is a discotheque playing somewhere every night of the week. A couple of miles south is the completely different Driftwood Club (Box 62) cheap, not taking package tours, with simple chalets, dancing under the moon, small boats and a qualified scuba-diving instructor.

Shops

Curio shops have boomed in Malindi, the best is Nafisi's Store with its genuine Arab silver and Lamu chests. The Rose Boutique, by the East African Airways office, is excellent and there are chemists, a bookshop and so on. The town has a resident European doctor.

Golf

For relaxation there is horse riding and a 9 hole golf course. You can manage perfectly well without a car, and bicycles are popular, unless you want to make long excursions. Several firms hire out cars. Kenya Airways run two flights daily from Nairobi, or you can use the cheap Peugeot taxis service which operates between Malindi and Mombasa. For local tours, consult United Touring Co (Box 365),

Tours

Southern Cross Safaris Ltd (Box 33) and Kingfisher Safaris (Box 29).

The obvious local trips are to Watamu, already described, and to Mambrui, 13 km (8 miles) a small fishing village of the Bajun tribe, with an old Arab mosque and its attractive new replacement. Further on you could go to Ras Ngomeni, where beachcombers find a paradise of tide-shaped driftwood, but you need four-wheel drive. Offshore there is an Italian–American rocket launching platform.

Robinson Island

Further on, reached by a turn-off from the road to Garsen, is Robinson Island, signed at some 20 km north of Malindi. You then drive 7 km to the shore, where there is a car park—and a boat. The island has a seafood restaurant in a beach hut. Lunch is Shs. 85/– including the boat trip and the season is August to April.

Garsen

Garsen itself is a small town on the Tana River, populated by Somali, Orma and Pokomo people. From here the murram road goes on to Lamu via a ferry, but it can be impassable in the rains. Near Garsen is a heronry, where breeding birds can be seen from May to September.

Tana River Primate Reserve

A diversion up-river from Garsen, turning left before the ferry, takes you to Wenje (58 km, 36 miles) and the Tana River Primate Reserve, created in 1973, an area of riverine forest, in which two rare species of monkeys survive, the red colobus and the crested mangabey. There are also rhino, oryx, topi and buffalo. Not far from Wenje, on the river bank, is the Baomo lodge, which charges Shs. 550/– per person full board inclusive of game drives. Canoe trips on the river show you hippo, crocodile and a profusion of birds. Wenje has an airstrip and Thorn Tree Safaris (telephone Mombasa 311970) arrange flying tours.

Arawale Reserve

Lamu

Further up the Tana is the new Arawale Game Reserve, designated to safeguard the Hunter's antelope, but still undeveloped. Now to Lamu, which with the sister islands of Manda and Pate, has been inhabited for a thousand years. Lying 130 km (80 miles) north east of Malindi by air, but 138 miles by road, Lamu has few 20th century houses and is reminiscent of Zanzibar. Various city states within the archipelago dominated each other in turn, being defeated in wars which reputedly would be interrupted if the tide brought in a big run of fish. Today Lamu has a relaxed and friendly atmosphere, whilst continuing to practise traditional crafts, such as produce the town's elaborately carved doors. On the waterfront mangrove poles lie awaiting shipment to Arabia, where they are still used for building because of their imperviousness to white ants. Dhows lie at anchor —Lamu dhows originally became famous as the "sewn boat", the *mtepe*, literally sewn because the people were suspicious of iron. Today fine model dhows are made for sale, as are traditional carved wooden plates and silver jewellery.

Two good books on Lamu are *An Historical Guide to the Lamu Archipelago* by Esmond and Chrysee Martin and *Lamu Town,*

Museum a *Guide* by James de Vere Allen, who established the museum, a veritable jewel of a place. The prize exhibits are two brass and ivory ceremonial horns, or *siwas.*

Hotels Lamu island has two Grade B hotels. Petley's Inn (Box 4, Lamu) is on the waterfront, while the Peponi (Box 24) is out on the unspoilt Shela beach. A third, the Ras Kitau Hotel, bookable through Archer's, Box 40097, Nairobi, is on a fine stretch of beach on Manda Island, on another part of which is the airfield. Cars are not allowed on Lamu and the best way to arrive is by air from Malindi.

Dodori Reserve A short way north of Lamu on the mainland is the new Dodori National Reserve, still undeveloped and inaccessible without four-wheel drive. Elephant, greater kudu and topi are among species here, while hippo can be seen at Kibokoni.

South of Mombasa, Diani Beach

The south Kenya coast is deservedly coming into its own. The fine white coral beaches here are mostly better than those north of Mombasa and the natural delights are swimming, goggling and big game fishing, though there is less marine life along the reef, not least owing to the depredations of shell and coral souvenir sellers. Although you have to cross Mombasa harbour on the Likoni ferry, which runs every ten minutes, you are then on a good tarmac road.

Just south of the ferry at Likoni is the enlarged Shelly Beach Hotel (Grade B, Box 80030, Mombasa), a pleasant place to go for a drink or

Dhows lying off Lamu

a meal. The reef is more interesting here than further south, though the swimming is not so good. Specimens you can expect to find in the clear greeny-blue water around the reef include brittle stars, a kind of starfish whose arms break off but grow again, and a variety of conch shells, among then the rare foot-long giant spider conch. Along Shelly beach there are also a children's resort centre and a camping site.

Shimba Hills Reserve

Between the village of Waa and Tiwi a road branches off inland to the village of Kwale and the Shimba Hills Reserve, known for its handsome sable antelope. The main gate is 17 km (10½ miles) from the turn-off and takes half an hour, going through the village of Kwale, where you are 1,200 ft above sea level. It's better not to take the earlier entrance, before Kwale, as it does not lead into the main circuits of the reserve, which are well signposted. The area is largely thick forest, inhabited by many animals including the small forest elephant. However we only saw herds out on the Lango plains near Giriama point, where the trees give way to rolling parkland along an escarpment. This is one of the few Reserves where you are allowed out of your car, but forest elephant have a reputation for ill-temper, so keep your distance. Camping sites are available (ask at the gate) but there is no lodge. All the beach hotels arrange day tours.

Tiwi

Along Tiwi beach, as further down the coast, there are beach cottages to rent at anything from Shs. 120/– a day for two bedrooms in simple style, to Shs. 500/– for luxury with servants included. There is no one agent, so the best plan is to book through one of the major Nairobi tour operators, such as UTC.

Tiwi beach is separated from the celebrated Diani beach by the estuary of the Mwachema river. On the south side, close to the sea, is a well preserved ancient Persian mosque in a grove of giant baobab trees. Persian, Arab and Portuguese ships all used the estuary for shelter if they could not reach Mombasa. A word of warning, however, do not walk here or anywhere away from the hotels either alone or carrying valuables. There have been many robberies.

Diani Beach

Diani beach, a magnificent five-mile stretch of white sand runs down to around a group of cottages called four twenty south after its latitude. A tarmac access road, signposted off the main road before Ukunda, serves a growing number of beach hotels, largely devoted to Germans, Swiss and Italians. About the most attractively designed is the Leopard Beach (Grade A, Box 34, Ukunda) though English speaking visitors might feel more at home at the Trade Winds (Grade C, Box 8, Ukunda) or the Two Fishes (also Box 8). All the hotels have discos or bands, arrange car hire, run buses to Mombasa and so on. A taxi to the city costs Shs. 200/– and to the airport Shs. 230/–.

By the side road to the Trade Winds stands an extraordinary baobab tree estimated to be 500 years old and with a girth of 21.69 metres (71 ft 2 ins). This giant specimen of a tree you often see in the coastal region is protected. Cashew nut trees are also common down here while in the nearby Jadini forest you will find innumerable butterflies, birds and monkeys. Look out specially for the black and white colobus monkey, with long white hair round its head and shoulders.

Big game fishing

However the real big game attractions down here are out in the Indian Ocean, where black and striped marlin, sailfish, barracuda, shark, tunny, five-fingered jack, kingfish, wahoo and bonito cruise in the almost unexploited deep water beyond the reef. The main Diani fishing expert, with several boats and full tackle, is John Bland (Box 47 Ukunda, telephone Diani Beach 2087), who operates from the Jadini Hotel. Other boats are run by Nomad Safaris, who have a luxury tented camp and *makuti* thatched restaurant on the beach near the same hotel. Costs are around Shs. 165/– per hour per boat. Count on at least four hours. John Bland also hires out diving equipment, has a glass bottomed boat for viewing the reef, and organises parasailing on the beach and clay pigeon (skeet) shooting.

To continue down the coast you must return to the main road at Ukunda. Pending much talked of new developments, there is little noteworthy except fine beaches near Gazi and on Funzi bay until

Shimoni

some 66 km (40 miles) from Mombasa you reach a sign for Shimoni. The side road leads to a coast village near which is the famed Pemba Channel Fishing Club (Box 54, Ukunda). Though graded D for its accommodation, and very reasonably priced, its *raison d'être* is that the offshore Pemba Channel offers some of the finest fishing in Africa, from which many record catches have come, especially marlin. A boat for four for 7 hours costs up to Shs. 1,300/–. Boats can also take you to goggle (ie snorkel) among the coral gardens of four

Kisiti Marine Park

reef islets which constitute the Kisiti National Marine Park. They are offshore of a larger island, Wasini, which lies opposite Shimoni and has a restaurant run by Thorn Tree Safaris. A dhow makes the short trip across for lunch.

The main road goes on to Tanga in Tanzania, but at the time of writing the frontier was closed.

Useful Facts—KENYA

Banks

Banking hours are 9 am to 1 pm Monday to Friday and 9 am to 11 am on Saturdays. The principal banks are Barclays Bank International, Kenya Commercial Bank, Commercial Bank of Africa, and the Standard Bank Ltd. Banks in Mombasa open 30 minutes earlier.

Currency

The Kenya shilling is tied to the US dollar and is officially at par with Tanzanian and Ugandan shillings—see General Information. In practice it is a "harder" currency than the others.

Customs Duties

See General Information section.

Diplomatic Representation

There are Kenyan diplomatic missions in Addis Ababa, Bonn, Cairo, Kinshasa, Lagos, Lusaka, London, Mogadishu, Moscow, New Delhi, New York, Paris, Stockholm and Washington.

Countries with diplomatic missions in Nairobi include—Australia, Austria, Belgium, Brazil, Bulgaria, Canada, People's Republic of China, Colombia, Cyprus, Czechoslovakia, Denmark, Ethiopia Finland, France, German Federal Republic, Ghana, Great Britain, Greece, Hungary, India, Iran, Ireland, Italy, Japan, Korean Republic, Kuwait, Lesotho, Liberia, Malagasy Republic, Malasia, Malawi, Netherlands, Nigeria, Norway, Pakistan, Poland, Rumania, Rwanda, Somalia, Spain, Sri Lanka, Sudan, Sweden, Switzerland, Swaziland, Thailand, Turkey, UAR, USA, USSR, Yugoslavia, Zaire and Zambia.

Immigration

All visitors must have a Visitor's Pass which can be obtained from Kenya Embassies abroad or on arrival, subject to the possession of a valid visa. However visas are not required by nationals of Commonwealth countries, Denmark, Ethiopia, Italy, Norway, San Marino, Spain, Turkey and Uruguay.

Public Holidays

Public holidays, when banks, shops and Government offices close, are Christmas Day, Boxing Day, New Year's Day, Good Friday, Easter Monday, Labour Day (May 1), Madaraka Day (June 1 or the following day if June 1 falls on a Sunday), Kenyatta Day (October 20), Jamhuri (Independence) Day (December 12). Additionally the Moslem holidays of Id-ul-Fitr and Id-ul-Azha are observed by all people of the Islamic Faith.

Weights and Measures

Kenya has converted to the metric system.

TANZANIA

LAND OF KILIMANJARO

THE GREAT SERENGETI PLAINS
It contains the greatest and most spectacular remaining concentration of plains game in Africa ... on a scale which has no parallel anywhere else in the world!

MAGNIFICENT MOUNT KILIMANJARO
Tanzania's pride and a longstanding attraction for tourists on leisure and those on business.

SERENGETI
NGORONGORO
MT. KILIMANJARO
LAKE MANYARA

THE NGORONGORO CRATER
The second largest extinct crater in the world ... it is unique ... it is in Tanzania.

LAKE MANYARA ... A BIRD WATCHER'S PARADISE
Witness the remarkable sight of thousands of pink flamingos on the shores of lake Manyara.

ZANZIBAR

ZANZIBAR ... THE ISLAND OF SENSATIONS
Make your visit to East Africa real and complete ... visit Zanzibar ... an exotic pearl of Tanzania coast. The spice island has more to offer than its famous cloves.

MAFIA

MAFIA ISLAND ...
A SPORTSMAN'S AND FISHERMAN'S PARADISE
Mafia's vast expanses of practically unfished waters offer goggling, deep sea and bottom line fishing. The Mafia island lodge designed as a fisherman's haunt, stands amidst tall palms to provide you with a peaceful atmosphere.

For more information
contact T.T.C. today
P.O. Box 2485. Tel: 27671-4
Telex: 41061. Cable: Tantour
Dar Es Salaam Tanzania

Tanzania Tourist Office,
43 Hertford Street,
London, W1Y 7TF,
England.
Tel: 01-499 8951

Lions taking their siesta near Lake Manyara

Tanzania

The Mainland – formerly Tanganyika

The Country

The highest, the longest, the deepest, the most vast, the most numerous, all these adjectives can be applied to the many attractions which Tanzania, the largest of the three East African countries, offers to the visitor. The first recorded mention of it occurs in the *Periplus of the Erythraean Sea*, a detailed mariner's guide to the East African coast dating from the first century AD. This document refers to the island of Menouthias, probably Zanzibar or Pemba, and the mainland town of Rhapta, possibly Pangani or another town in the Rufiji river delta.

A number of settlements were made on the coast by Arabs and possibly Persians, the most famous and best preserved being Kilwa in the south. Bagamoyo, a small town just north of Dar es Salaam, was the favourite jumping-off spot for the nineteenth-century explorers, including Livingstone, Stanley, Burton and Speke, as well as being the start and end of the great slave caravans from the interior.

Within Tanzania's borders lie Africa's highest mountain, Kilimanjaro; its deepest and longest freshwater lake, Tanganyika; and the largest Game Reserve in the world, the 16,000 square mile Selous, as well as the finest concentration of wildlife in the world. The country's 900,000 square kilometres are the home of over 120 different tribes, the largest being the Sukuma. The total population is 17.5 million (1978), including a small percentage of Arabs, Asians and Europeans.

Tanganyika became a sovereign state on December 9, 1961. Previously it had been a German colony from the 1880s until 1916, and after that a United Nations Trusteeship administered by Britain. It became a republic within the Commonwealth exactly a year after *Uhuru* (Swahili for independence), under the Presidency of Dr Julius Nyerere, who was the country's first Prime Minister. Then on April 27, 1964, a union was formed between Tanganyika and the islands of Zanzibar and Pemba (see under Zanzibar), taking the name of the "United Republic of Tanzania". Mwalimu Dr Nyerere became President of this new state.

A new capital city is currently being laid out at Dodoma, for completion in the mid-1980s, but Dar es Salaam will remain the commercial centre.

The most convenient way of describing the wide variety of attractions for visitors is to divide the mainland into the areas listed in the Contents. First, however, we give information on the National Parks and on hotels, lodges, and transport.

National Parks and Game Reserves

President Nyerere's Arusha Manifesto of 1967 was a landmark in African game conservation, "Wildlife is an integral part of our resources," he said. Today three per cent of the country's area is devoted to National Parks. A full list is given in the index and all are mentioned in the text. The most famous ones are:

ARUSHA NATIONAL PARK

116 sq km (45 sq miles). Combines three formerly independent sanctuaries—the 1½ mile wide Ngurdoto crater, the Mount Meru crater, and the Momella lakes, scene of many films. Elephant, rhino buffalo and smaller game. Open all the year. See page 86.

LAKE MANYARA NATIONAL PARK

318 sq km (123 sq miles) in the Rift Valley south-west of Arusha. Noted for its 340 species of birds and for the lions that take their siestas in its trees. Open all the year. See page 88.

THE MIKUMI NATIONAL PARK

1295 sq km (500 sq miles). In the coastal belt 288 km from Dar es Salaam. Plentiful cross-section of game. Open all the year. See page 101.

THE NGORONGORO CRATER

The floor area of this fantastic 2,000 ft deep volcanic crater is 113 sq km. It is the centre of a 8,290 sq km (3,200 sq mile) conservation area which is a pioneer experiment in reconciling the interests of wildlife and forests with the needs of the local Masai tribe. Large herds of plains game. See page 89.

THE SERENGETI NATIONAL PARK

About 14,760 sq km (5,700 sq miles) in Northern Tanzania. Contains the most spectacular concentration of plains game anywhere in the world. Open all the year. Lodges. See also pages 90–91.

Hunting

Entry fees to the National Parks are between Shs. 10/– and Shs. 20/– per adult per day for non-residents. Ranger guides are well worth hiring. In Tanzania's Parks and Game Reserves hunting is permitted from July to December under the control of Tanzania Wildlife Corporation (Box 114, Arusha), a Government-sponsored organisation which has been introducing special types of cheaper hunting safari as well as photographic and game viewing tours.

No special permission is required to travel in the Game Reserves which are administered by the Game Division of the Ministry of Natural Resources and Tourism. The entry fee is Shs. 20/– per 24 hours and ranger guides can be hired for Shs. 30/– a day. The use of campsites in the Parks and Reserves costs Shs. 40/– per night.

Hotels and Lodges

A chain of hotels and game lodges is run by the Tanzania Tourist Corporation, who run a centralised booking system through their Dar es Salaam office (Box 2485, telephone 27671/4, telex 41061). These hotels are indicated by (TTC) in the text. They maintain high standards. Prices at the time of writing (1979/80) ranged from Shs. 215/– to Shs. 275/– single with bed and breakfast and up to Shs. 385/– double. Lodges normally offer full board. There are special cheap low season rates at the lodges and beach hotels from April 15 to June 30. A hotel levy of 12½ per cent is included in these prices.

Other hotels, especially in provincial towns, often charge less and it is often possible to stay a night for Shs. 100/– or so. Addresses for booking non-TTC hotels are given in the text, but no prices since these are so subject to change.

Meals

The cost of meals varies widely. Outside Dar es Salaam and Arusha, menus are likely to be simple, except of course in the game lodges. A snack will cost up to Shs. 20/–, while a full meal in a good restaurant will be Shs. 50/– or more. Wine is obtainable and Tanzania has also started making her own Dodoma rosé and red.

Safaris and Transport

Air Charter

In addition to the scheduled services of Air Tanzania Corporation, the airline offers air charter, as do Tanzania Aviation Ltd, Tanzanair and Flight Service International, all based at Dar es Salaam.

Car Hire

Car hire is available in large towns, but seldom on a self-drive basis. However the cost of the driver is modest. Typical standing charges are Shs. 150/- a day plus Shs. 3.50/– per kilometre.

Buses

Extensive, cheap local bus services operate, but they are usually crowded.

Trains

Trains run on both the original railways system linking Dar es Salaam with Arusha, Mwanza and Kigoma, and the intermediate towns, while the Tazara railway from Dar to Zambia passes through Mbeya. Train tickets are cheap.

State Travel Service

Information

Whilst there are private safari firms and tour operators listed in the text, the major firms are the government owned State Travel Service (Head Office, Box 3100, Arusha), represented overseas by TTC, and Bushtrekker Safaris (Box 88, Arusha and Box 5350, Dar es Salaam). Hunting is organised by the Wildlife Corporation and its subsidiaries. For information on any of these consult the TTC, which has offices in London (43 Hertford Street, London W1Y 7TF), New York (201 East 42 Street, New York 10017: 8th floor) and in Frankfurt and Milan. The Head Office is Box 2485, Dar es Salaam.

Northern Tanzania, Arusha, Mount Kilimanjaro, Lake Manyara, Ngorongoro, the Serengeti

The north has often been described as a microcosm not just of Tanzania but of East Africa as a whole. Its scenery ranges from the vast, golden plains of the Serengeti to the snowcapped peaks of Mount Kilimanjaro, from wild bush country to neatly tended farms and plantations, from tumbling mountain streams to lakes pink from the flamingoes flocking round them, over rolling grasslands and through tropical rainforests. Among the people are prosperous African and European farmers, operating highly mechanised farms, peasant cultivators still using the primitive digging stick, pastoral nomads like the famous warrior tribe, the Masai.

The main attraction is, of course, the unsurpassed concentration of wildlife, the greatest in Africa. Almost wherever you go, even on the main highways, you can generally expect to see zebra, wildebeeste, ostrich and antelope. In fact, one of the most frequent road signs on the Arusha–Moshi road is "Danger—game area", illustrated by a leaping buck. Furthermore, visits to the incomparable Serengeti plains, Kilimanjaro, Lake Manyara and the Ngorongoro and Ngurdoto Craters can be made without strain in a short tour, since they are not far apart and the roads are good.

The Kilimanjaro International Airport at Sanja Juu, 56 km from Arusha, means that visitors can fly straight from overseas into the heart of Tanzania's safari country.

Climate

Northern Tanzania is a semi-temperate region with two rainy seasons a year, the long rains in April and May and the short rains in either October or November. Mean temperatures vary between 62°F. and 85°F. and there is frost and snow on high ground. The nights are cool. In the evenings, especially from June to October and during the rainy seasons, warm clothing is necessary. There is low humidity and the area is virtually free from mosquitoes, though mosquito nets are provided in some hotels.

Moshi

The 19,340-foot Kibo peak of Mount Kilimanjaro dominates Moshi, the life of which is closely linked with its mountain. The town is slightly larger than Arusha and is connected with Nairobi by rail, while a branch line runs from it to Arusha. Fine views of the snows of Kilimanjaro can be had from the Moshi Hotel, a large, airy hotel, built only a few years ago. There is a hairdresser in the hotel. Other, cheaper, places to stay are the Coffee Tree Hostelry and the Waremi Hotel, while the YMCA on the Moshi–Arusha road is very active. It has a swimning pool, tennis, and organises mountain climbs.

Tours

Land Rovers, minibuses and cars can be hired through the State Travel Service office in the Moshi Hotel. Reliable taxi services are operated by Aziz Taxis and Kilimanjaro Tourist Cabs. Air charters can be arranged through the travel agents, Emslies Ltd (telephone Moshi 2071). There are daily scheduled flights to Dar es Salaam by Air Tanzania.

Sport

The Moshi Club has an excellent golf course facing Mount Kilimanjaro, and there are tennis courts at the Gymkhana Club.

Moshi is the principal centre of the Tanzania coffee industry, and buyers from all parts of the world attend the coffee auctions there. It is also the administrative headquarters of the Kilimanjaro region, with almost one million people, mostly from the Chagga tribe, who run notable coffee-growing cooperatives. The Chagga are known for the beauty of their women. In fact they live at one end of what has often been described as Tanzania's "belt of beauty" stretching from the Chagga of Kilimanjaro to the Wabondei of Tanga, with the Wapere of Pare in between.

The Chagga

Mount Kilimanjaro

Many people are drawn by the magnificence and mystery of Africa's highest mountain, Kilimanjaro, lying only three degrees south of the Equator yet crowned with a permanent icecap. Often the only visible sign of the mountain is the great, snow-mantled shoulder of Kibo (19,340 feet) and the rugged crags of Mawenzi (16,890 feet) thrusting through a ring of cloud. The lower slopes and forests are hidden.

The Roof of Africa ranks among the highest volcanic mountains of the world, consisting of three separate volcanoes of different ages which have been welded into one great mass covering an area of 89 km by 61 km (56 miles by 38 miles). The oldest of these volcanoes, known as Shira (13,140 feet), is 12 km (7½ miles) to the west of Kibo, while Mawenzi is 28 km (17½ miles) to the east. Kibo is the youngest of the volcanoes.

Climbing Kilimanjaro

The first European to see Kibo was Johannes Rebmann in 1848 and the first to reach its highest point was Hans Meyer, in 1892. Climbers traditionally follow the route taken by most of the early explorers. They start from Marangu—which means "many waters"—where the Kibo Hotel (Box 102, Moshi) and Marangu Hotel (Box 40, Moshi) are situated, 5,000 feet up and 40 km (25 miles) from Moshi. Neither hotel is expensive.

In the area of the hotels there are plantations of coffee, maize and bananas. From here, climbers pass through the forest belt which ends at 10,000 feet. The first night stop is made at Mandara Hut (9,000 feet). Then they emerge on to the grasslands, near a volcanic cone known locally as "Kimangi Marangu"—"the small chief of Marangu"—which until not long ago was the site for rainmaking ceremonies.

The second stop is made at Horombo Hut (12,300 feet), near the start of the moorlands, glaciers and snow. Dotted around are giant lobelia and groundsel. On the third day, climbers reach Kibo Hut, 3,000 feet below the summit. The final ascent usually begins about 3 am so that Gillmans Point (18,635 feet) can be reached by about dawn, when there is a good chance of a clear view of the plains below and of the glorious sunrise behind Mawenzi.

One of the main attractions of the ascent of Kilimanjaro is that it does not require mountaineering experience, nor is any special climbing equipment needed for Kibo if the normal route is followed. The climb can be done by any normally healthy person, though considerable physical endurance is required over the five days needed to make the ascent.

Furthermore new routes up have been developed. For instance one can drive up to 15,000 ft on the Shira plateau, seeing the game in the National Park, then climb this "plateau route".

Mawenzi, however, should only be attempted by experienced mountaineers, using normal Alpine climbing gear. Advice for those wishing to attempt this climb can be obtained from the Kilimanjaro Mountain Club, Box 66, Moshi, the TTC, or the Director of National Parks (Box 3134, Arusha).

The mountain can be climbed in almost any month except during the long rains in April and May, but the best months are January February, September and October, when there are very often cloudless days.

Both the Kibo and Marangu hotels have been arranging safaris for more than 30 years. Costs are reasonable, with reductions for larger parties. This includes everything from guides downwards, though clothing, which the hotels can provide, is extra. The guides—absolutely essential for any safari—and porters are very experienced many having made more than one hundred ascents each.

Many places of interest can be visited from Marangu, such as the Ura river with its spectacular waterfalls and the Msumbe Spring, said to have been the home of a snail endowed with powers to revive warriors killed in battle. There are fine walks and visitors often find themselves being accompanied by friendly Chagga children, who like to invite their newfound friends into their homes.

Fishing

Fishermen can find plenty of sport in the mountain streams and trout rods can be hired from either of the hotels.

Kilimanjaro, the shining mountain, has its legends, like all other mountains, Kibo, pronounced by the old people "kiboo" as an exclamation of wonder, has a cave at its foot known as "Nyumba ya Mungu"—"The House of God".

The ancient stones of Umbo, situated at Machame and Uru, pillars about six feet above ground level and rammed deeply into the earth, are said to have been places of initiation. The story is told at Uru that they were put in by white people with broad shoulders who reached Kilimanjaro from the west in great numbers, searching for cedarwood and ivory with which to build and decorate the palace of their king, Semira. The story goes that they found cedar at Nanjara in Usseri near the eastern part of Kilimanjaro and that the king was actually Solomon and his palace the temple at Jerusalem.

Kilimanjaro National Park

A wide variety of animal life, including elephant, buffalo, rhino, eland, colobus and blue monkeys, and the rare Harvey's and Abbott's duiker can be seen in the 1,665 sq km (643 sq mile) Kilimanjaro National Park, which includes rainforest, moorland, tundra and the extraordinary giant plant growths that characterise the East African mountains. Like the Arusha National Park, this Park also protects vegetation and is used for research. Elephant have been seen at 16,000 ft, and the skeleton of a leopard found above the snowline, where there are known to be wild dogs too.

The tarmac road from Moshi to Arusha stretches across the Sanya Plains, and several species of game are usually seen on the drive between the towns. About 21 km (13 miles) from Arusha is the turn-off for the 116 sq km (45 sq mile) Arusha National Park, which includes the Momella Lakes, the Ngurdoto crater, and the former Mount Meru Crater National Park. The Park can easily be visited from Arusha in half a day, being only 45 minutes' drive from the town, and is open throughout the year. The best months are July to March.

Arusha National Park

Momella

Momella was formerly a game farm run from 1907 by the Trappe family. The remarkable Mrs Trappe was the first woman to become a professional hunter in East Africa. She made Momella into a sanctuary in German times and it became a National Park in 1960. It is a most beautiful area that includes five large lakes, tranquil and untypical of Africa, with a tremendous amount of birdlife and a heavy concentration of wildlife, including elephant, buffalo, rhino, giraffe, waterbuck, bushbuck, hippo and colobus monkey. It lies in a saddle between Mount Meru in the west and Kilimanjaro in the east and is spectacularly lovely on a clear day when the mountains can be seen high in the sky. The Mount Meru crater, an extinct volcano like Kilimanjaro, and its splendid surroundings is one of the best places to see colobus monkeys. Camping is permitted on Mount Meru at Shs. 40/– per night and you can book through the Park Warden (Box 3134, Arusha) or the State Travel Service.

Ngurdoto

Ngurdoto is a beautiful miniature crater about one and a half miles across and a few hundred feet deep. A ring road gives access to several vantage points on the crater rim but visitors are not allowed into the crater itself. The crater walls are heavily forested and on the well-watered floor almost every type of animal can be seen while the visitor picnics in glades on the wooded rim. It has been described by Sir Julian Huxley, the naturalist, as "a gem of a park".

The Arusha National Park is served by a rustic hotel, the Momella Game Lodge (Box 418, Arusha, radiocall Arusha 4648), originally a £30,000 set for the Paramount film *Hatari* and now rebuilt. It is partly owned by film star Hardy Kruger. On a nearby lakeside, Edward G. Robinson, as the illicit diamond miner, "Cocky" Wainwright, in *Sammy Going South*, built his hut and excavated his mine. The charges are from Shs. 220/– per person, full board. The lodge is an excellent spot for the person who does not want the strain of a strictly scheduled tour but prefers to have a base from which to make sorties into the surrounding areas as the mood takes him.

Mount Meru Sanctuary

Approximately 20 km (12 miles) from Arusha on the Arusha–Moshi road is the Mount Meru Game Sanctuary, where Dr von Nagy welcomes visitors to look around his natural zoo, open 1030 to 1900. The small Sanctuary Lodge (Box 659, telephone Usa River 43) charges around Shs. 195/– per person full board.

Returning to the tarmac highway, eight miles from Arusha there is a turn-off for Lake Duluti, a very pretty and fairly deep crater lake, where facilities for fishing, swimming and water-skiing are available at the Aqua Sports Club, run by the Arusha Gymkhana Club. A motor-boat can be hired. Tilapia fishing is free. A fair number of waterbirds can be seen on the lake and in the reeds.

Lake Duluti

Arusha is an old trading post that is now the most important town in Northern Tanzania, the administrative headquarters of its region, and the place where President Nyerere set out the famous "Arusha Manifesto" on game preservation. Its position on the Great North Road, halfway between Cairo and the Cape, is marked by a plaque near the New Arusha Hotel, and it is also the exact geographical centre of East Africa.

Arusha

Despite its recent rapid growth it has managed to retain a pioneering air, yet in places is paradoxically reminiscent of an English town. Behind it tower the slopes of Mount Meru. Its avenues are riotous with Nandi flame trees and blue flowering jacarandas, while brightly dressed Africans walk proudly through the busy streets, gathering in the markets, where they will usually consent to be photographed—for a small fee.

The Meru Hotel (TTC) is set in beautiful grounds half a mile from the centre of the town, overlooking Mt Meru. It has a swimming pool and is adjacent to a golf course. The Hotel Seventy Seven (TTC) is constructed like a village, with tennis, swimming and golf, while the New Arusha Hotel (Box 88, telephone 3241) also has a pool and gardens stretching down to the river. The less expensive New Safari Hotel (TTC) is famous. In the bar innumerable photographs of game, leopard skins, Masai shields and spears, and the long, shining copper bar top, create an atmosphere well known to Ernest Hemingway on his visits. The hotel was extended and modernised in 1978. Other places to stay include the Hotel Equator (adjacent to the New Arusha and under the same management), the attractively positioned Tanzanite Hotel (Box 3063, telephone Usa River 32) six miles out on the Moshi road, and the YMCA, which is behind the New Safari Hotel.

Hotels

Arusha has modern shops in the north of the town and a bustling, colourful bazaar, used mainly by the Asians and Africans. The range of shops, which are generally open between 8.30 am and 5.30 pm, include tailors, dressmakers, safari outfitters, shoemakers, chemists, photographic, gifts and curios. Carvings, skin articles and trophies are among the good buys. A safari outfit can be made in 24 hours for Shs. 600/– to 800/–. This would include two pairs of trousers, two bush jackets, two shirts and a pair of boots. Ready-made clothes are generally more expensive than in Britain, often by as much as 25% Meerschaum pipes, known throughout the world, are manufactured in Arusha and can be bought in the curio shops. The National Bank of Commerce has branches in Uhuru Road and Clock Tower Square,

Shopping

Hairdressers

and a Mt Meru branch downtown. There are good ladies' hairdressers in the Mt Meru Hotel, the New Arusha Hotel and in India Road.

Tour Operators

The main tour operators include the State Travel Service (STS) (Box 1369), Tanzania Wildlife Safaris Ltd, Subzali Tours and Safaris (Box 3061), Twiga Tours in Uhuru Road, and Emslies (Box 24). All these can arrange car hire. For official tourist information consult the STS.

Local sports include fishing for trout in the Temi River for which a licence has to be obtained from the New Arusha Hotel. There is a 9-hole golf course at the Gymkhana Club. Mountaineering enthusiasts can tackle Mount Meru (14,978 feet) in a day, starting from an advanced point reached by car, or they can do it at a more leisurely pace, taking three days. The climb is little more than a stiff scramble.

Safaris

Arusha is a major starting point for hunting and photographic safaris. In fact, 21 of the 29 species of game which may be shot by the holder of a general game licence are to be found in Northern Tanzania, while some of the rarer species are more easily obtained here than anywhere else in East Africa, especially the greater kudu and the sable antelope. The hunting season is from July to December. Complete hunting or photographic safaris are organised by Tanzania Wildlife Corporation (Box 602, Arusha) who handle taxidermy and the shipping of trophies. For prices write to them.

Lake Manyara National Park

Travelling westwards on an excellent road, your first stopping place would be the Lake Manyara National Park, 127 km (73 miles) from Arusha. This 318 sq km (123 sq mile) Park was once one of the most popular hunting grounds in East Africa because of its profusion of wildlife. Protection means it still contains a spectacular concentration for such a small area. The lions in Manyara have the habit of spending most of the day spread out along the limbs of acacia trees, ten to twenty feet from the ground, perhaps because it's cooler than being on the ground. The Park gates are open from 1600 to 1900 daily. It is well worth hiring a guide at Shs. 30/– per day, and best to start your visit early in the morning. You should see at least three of the "Big Five" in one day.

Manyara is as famous for its birds as its animals, and a small hide has been built on the edge of the soda lake for the use of enthusiastic birdwatchers. At certain times of the year, thousands of flamingoes form a solid line of shimmering pink, stretching many miles down the lake while among the 340 species are duck, waders, jacanas, egrets, ibises and storks. In the acacia woodlands and along the open grasslands are kingfishers, plovers, coursers, larks and wagtails. The Park includes five vegetation areas—from forest with high mahogany trees, through marshland, parkland and scrub to open grass plains. It has an airstrip by the hotel. This luxurious Lake Manyara Hotel (TTC) is perched on the edge of the Rift Wall with a magnificent view overlooking the park, and rhino, buffalo, elephant and other animals can be seen from the hotel grounds. There is a swimming pool, gift shop and beauty salon. Land Rovers and minibuses can be hired and guides are available at the Park gate. There are also campsites which can be booked through the Park Warden and a hostel at the gate.

Tarangire National Park

From Lake Manyara you can either return to the main road and head south or continue westwards to Ngorongoro and Serengeti. The first route which leads to Dodoma and Southern Tanzania brings you to the Tarangire National Park, an area of more than 700 square miles, designated as a Park particularly to protect rhino, oryx and lesser kudu. There is a tented camp with full catering facilities, and bookings may be made through Box 437, Arusha. Other big game are plentiful and include elephant, buffalo, lion and greater kudu. The Park lies due south of Lake Manyara, the entrance being 107 km (67 miles) from Arusha on a tarmac road. Eight miles further on there is a permanent tented camp with full catering facilities, a petrol station and airstrip. Charges are from Shs. 195/– per person full board. Bookings through Tarangire Safari Camp (Box 1182, Arusha, Telephone 3265).

Rock paintings

This part of Tanzania is noted for neolithic graves and rock paintings. Some of the best and most accessible paintings are at Kolo at the foot of the Rift Wall. Kolo is 249 km (156 miles) south of Arusha on the Great North Road. Visitors must be accompanied by one of the Government guides who are there. There are eleven protected sites in the area, out of more than a thousand, many not yet fully examined.

The paintings, associated with various Stone Age cultures, are usually dark red and depict animals, hunting scenes and various symbols. At least a dozen styles are discernible and the earliest work is perhaps three thousand years old, the newest only two hundred. But no one knows for sure who did the paintings. A good selection can be seen in a day before driving on to Dodoma.

Dodoma

Once merely a small town on the Great North Road, Dodoma is being rebuilt as the capital of Tanzania and the seat of government. Lying in a natural bowl, surrounded by hills, it is being extensively planted with trees and shrubs and will become most attractive, especially as it has a pleasant dry climate. The Dodoma Hotel is recommended. The road to Morogoro is being tarmaced and this will improve access from the capital to the Mikumi National Park, described under Southern Tanzania. It is also near the Ruaha National Park.

Ngorongoro Crater

Returning to the Lake Manyara area, from which a visit to the new capital is a substantial detour, the road to the world famous Serengeti plains winds up a mountainside through spectacular scenery past the Ngorongoro Crater, the heart of a 8,290 sq km (3,200 sq miles) conservation area that contains the greatest *permanent* concentration of wildlife in Africa in a setting of unequalled grandeur. Some 10,000 Masai live near Ngorongoro with their 100,000 cattle, sharing the land with the wildlife. The fantastic crater itself, a caldera or "collapsed" volcano, is 2,000 feet deep and its flattish floor is 18 km (10 miles) wide. You need four-wheel drive to go down into it, but once there you find one of the wonders of Africa, where approximately 14,000 wildebeeste, 5,000 zebra and hundreds of gazelle graze, while the Ngorongoro lions are almost as famous as those of the neighbouring Serengeti. With luck an early morning visitor will see at least one lion and his mate tearing at a kill of wildebeest or zebra, with the attendant scavengers, hyena, jackal and vultures hovering nearby. The State Travel Service operates Land Rovers into the crater, charging Shs. 550/– a half day or Shs. 850/– a full day. Consult them or the Conservator about taking your own vehicle down and about camping.

Ngorongoro Crater Lodge sits on the lip of the crater. It has a log-style dining room, lounge and bar. Most other buildings are of log construction, their rural aspect contrasting strongly with the high standard of comfort inside. Warm clothing is advisable for early mornings and evenings as the lodge is nearly 8,000 feet above sea level. The full day tariff ranges from Shs. 265/– single, bookings through Box 751 Arusha, telephone 3530. Another place to stay is the comfortable Ngorongoro Wildlife Lodge (TTC), similarly overlooking the crater. More simple accommodation is available at the Ngorongoro Forest Lodge (Box 445, Arusha).

From Ngorongoro, it's worth going on to the Seronera Lodge (see below) in the middle of the Serengeti Plains, 144 km (90 miles) away over a gravelled road. Travellers arriving from the Crater come, after 57km (36 miles), to the cradle of mankind, Olduvai Gorge. Here very early human remains, 1¾ million years old, forming what has become known as the Nutcracker Man, were found by Dr L. S. B. Leakey. The skull of *Zinjanthropus boisei*, to give it is scientific name, is now in the National Museum in Dar es Salaam. In late 1963, Dr Leakey and others found remains which are believed to be even older than the Nutcracker Man. Fossils were first seen here by a German butterfly collector in 1911. There is a small museum where guides and publications are available.

Olduvai Gorge

Serengeti National Park

The Serengeti National Park encompasses the largest migratory concentration of plains game to be found anywhere in the world. The northern boundary adjoins the famed Mara game country of Kenya, while to the west the Park stretches in a long "corridor" to within two miles of Lake Victoria. On the eastern boundary lie Masailand and the Ngorongoro Crater.

The terrain within the park varies from the treeless, central Serengeti Plains to savannah-type stretches dotted with flat-topped acacia trees and interspersed with magnificent rock outcrops, while riverine bush, thick scrub and forest grow in the north and along the Mara River.

Although the Serengeti is best known for its magnificent lions, it contains over 35 species of plains game as well as some 350 species of birds. A wildlife population of more than 1½ million large mammals has been recorded. According to recent estimates, there are more than 350,000 wildebeeste, 180,000 zebra and 500,000 gazelle.

Game migration

The annual movement in May or June of wildebeeste and zebra from the central plains to the permanent water of the western corridor and their return in November or December is one of the most remarkable and inspiring sights of Africa. The great herds gather in the central plains in May or June and then move steadily westwards, six or seven abreast and often several miles long. At the tail end of the procession come the cripples and those too old to keep up, with the inevitable following of lion and other carnivores. Thousands and thousands of wildebeeste and zebra pass through the central Itonjo Range, gradually dispersing throughout the length and breadth of the corridor until many are up in the northern Serengeti, bordering the Mara in Kenya.

The classic book on the Park is *Serengeti Shall Not Die*, by Dr Bernhard Grzimek, the Director of the Frankfurt Zoo. Indeed the Serengeti manages to retain the wild, untamed atmosphere of Africa as it always was, leaving even the most blasé visitor with a haunting memory of its primeval beauty.

Seronera

There are several excellent lodges in the Serengeti and many camping sites. The Seronera Wildlife Lodge (TTC), pretty well in the centre of the Park, is pleasantly built of stone, with swimming pool, shop and airstrip. The game viewing round here is renowned and at night you can hear lions roaring nearby. Land Rovers can be hired from STS and ranger guides are available. About 64 km (40 miles) from Seronera towards the Kenya border is Lobo Wildlife Lodge (also TTC), ingeniously set on a natural rock promontory, with a swimming pool, shop, airstrip and good game viewing. Fort Ikoma, a remarkable "Beau Geste" type of fort built by the Germans in 1904, north-west of Seronera, was made into a lodge but has now reverted to military use. Finally there is the Ndutu Safari Lodge, 24 km (15 miles) off the Ngorongoro–Seronera road.

Lobo

Constant improvement of the game viewing circuits in the Serengeti is being achieved, with new roads, whilst a unique foundation, the Serengeti Research Institute, can be visited. This internationally staffed centre studies the wildlife and vegetation of the area, plots the migration of animals, and improves conservation methods. It is situated two miles east of the Seronera Wildlife Lodge.

Dar es Salaam

The former capital of the United Republic is a comparatively small city, attractive in appearance, with a leisurely air that belies the tremendous amount of activity going on. It has a beautiful, palm-fringed, land-locked harbour from which it takes its name, Dar es Salaam, the Arabic for "the haven of peace", but is at the same time a busy commercial port with modern facilities, visited by the vessels of many nations. As well as serving Tanzania, the port is the shipment point for the Tazara railway to Zambia, completed with the help of the Chinese, and also known as the Great Uhuru Railway.

Dar is a town of tree-lined avenues, Independence Avenue being a brilliant sight around Christmas time when the colourful acacias are in full bloom, full of contrasts. Modern office buildings rise next door to black and white painted, wood-beamed German buildings, new

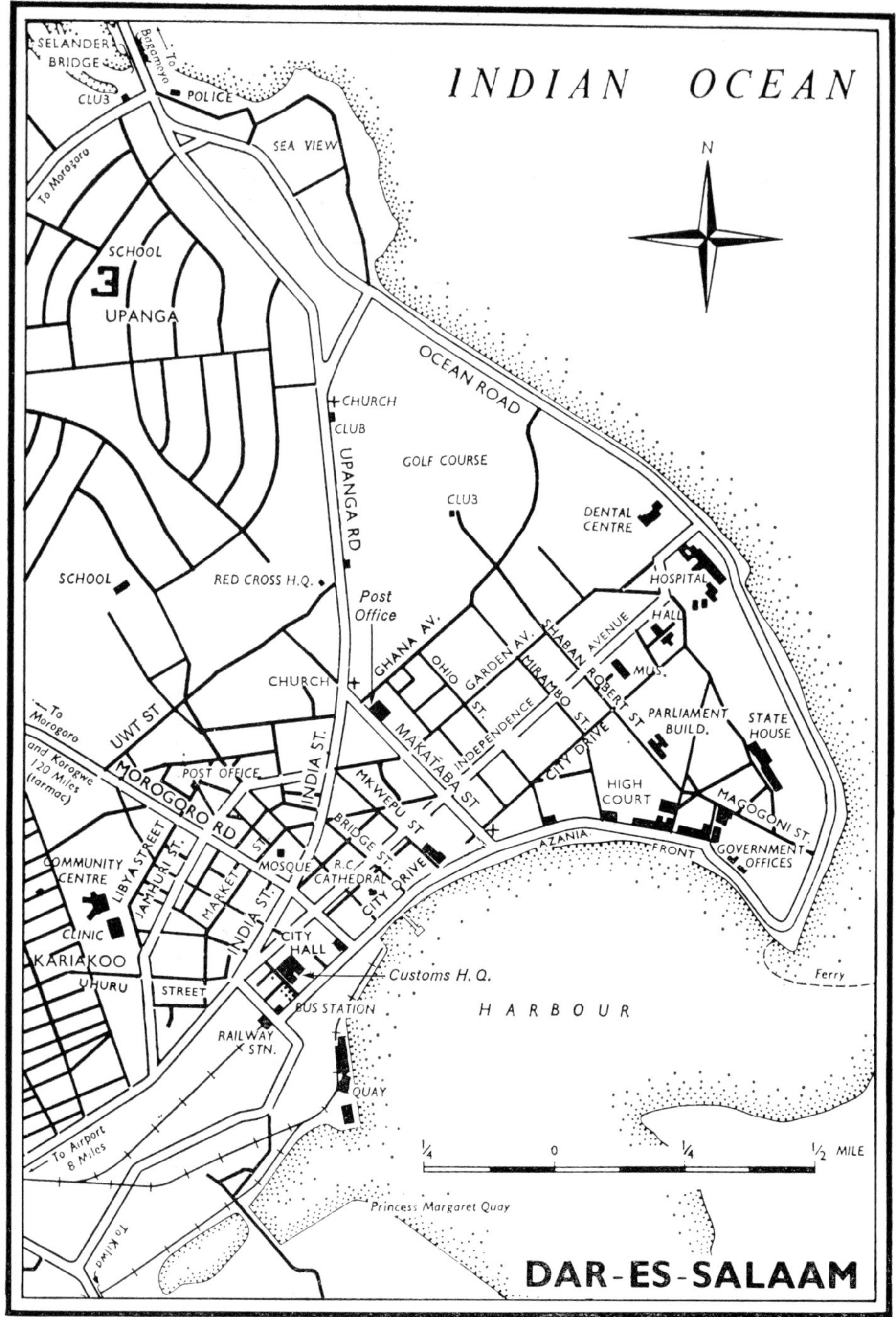

Reprinted with grateful acknowledgments to Caltex (East Africa) Ltd.

shops trade next door to the old shoemaker sitting on his step surrounded by pieces of leather. The city is rapidly changing and expanding, with new roads and modern buildings, but as recently as 1954 lions were roaming freely in the area which is now the exclusive residential suburb of Oyster Bay.

Although Dodoma is becoming the new capital, Dar will remain the country's commercial centre and also retains the official residence of the President, State House. This lovely white Arab influenced building was the Governor's house in colonial days and stands in spacious grounds near the harbour entrance. The President has founded a private zoo in the gardens and as a result peacocks stray around the area. Note that it is forbidden to photograph any part of State House.

Other historic buildings include the German administrative buildings along the waterfront, the former German club, next to the Kilimanjaro Hotel, and the small house now containing the British Council library on Independence Avenue. The old hospital on Ocean Drive is also remarkable.

The focal point of the city centre is the Askari memorial at the junction of Independence Avenue and Makataba Street, and a stone's throw from the popular open air terrace bar of the New Africa Hotel. Most of the good shops are round here, so are the airline offices and banks. *Shops* The main Post Office is a couple of hundred yards along Makataba Street. There are several chemists, including the Mahen Pharmacy, hairdressers in the Kilimanjaro Hotel and in Independence Avenue, an excellent bookshop in Independence Avenue close to the memorial, and a variety of curio shops. The great speciality of these is the carving of the Makonde tribe of southern Tanzania, who make unique pieces in ebony, both traditional and modern. The Tanzania Handicrafts Marketing Corporation's shop in the arcade of the IPS building has a very fine display at prices from Shs. 100/– to Shs. 3,000/–, which are excellent value. You could pay ten times as much in Nairobi. If you become interested you should also see the Makonde ritual masks in the Museum. Another speciality of curio shops is the traditional Zanzibar brass bound chest. And of course there are game trophies. Most shops close for lunch from 12.30 to 2.00 pm (1400).

The National Bank of Commerce has branches in Independence Avenue and Makataba Street, while the sub office in the Kilimanjaro Hotel remains open in the afternoons.

Hotels

The Kilimanjaro Hotel (TTC, telephone 21292) stands on the Azania Front with a magnificent view over the harbour, its own swimming pool, and a nightclub. Rivalling it is the twice enlarged New Africa Hotel (TTC, telephone 29611), originally one of three lodges built for a visit by the Kaiser before the Great War, though he never came in the end. Alas, nothing remains of the lodge, but the hotel is first class. Other modern hotels include the Twiga, the Motel Agip, and the Skyways, these being less expensive, though air-conditioned. It is essential to book city centre accommodation in advance. A pleasant, small hotel in the picture postcard setting of a tropical, palm-fringed beach, is the Oyster Bay Hotel, 6½ km (4 miles) from the centre.

Restaurants

For eating out we recommend the Simba Nightclub at the Kilimanjaro, which has a cabaret. It is certainly the most expensive restaurant in Dar es Salaam but has plenty of atmosphere, and the menu is both extensive and exotic. A more moderate and pleasant evening, particularly at the hottest time of the year, can be had in their roof-top restaurant which has a discotheque. The Agip Motel restaurant is good, and for a reasonably priced evening out, the Twiga roof-top open-air restaurant provides oriental food, with dancing two nights a week. Oyster Bay Hotel and Palm Beach Hotel specialise in seafoods. For people who like a real Indian curry, there are two restaurants, the Sheeshmahal restaurant and the Hindu Lodge at the City Hotel, which will satisfy the connoisseur, though first impressions may not be inviting; for those who prefer a Chinese meal, there is an excellent, though seemingly unnamed, restaurant in the basement of the NIC Investment House. There are snack bars in the Kilimanjaro Hotel and at the Agip Motel.

Car Hire

Among car hire and taxi firms are STS, Co-Cabs, Valji and Alibhai, and Subzali Tours.

Tours

The major tour operator is also STS, together with Bushtrekker Safaris (Box 5350, telephone 31957) and Kearline Tours (Box 1638, telephone 20607). Tour operators also have offices in the hotels, but it's worth shopping around for value among the local city tours and visits to such places as the old slave port of Bagamoyo (see page 99). Another favourite tour is to the Mikumi National Park, some three hours' drive, while in the high season daily air excursions are available to Zanzibar (see below). For Air Charter see Useful Facts section.

Information

Up to date information on what's on can be obtained from the Information Office of TTC on Independence Avenue.

Cultural Centres

As well as the British Council Library, already mentioned, there is an American Library on Independence Avenue and a West German Goethe Institute. The University of Dar es Salaam is very active though outside the city.

Museums

The fine National Museum in Shaaban Robert Street has relics of Chinese, Arab and Persian coastal civilisations as well as archaeological finds from Olduvai Gorge. To understand more about African life visit the traditional African village which has been built off the Bagamoyo road, showing the various types of houses found in different parts of the country. You can often see Makonde craftsmen doing carvings, and men at work on the houses. The village is open daily, all the year, from 9.30 am to 3 pm.

National Festival

Every year from July 1 to July 7 a National Festival Farmers' Week is held in Dar es Salaam, to coincide with the celebrations of the founding of the political movement which led Tanzania to Independence, now called the CCM, or Revolutionary Party. There are displays of tribal dancing, varying from the snake dancers of Mwanza, who use live snakes, to the weird stilt dancers of the Makonde.

Sport

There is golf, tennis and cricket at the Dar es Salaam Gymkhana Club. Fishermen should contact the Deep Sea Angling Club Secretary at the Yacht Club which is about six miles north of Dar es Salaam. Riding is available at the Sunny Horse Ranch (telephone 67046) just past the village of Kigogo, at Leopard Cove.

There are safe bathing beaches near the city, the most convenient being at Oyster Bay 6½ km (4 miles) and at Silversands 19 km (12 miles) to the north, and at Mjimwema south of the city for which you must cross the harbour entrance by ferry. Or there are the beaches at Bahari and Kunduchi described below.

The Coast

Big Game fishing

The two main attractions of the coast are magnificent coral beaches and big game fishing. More beach hotels are built every year. We describe the coast line as it runs south of the capital, and then north. But first the fish. Marlin and tunny of medium size are often caught near Dar es Salaam, Tanga, Lindi and Mtwara, as well as barracuda, kingfish and large rock cod, and provide plenty of sport for those who are not interested in the bigger game fish. Trolling is the usual method of fishing.

For the big game fisherman, there is as great a variety of big fighting fish as can be found in the better known game fishing areas of the world. The best areas are around Pemba Island, in the vicinity of Mafia Island, off Ras Kankadya and Bongoyo Island, and in Lindi Bay. There have been some fine catches in the Mafia Channel, including a 500 lb rock cod, 75 lb dolphin, 80 lb horse mackerel, 100 lb sailfish, and American jack and marlin of up to 150 lb. The big migratory fish, the sailfish and swordfish, usually run between December and March, together with the yellow-finned tunny. In general the fishing season is from September to March. Seafaris, Box 9500, Dar es Salaam, telephone 281281, which is a TTC subsidiary, operates big game fishing boats from the beach hotels and at Mafia Island. Rates are up to Shs. 500/– per day for four persons.

Mafia Island

Mafia Island is 170 square miles in size and lies on the edge of the Continental shelf 128 km (80 miles) south of Dar es Salaam. The fully air-conditioned Mafia Island Lodge (TTC), situated on Chole bay, provides a base for every kind of fishing. Scuba and underwater "goggling" equipment can be hired. Guests can be met at the airport, which has scheduled air services by Air Tanzania from Dar es Salaam (45 minutes flight). Air charter firms will also quote rates. The voyage by schooner takes 12 hours, contact Mwambao Shipping Co, Dar es Salaam (Box 393, telephone 23097).

South of Dar es Salaam

Some 320 km (200 miles) south of Dar es Salaam is the town of Kilwa, where relics of the colonisation of the coast by Arabs, and possibly Persians, are found. The surviving ruins date mostly from the thirteenth century but settlements are known to have existed since the first century AD. There is plenty of archaeological interest here.

Kilwa

There are in fact three towns of Kilwa; the first is Kilwa Kivinje (Kilwa of the casuarina trees) which has a picturesque Arab appearance. It was originally built in 1830 by the inhabitants of Kilwa Kisiwana who fled there to avoid the British gunboats cruising in nearby waters to suppress the slave trade. Kilwa Kisiwani (Kilwa on the island) contains the ruins of the capital of the sultans of Kilwa (the "Quiloa" of Milton's epic poem *Paradise Lost*) with a large palace, several mosques and a castle, probably of Portuguese origin, dating from 1505. The Great, or Friday, Mosque is the largest and best preserved in East Africa and dates from the fourteenth and fifteenth centuries. The third town of Kilwa Masoko (Kilwa of the markets) is beautifully situated on a promontory projecting into the harbour. Kilwa can be reached by road only during the dry season but there are regular air services.

Lindi

Lindi was the main port of the southern province before Mtwara was constructed, but shipping does not now use the harbour. The Beach Hotel is small but adequate and fishing and bathing on nearby beaches is good.

Mtwara

Mtwara was planned and built as a result of the ill-fated groundnut scheme and has two deepwater berths, deep enough for the largest ships afloat. It is situated on the southern shore of a magnificent natural harbour, which is almost completely landlocked. The hotel is the Mtwara Beach Hotel and swimming and goggling is possible from the beaches. There are regular air services.

Mikindani

Seven miles south of Mtwara by road stands the old Arab seaport of Mikindani, with narrow streets lined with small shops and mosques, framed in a background of palm and flamboyant trees. The port is still a busy centre for dhows.

Makonde

Down here, both in Tanzania and northern Mozambique, live the Makonde people, famous for their carving and their weird stilt dances. They inhabit the dense bush in the highlands of the interior. One of the most interesting points about their ebony carvings is that they are influenced both by African art from other parts of the continent, and by European sculpture, whilst retaining their own distinct character.

North of Dar es Salaam

Kunduchi

Twenty-two km (14 miles) north of Dar es Salaam is Kunduchi, with superb beaches and the site of the tomb of Sharifu Musa at Kondo who, it is said, is a descendant of Mohammed the Prophet. This holy man had such a presence of good, and was so well known along the coast, that when he died his body was distributed in seven places and interred in Zanzibar, Mkarja and Moa (Tanga), Kondo (Kunduchi),

Kilwa Kivinje, Lindi and Mikindani—the graves being spread 500 miles up and down the coast. Today Kunduchi is better known for two beach hotels and as an integral part of the coastal tourist circuit. The Kunduchi Beach Hotel (TTC) can justifiably be called one of the best designed in Africa. Situated on a long, sandy beach, it was inspired by early Arab architecture and its cool white arches and terraces make a magnificent contrast to the palm trees and tropical plants around it. There is a pool-side restaurant and all rooms are air-conditioned. Close by is a local fishing village on a lagoon. Further down the beach is the brick and thatch Rungwe Oceanic Hotel (Box 5659 Dar es Salaam, telephone 47021).

Bahari Beach

Beyond Kunduchi is the equally fine Bahari beach, with the Bahari Beach Hotel (TTC), based on native African designs and with one of the longest thatched roofs ever made. Its buffet food has a good reputation.

Five km (3 miles) further on is the Africana vacation village with thatched-roof bandas. The atmosphere is casual and relaxing and an interesting feature is the swimming pool bar, built half in and half out of the water. All sea sports and riding are available, and there is a small zoo. For reservations contact Hotel Africana, Box 2802, Dar es Salaam, telephone 81231.

Bagamoyo

About 64 km (45 miles) north of Dar es Salaam is Bagamoyo, which was the terminus of the slave caravan route from Lake Tanganyika and the port of embarkation for thousands of slaves and hundreds of tons of ivory. You can still see the old stone pens where slaves were kept, and there is a shackle ring, for securing slaves, embedded in a fine old baobab tree. Several famous explorers, including Burton, Speke and Stanley, began their expeditions into the interior from here, and there is a memorial to Burton and Speke.

In a little chapel behind the mission church of Notre Dame de Bagamoyo the body of David Livingstone oncel ay, after being carried across country by faithful African followers. The town, once the capital of German East Africa, is famous for carved Arab doors.

Kaole

Five km (3 miles) south of Bagamoyo is the picturesque village of Kaole, near which are the ruins of a mosque and pillars believed to be 800 years old.

Tanga

Tanga is the second largest town and second port of mainland Tanzania. There are several hotels, the best being the new Mkong Hotel, with all rooms air-conditioned. The Planters Hotel (Box 242, telphone 2071) used to be the scene of marathon gambling sessions during which whole sisal estates and plantations acquired new owners. The town is the principal centre of the sisal industry, Tanzania being the world's largest supplier of the fibre. Conducted tours are available at the Amboni estate. Other interesting local places include the Galanos Sulphur Springs and the Persian 13th century ruins at Tongoni some 20 km (13 miles) out on the Pangani road. In Tanga itself there are various relics of German days, including a splendid small obelisk commemorating a German naval death.

Mkomazi Game Reserve

From Tanga you could drive inland to visit the 2,850 sq km Mkomazi Game Reserve, an important elephant migration area in typical savannah country; or down the coast to Pangani, a small Arab port, past a delightful "Painted Village". This village, called Kigombe, has murals covering the outside walls of its houses, painted by the villagers and showing Tanzanian scenes and people.

Usambara Mountains

Visitors often find the magnificent scenery of the Usambara Mountains, behind Tanga, reminiscent of the Swiss Alps, only without the snow. Their narrow roads wind steeply round the mountainsides, giving breathtaking views into the valleys below. The Usambaras are also a centre of the tea-growing industry in Tanzania and from Amani the tea gardens stretch for many miles. The climate is cool and sunny throughout the year, the hills being between 5,000 and 10,000 feet up.

Lushoto

At Lushoto, a former German hill station, there are two hotels. The Lawns (Box 33) and Oaklands (Box 41) charge around Shs. 110/- per person full board. Lushoto lies at the head of a sheltered valley in the Usambaras, surrounded by hillsides covered with forest, plantations of eucalyptus, cedar and wattle. Flowers found in Europe grow in profusion, as well as African varieties, and the countryside is always green. Tennis, golf, fishing and riding are available, as well as swimming in the mountain streams. Twenty-one miles away at

Shume

Shume is the popular site of Jiwe la Mungu—the stone of God. It is a large natural stone which is believed to be the highest point in the Usambara mountains, and from it you can get a magnificent view of the valleys and plains below.

Southern Tanzania, Mikumi, the Selous Reserve, Ruaha, Mbeya

South-western Tanzania has been opened up by the Tazara railway, linking Dar es Salaam with Zambia via Mbeya, and by a tarmac road running roughly parallel to it. The road, though not this railway,

Morogoro

passes through Morogoro, a small town 193 km (120 miles) from Dar and beautifully situated at the foot of the blue mountains of Uluguru, where there are excellent trout streams, particularly the Mgeta river, as well as bird shooting. The climate is cool and pleasant and there are two hotels, the Acropol (Box 78) and the Savoy. Neither is expensive.

Mikumi National Park

A further 96 km (60 miles) on from Morogoro the road runs smack through the Mikumi National Park, which covers 500 sq miles of open plains and wooded hills, some 1,800 ft above sea level. Large herds of elephant feed by the Mkata river, and lion, buffalo, hippo, giraffe

Opposite top: Samburu moran of northern Kenya
Bottom: Herding goats and camels on the Tana river near Garissa, Kenya. Photos Richard Cox

and many other species can be seen, including an occasional sable antelope and greater kudu. June to November is the best time for a visit, this being the dry season, though the Park is open all year round. It is recommended to hire a guide from the National Parks staff. In the centre of the Park, close to the main road is the Mikumi Wildlife Lodge (TTC) with swimming pool and nearby airstrip. Another seven km brings you to a tented camp which is fully equipped, with a restaurant and bar service, operated by Oyster Bay Hotel, Box 1907, Dar es Salaam. The visitor can have all the thrills of camping out in the African bush, yet with a high standard of comfort, only three and a half hours' drive from Dar. The hippo pool is a ten minute drive from this camp. Land Rover trips are available through the Park authorities. For those who wish to use their own tents or motor caravans, a campsite can be booked at Shs. 30/– per night through the Chief Park Warden, Box 642, Morogoro.

Selous Game Reserve

The largest Game Reserve in the world, to which the Mikumi National Park is adjacent, the Selous in south-eastern Tanzania, has some of the finest virgin bush left in Africa, where the last of the really big-tusked elephants and large-maned lions still roam. It supports around one million head of game.

These 41,440 sq km (16,000 sq miles) are named after Frederick Selous, who hunted elephant on horseback with muzzle-loading rifles and was a naturalist, explorer and soldier too. It is claimed that he shot as many as 30 elephants in a day and when his horse could no longer follow the herds, he would pursue them on foot, clad only in a shirt and a pair of sandals, which he said was the most suitable garb for running after elephants. His grave lies near where he fell during the First World War, close to the Mbuyu safari camp. The area is dominated by the Great Ruaha and Kilombero rivers, which join to form the Rufiji. This river then meanders through creeks to the Indian Ocean, and was the scene of the legendary British pursuit of the German battleship *Königsberg*, which inspired Wilbur Smith's novel *Shout at the Devil*. The wreck of the *Königsberg* is still visible in the creek where it was sunk.

The Selous was largely inaccessible until in the mid-1960s the government began to open up the area through what is now the Tanzania Wildlife Corporation. The venture has been successful, with clients from many parts of the world. Half a dozen airstrips have been constructed by the Game Department, and there are 900 miles of hunting tracks in the Selous Reserve. But the safaris most worth special mention are those to the upper Kilombero River Valley, which lies south of Iringa. From March to May floods sweep this valley, forcing the game on to "islands" of higher ground, where elephant, buffalo, lion, leopard, crocodile, puku, buck, eland, sable and others concentrate. Safari parties fly in, then continue by canoe and on foot. The Great Ruaha river which joins the Kilombero to form the Rufiji

Opposite top: Luo fishing boat in the Kavirondo Gulf of Lake Victoria. Photo Richard Cox
Bottom: Buffalo by a waterhole

river, flows through the northern Selous. The Mbuyu camp has been established on the bank of the Rufiji, with views of the swamp areas where hippo wallow, and a great variety of birds. It has a 20 ft high viewing platform mounted in a baobab tree (called *mbuyu* in Swahili). Bookings through Bushtrekker Safaris, Box 5350, Dar es Salaam, who can arrange air charter to a nearby strip. Two nights and three days for two people, flying down, would cost Shs. 3,466/– each all inclusive. The basic accommodation charge is Shs. 303/– a night.

The western part of the Selous has been opened up by the Tazara railway's proximity and the tarmac road, which has a spur to the corner of the Reserve on the Great Ruaha river.

Iringa

The main road then continues to Iringa, a town that is as nearly in the centre of Tanzania as anywhere. Situated on top of a lofty escarpment, it has wide streets lined with jacaranda trees. There are two hotels. The Iringa Railway Hotel (Box 230, telephone 2039) has recently been modernised. The town is served by regular Air Tanzania flights.

Hehe tribe

Iringa district is the home of one of Tanzania's most famous warrior tribes, the Wahehe, reputedly so called owing to the manner in which they expressed heightened feelings—"He! He!" Their chief, Mkwawa, was renowned throughout East Africa and successfully resisted German troops for many years, on one occasion annihilating a German column 1,000 strong. The present chief of the Hehe, Chief Adam Sapi, is the Speaker of the Tanzania National Assembly, and Chairman of the TTC and of the Tanzania National Parks' Trustees. Iringa is famous for its elephant. Many excursions can be made from the town, and Lake Ngwazi at Mufindi, 96 km (60 miles) away, is a paradise for ornithologists.

Ruaha National Park

The road from Iringa to Mbeya passes the Ruaha National Park, 13,000 sq km (5,000 sq miles) of mostly undulating plateau 3,000 ft above sea level. Driving from Iringa you should fork right at Mloa, avoiding the low ground around Tumgamulenga. Allow 4 hours to cover the 128 km (80 miles) to the Park as you must cross the Great Ruaha river by ferry. Game in the Park includes large herds of elephant and impala, greater kudu, buffalo and some sable and roan antelope. The gorges of the Great Ruaha river are particularly beautiful while its pools and shallows, inhabited by hippo, crocodiles and turtles attract a concentration of wildlife during the dry season, including a great variety of birds. During the dry season most tracks are passable to ordinary saloon cars, but during the wet season from January to March the access roads to the Park are poor.

The best months for a visit are July to November. There is no Lodge in the Park, but there is a do-it-yourself visitors' camp at Msembe on the west bank of the Great Ruaha river 84 km (52 miles) north-west of Iringa. Accommodation is in fully-equipped thatched rondavels, but you must bring your own food. Bookings can be made through the Park Warden (Box 369 Iringa), or through Bushtrekker Safaris (Box 5350, Dar es Salaam). Private camping at a variety of places can be arranged through the Park Warden. Campers must bring all their own equipment, including food and drinking water. Alternatively you can stay at one of the two proper hotels in Iringa. Ranger guides are often available through the Warden's office at Msembe. The Park, incidentally, was formerly part of the Rungwa River Game Reserve, in which three dams were built to attract game.

Rungwa River Reserve

Past the Park the Mbeya road runs through the high mountains and hills and plunging valleys of the southern end of the Great Rift Valley, which in parts looks very much like the Scottish moors. There are many waterfalls and rapids on the innumerable streams and 81 km (51 miles) from Mbeya is the Chimpala scarp road with delightful views of the Usangu Plains. From November onwards some of the loveliest wild flowers in the African tropics can be seen on the mountainsides.

Mbeya

Lying in a gap between two mountain ranges and between two arms of the Great Rift Valley, Mbeya is an ideal centre for visiting some of the most beautiful countryside in East Africa. It owes much to the interest in gold mining on the nearby Lupa. Fishing is a very popular pastime in the trout streams of the Mporoto Mountains. The Mbeya Hotel and the Mbeya Guest House provide full board while at the time of writing a new hotel, the Highlands, was under construction. North-west of Mbeya is Lake Rukwa, a magnificent game area, where incidentally two oddities have been seen—an albino giraffe and a spotted zebra.

Lake Rukwa

Western Tanzania and the Lakes

The west of this vast country—it is easy to forget just how large Tanzania is—lies nearer to Zaire and Zambia than Dar es Salaam. Here the western branch of the Rift Valley creates a natural frontier in the shape of Lake Tanganyika, and the great plains terminate in the foothills of the mountains of Burundi.

Tabora

Tabora on these plains is best reached by air or rail. It grew up as a station on the old caravan route from the coast to Lake Tanganyika and was a centre for the slave and ivory trades. Along the main road from Tabora to the lake is a virtually unbroken line of mango trees, sometimes reaching a width of one mile, which is said to have been caused by the slaves throwing away the stones of the mangoes they had eaten as they marched. The ruins of the houses of the old Arab traders can still be seen near the town. About four miles out is a reconstruction of the house where Livingstone and Stanley lived intermittently in 1871 and 1872, containing relics of the explorers. From here Livingstone set out on his last journey. Tabora has a hotel (Box 147, telephone 47) and remains a centre of communications. One route goes north to Mwanza on Lake Victoria (see below). Another goes direct by rail, but circuitously by road, to Kigoma on Lake Tanganyika. It is not unknown for people in a hurry to forsake the road and drive straight through the bush. But we do not advise it.

Ugalla River Game Reserve

The road south towards Mbeya passes near the Ugalla River Game Reserve, which occupies 4,773 sq km (1,843 sq miles) of bush some 160 km (100 miles) south-west of Tabora. The main characteristic of this reserve is its river valleys running through miobo woodland and it is noted for its sable antelope.

Katavi Plain National Park

Further south-west of Tabora, but accessible only from the main road from Kigoma down to Zambia, unless you motor direct along unpaved tracks, is the Katavi Plain National Park. Situated near the small town of Mpanda, its 1,935 sq km (747 sq miles) shelter the country's largest herd of buffalo, reputed to number 1,600, as well as elephant, hippo, crocodile and roan antelope. There is a resthouse belonging to the Game Division and an airstrip.

Lake Tanganyika

Lake Tanganyika is the second deepest lake in the world and in places the bottom is several thousand feet below sea level, even though its surface is 2,534 feet up. Tanzania Railway Corporation operates an eight-day round trip of the lake by steamer. The lake also provides excellent fishing, containing over two hundred known varieties of fish up to 100 lb or more in weight. Trolling is the method normally used but sport may also be obtained—for example at Kigoma—from piers, wharves and rocky promontories. The most common fish are Nile perch, tiger fish, yellow bellies and tilapia.

Kigoma
Ujiji

The main town on the lake is Kigoma, where there is an hotel. Five miles to the south is Ujiji, where a plaque marks the site of the mango tree beneath the shade of which Stanley met "Dr Livingstone, I presume", on 10 November, 1871, after coming from Tabora on his long search for the doctor. This part of Tanzania has many graves of missionaries, and many Mission Stations, both active and abandoned.

Gombe Stream National Park

Twenty-four km north of Kigoma, by the lake shore, is the Gombe Stream National Park, an area of 65 sq km (25 sq miles) which provides unique chances for observing chimpanzees in their natural habitat. It is not yet known how many live in the Park; only the Kasakela chimps, on which Dr Jane Lawick-Goodall has done outstanding scientific and photographic work, are well known and have become very tame. There are now plans to accustom another group to the proximity of human beings. However, because chimpanzees are very susceptible to human ailments the Park is only open to officially recognised researchers.

Biharamulo Game Reserve

Here you are almost in Burundi, the capital of which, Bujumbura, stands at the head of the lake between dramatic ranges of hills. You are likely to notice Hutu people from Burundi with their cattle if you take the road up to Bukoba, in Tanzania's West Lake region—so called because it lies west of Lake Victoria. On the way you pass near the Biharamulo Game Reserve, formed to protect game in an area that is rapidly becoming settled. It is actually on the road from Biharamulo to Nyamirembe, on the lakeshore, and covers 116 sq km (450 sq miles). Its rare animals include sable antelope, Sharp's grysbok and Lichtenstein's hartebeeste. Rubondo Island, close by in the lake, is also a game sanctuary, and designated a National Park.

Rubondo Island

Another Reserve in the West Lake Region is the Rumanyika Orugundu Game Reserve, the 775 sq km (300 sq miles) of which lie mostly in the Kishanda Valley of the north Karagwe District. This is basically a rainforest reserve among high mountains, but with the added attraction of one of the largest concentrations of rhino anywhere in Tanzania. It has no lodge or hotel, however.

Rumanyika Orugundu Reserve

Bukoba is situated on a hillside on the western shores of Lake Victoria, in what some people consider to be the loveliest surroundings in the whole country. The climate is very damp and the vegetation dramatically tropical. Hippos often come into the town at night and motorists need to keep a look-out for them. There are two hotels, the Lake (Box 66) and the Coffee Tree Inn. You see the long-horned cattle of this part of Central Africa, and feel in a different country. A good way of reaching Bukoba, apart from the flights from Mwanza and Entebbe, is by the Lake Victoria steamer service which calls about twice a week.

Bukoba

Travelling from here or from Tabora to the East Lake region visitors can go via Shinyanga and visit the famous Williamson Diamond Mines at Mwadui, though arrangements must be made well beforehand with the company. Mwadui is 137 km (86 miles) from Mwanza by road but can also be reached by air charter. Not that diamonds are Tanzania's only gems. Local stones include rubies, sapphires,

Diamond Mines

Sukuma dancers of Tanzania

zircons, moonstones, tourmalines, garnets and tanzanite, a beautiful blue semi-precious stone.

Mwanza

Mwanza is a thriving commercial town on the shore of Lake Victoria, with low hills behind it. It is one of the principal ports of the lake and steamers call regularly. The climate is hot but not so humid as on the coast. A well-known sight near Mwanza is the Bismarck Rock, a huge rock which has been poised as if about to fall for as long as anyone can remember. There are two hotels, the New Mwanza (TTC) and the Lake (Box 910, telephone 3263), while a cheaper place to stay is the Mwanza Guest House (Box 971).

Saanane Reserve

Half a mile from Mwanza, and a short boat trip away, is Saanane Island, a game sanctuary where many species of animals can be seen at close quarters. Rhino and buffalo are kept separate from the public, but antelope and other non-dangerous game are allowed to roam freely. Speke's Gulf near Mwanza is named after the explorer, who caught his first glimpse of the lake from the village of Mwanza in 1858.

Sukuma Museum

A growing attraction in the area is the Sukuma Museum at Bujora about 10 km (6 miles) from Mwanza. This is the first of Tanzania's tribal museums and it has many fascinating mementoes of the Chiefs and the traditional rites of the Sukuma people, Tanzania's largest tribe. Furthermore once a year, just after Saba Saba Day in July, the tribe's most famous dancers gather at Bujora for a mammoth *ngoma* or festival.

Street in Zanzibar's Stone Town

Zanzibar

Republic of Tanzania

The Islands

Zanzibar is one of the world's legendary tropical islands, with a long, crowded history and a uniquely romantic atmosphere. Like its sister island, Pemba, it is part of a coralline reef that stretches down through the Indian Ocean as far as Mafia Island, south of Dar es Salaam. Being coral islands, both Zanzibar and Pemba have superb white sand beaches. They are not large—Zanzibar is only 85 km (53 miles) long and 38 km (24 miles) across at its widest, while its highest point is only 390 feet above sea level—but they have had a considerable influence on the mainland territories of East Africa. There is an old saying, "When they pipe in Zanzibar, people dance on the Lakes"—meaning Lakes Victoria and Tanganyika.

History

You only have to glance at the map to see how Zanzibar lies smack on the route of anyone sailing down the African coast. Although the first recorded mention of the island is in the *Periplus of the Erythraen Sea*, the mariner's guide written around 50 AD, it is reckoned that it was known to the ancient Assyrians, Phoenicians and Greeks, as well as to the civilisations of Arabia. It was with the Arabs, the rulers of the Persian Gulf, and Indians that Zanzibar and Pemba were most entangled over the 1,200 years before this century. The famous Kilwa Chronicle (see also page 96) tells how in the tenth century there was large-scale emigration from Shiraz in Persia to the islands and how a struggle for supremacy ensued between the Shirazis and the Arabs, which was never fully resolved.

The Portuguese ascendancy started with Vasco da Gama's visit in 1499, and brought the building of the first church in what became Zanzibar Town. But the Portuguese were eventually evicted by the Arabs. In 1832 the Sultan of Oman transferred his court to Zanzibar, and later developed both Zanzibar Town and the all-important clove industry. The Sultanate lasted right through the suppression of the slave trade, brought about by missionary influence, and was confirmed when a British Protectorate was declared over the islands in 1890. At Independence on December 11, 1963, the former Sultan's descendant took over as a constitutional monarch and Zanzibar also officially gave the coastal strip of Kenya to the newly independent Kenyan State. This had belonged to Zanzibar before 1890 and throughout British rule the Sultan's plain red flag had flown over Mombasa—a curious relic of one time Arab power. Then a bare month after Independence on December 11, 1963, an overnight revolution deposed the Sultan, and Zanzibar and Pemba became a People's Republic. On April 22, 1964, the Republic was united with Tanganyika and the joint name of Tanzania was adopted for the two countries.

The people

Intermarriage has mixed the African and Arab populations, which total around half a million in the two islands. Swahili is the principal language and is considered to be at its purest in the Unguja dialect of Zanzibar Town, if you happen to be interested. Most public notices are in Swahili with an English translation alongside, and English is spoken in shops and hotels. The vast majority of the people are Moslems, and Moslem holidays are observed. Otherwise public holidays are as on the mainland of Tanzania. (See Useful Facts—Tanzania.)

Climate

During the north-east Monsoon from December to March the weather is hot and relatively dry (77°–91°F). In April and May it rains heavily and then from June to October the south-west Monsoon blows, bringing cooler days (71°–84°F). Humidity averages 78%.

Wildlife

Aeons ago both islands must have been connected to the mainland, since it is unlikely that leopards and colobus monkeys swam the 36 km (22½ miles) from the mainland to Zanzibar, or antelope crossed the 64 km (40 miles) of the Pemba Channel. Other animal inhabitants of Zanzibar include Sykes monkey, lemurs, bush pigs, civet cats, tree hyraxes, mongoose, duikers, and some 102 species of birds. There are also magnificent tropical butterflies. However, the wildlife is shy and the only Reserve is the 2¼-sq-mile Jozani Forest in the south of Zanzibar Island.

Transport

Zanzibar Airport has daily services by Air Tanzania from Dar es Salaam (20 minutes flight), Tanga, Kilimanjaro International (Arusha). Pemba has one service a day. Two steamers, the MV *Jamhuri* and the MV *Mapinduzi*, ply regularly between the islands and Dar es Salaam.

ZANZIBAR

The classic greeting that Zanzibar gives one is the pungent, spicy scent of cloves. There are clove trees growing almost everywhere—indeed Zanzibar is known as "the island of cloves", though in fairness Pemba ought to share the nickname. The clove is actually the dried, unopened bud of the tree, which grows as much as 50 feet high and blossoms with crimson flowers. The clove harvest lasts from July to December and during the season you can see the crop spread out on mats in the villages, drying out and slowly turning from a golden brown to a deep, dark brown. The annual crop averages 10,000 to 11,000 tons and is mainly exported to Indonesia and to India. You can watch the sacks being loaded in Zanzibar harbour, both on to ordinary ships and on to the dhows that come down on the trade winds from India and end their long voyage here.

Zanzibar Town

Conquest and trade developed Zanzibar Town out of a fishing village in the early seventeenth century. Originally it was on a small island, and Creek Road is the filled-in creek that divided it from the mainland. The "Stone Town", on the island, where the Arabs built stone houses, remains endlessly fascinating. Its high, whitewashed houses with their wooden balconies and ornate doors line narrow,

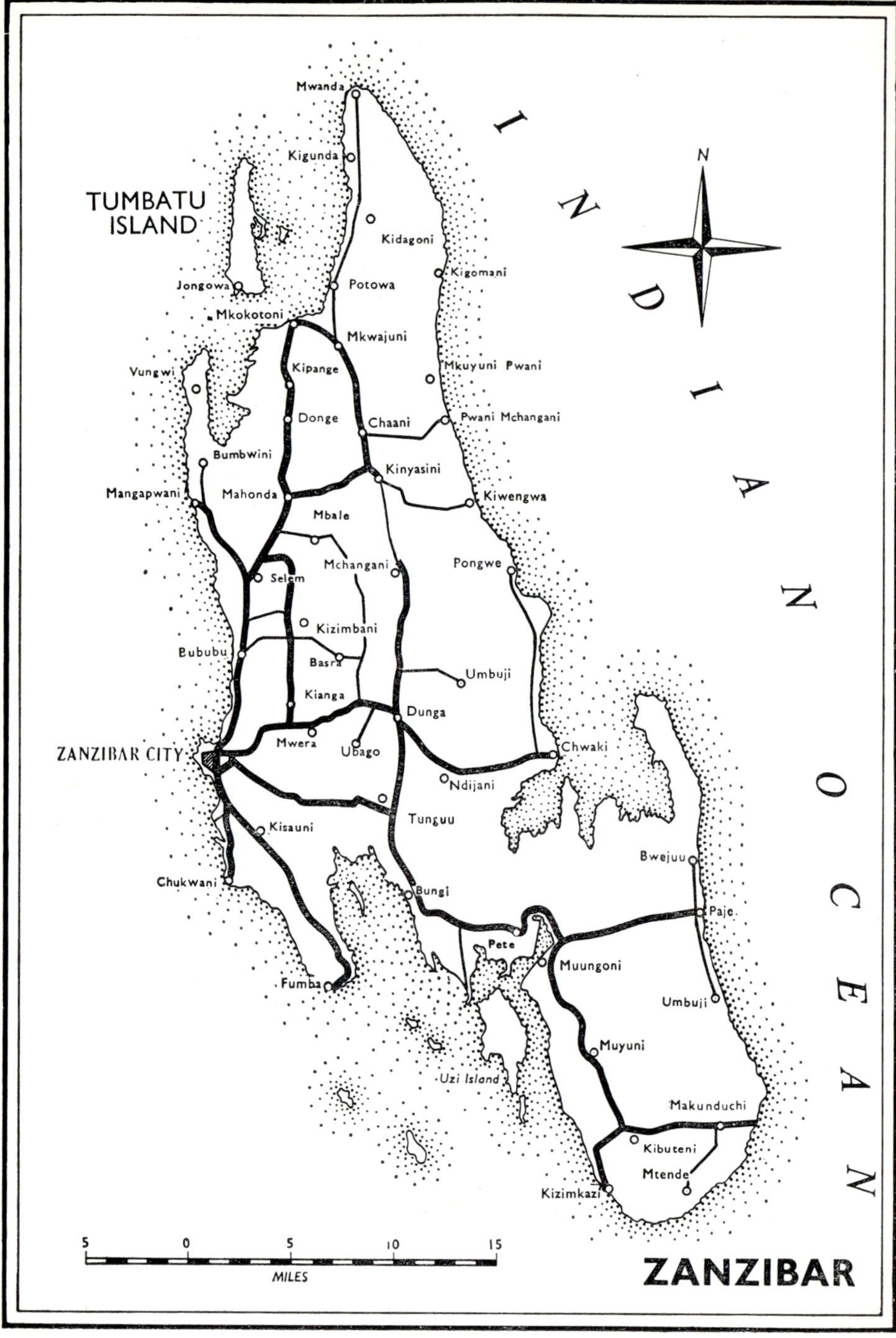

INDIAN OCEAN
N
TUMBATU ISLAND
Mwanda
Kigunda
Kidagoni
Jongowa
Potowa
Kigomani
Mkokotoni
Mkwajuni
Vungwi
Kipange
Mkuyuni Pwani
Donge
Chaani
Pwani Mchangani
Bumbwini
Kinyasini
Mangapwani
Mahonda
Kiwengwa
Mbale
Mchangani
Pongwe
Selem
Kizimbani
Bububu
Basra
Umbuji
Kianga
Dunga
ZANZIBAR CITY
Mwera
Ubago
Chwaki
Ndijani
Tunguu
Kisauni
Bwejuu
Chukwani
Bungi
Paje
Pete
Muungoni
Fumba
Umbuji
Muyuni
Uzi Island
Makunduchi
Kibuteni
Mtende
Kizimkazi
5
0
5
10
15
MILES
ZANZIBAR

winding streets that suddenly debouch into tiny squares and markets, or bring one blinking into the bright sunshine of the sea-front. These houses are a feature of Zanzibar and the Arabs used to vie with one another in the extravagance of their building. There is even one house where the sand and other materials are reputed to have been mixed with egg whites. The houses have very thick walls and the size of their rooms depended on the length of the mangrove poles that were obtainable for supporting the ceilings. These mangrove poles are still shipped out on the dhows from Zanzibar and Lamu today. They are impervious to white ants and are much in demand in Arabia. You can see how they were used in the finely preserved rooms of the Zanzibar House hotel.

But the most important element in these houses are their main doors, made of teak, set with great brass studs and with their surrounding frames and lintels elaborately carved. The favourite motifs of this carving are the lotus (symbolising reproductive power), the fish (symbolising fertility), the chain (symbolising security), the date (symbolising plenty), and the frankincense tree (symbolising wealth). The designs are stylised, but easily recognisable. A good place to look for them is in the lanes around the Zanzibar Hotel, where many have been renovated.

From the civic point of view the most important buildings are along the seafront by the lawns of the People's Gardens. Here stand the old Arab Fort, with its round stone towers; the white People's Palace (formerly the Sultan's Palace); and the great Beit-el-Ajaib, which means the House of Wonders, with cannon guarding its steps. In the town there are several mosques, most notably that of El-Jami, and it is well worth visiting the museum, where there are fascinating exhibits of local wildlife, of dhow construction and traditional carving, as well as relics of the great explorer and missionary, Dr Livingstone, including his medicine chest. The house that Dr Livingstone lived in stands at Ngambo by the Dhow Harbour and is a highlight of the guided tour of the town, as is the explorer Burton's house.

Dr Livingstone

The slave market

Zanzibar was the base for Livingstone's famous expeditions, as it was for many missionaries' activity in East Africa, especially against the slave trade. The Arab slave traders used to bring captured Africans to Zanzibar from all over the East African interior. The slave market itself is described as having been an irregular, oblong space some 50 yards by 30 yards, surrounded on three sides by thatched palm huts and on the fourth by stone buildings. Sales were held at 4 pm and the male slaves were made to sit in rows on the ground while female slaves stood apart. The number of slaves and buyers present often exceeded 600. This iniquitous market was finally closed in 1873 and the present Anglican cathedral was built on its site. Even now the horrors of the trade are still remembered by Africans, and the revolution of 1964 was seen by many as the final overthrow of the Arabs who had organised that inhuman business.

Shops

There are innumerable shops in the Stone Town, some dim and mysterious, selling all manner of silver filigree work and curios, as well as local sweetmeats and other delicacies. The modern ones are near the Post Office. The Government guide from the Tanzania Friendship Tourist Bureau who meets you at the airport will advise on shops, most of which are now co-operatives. The open air fruit and vegetable markets are worth seeing. Specialities of the island are copperwork, silverware, mats, baskets, china and carving. You can get all sizes of the traditional Arab beaked copper coffeepots right up to the enormous ones that the itinerant coffee-sellers carry round the town. Models of dhows and of outrigger canoes also make amusing souvenirs. One of the best shops for these is at the Tanzania Friendship Tourist Bureau itself (Box 216, telephone 2344, cables URAFIKI), by the People's Gardens on the seafront. In particular it sells local silver necklaces, bracelets, coffee spoons and cocktail sticks, baskets and pomanders.

Tourist Bureau

Pomanders

The pomander, which takes its name from the French *pomme d'ambre*, is a ball of aromatic substances contained in a cloth or gauze bag. Pomanders have been used since Elizabethan times to keep household linen fresh. Naturally the ones sold in Zanzibar are clove pomanders and they are as pleasant a reminder of the island as you could hope to buy. They cost between Shs. 5/– and 10/–.

Arab chests

Another traditional, but rather bulkier, souvenir is an Arab chest. These are brought in on the dhows from Persia, Surat in India, and Bombay, and come in many sizes. A good shop to get them from is the Handcraft Showroom (Box 1072, Zanzibar) near the old Arab fort. Usually they are made of teak, are bound and studded in brass and have two or more locking drawers underneath the main part of the chest, while inside there is a small lidded partition. Bombay chests often have a secret drawer as well. Finally you can buy triangular Pemba stools, with leather-covered seats.

Hotels

There are three botels on the island. Two are in Zanzibar Town, the Zanzibar House (Box 392) and Afrika House (Box 317). The former, in one of the alleyways near the centre, was originally one large Arab house which was the Sultan's guest house, plus two smaller ones. It is a beautifully preserved example of traditional Arab architecture, has 32 rooms, some with air conditioning. The Afrika House Hotel, formerly the English Club, is a dignified building with a view over the sea and is rather cheaper. The third hotel is the entirely modern Bwawani, with 130 rooms, all air-conditioned and with private baths. It stands two miles from the town, near the Zanzibar National Stadium. All bookings and enquiries should be made through the Tanzania Friendship Tourist Bureau (see above). There are plans for a beach resort near Kibweni, north of Zanzibar Town.

Restaurants

There are no restaurants except in the hotels. However you can get chappattis and cooked meats of various kinds from street sellers and these can be surprisingly good, though eating this way cannot be called sitting down to a meal.

Tours and Transport

All visitors are met by the TFTB, who are responsible for ground transport throughout their stay. Both half day and full day tours are available, which go round the town and to several beach resorts where snacks are available at small cafés. The main places seen are Uroa beach, Mangapwani beach, Nungwi beach, Mapinduzi, Makinduchi, the Jozani forest and Kizimbazi. The stop at each place is normally around one hour. Costs are from Shs. 150/– per person for a full day. Individual travel in the island is discouraged, though visitors can walk round the town. The TFTB may be able to arrange boat trips to the islands near the harbour.

Prison Island

These are Prison Island, where recalcitrant slaves used to be incarcerated, now well known for the giant tortoises that inhabit it; Bat Island, from which the flying foxes cross the water to Zanzibar every evening to feed on the fruit trees; and Grave Island, where a number of British sailors were buried during the 1914–18 war, and where small gazelle live.

For the sportsmen there are tennis courts and a golf course, but the main attractions of Zanzibar are its wonderful beaches and coral reefs, with the countless sea shells that you find among them, and the ruined palaces of former Arab rulers. The best beaches are along the east coast of the island, especially at Chwaka Bay, to which there is a good road from the town. However, practically wherever you go you will find a good beach, and all of them are kept free of sharks by the surrounding ledge of coral. The skin-diving, or goggling as it's known here, is superb. Do not forget the tides—they rise anything up to 15 feet, depending on the time of year. You will see dozens of canoes on the beaches, both simple dugout ones and outriggers. Canoe-building is an important craft in these islands, since fishing is a major industry. You may also notice the fish traps along the shore—long lines of stakes forming a V, with the wide end in the shallows. As the tide recedes, fish that have sum into the wide end are forced down into the trap at the narrow end and so are caught.

South of Zanzibar Town, Jozani Forest, Makunduchi

One good short trip is to go out past Mazizini to Chukwani, where there are coral cliffs. However the principal road south towards Makunduchi, leaves the town a different way. Thirty-five km (22 miles) out, near Pete, is the tiny primeval forest of Jozani, where there are leopards and monkeys. Further on, around 55 km (35 miles) you fork right for Kizimbazi, where there is an ancient Shirazian Mosque. This has been renovated in recent years but the northern wall has a fine original mihrab (equivalent to an altar) and two layers of Kufic writing, in which the date of the mosque is mentioned. When translated it comes to 1107 AD. Kufic writing, a form of very old Arabic script, is found on other mosques in East Africa, but this is the longest example. On the road to Kizimbazi you will pass through various villages and probably see both cloves and copra being dried. Near Makunduchi at mile 36 is an underground cave with formations of stalgamites.

Kizimbazi

The road to Chwaka Bay, due east of the town passes Dunga, where lie the remains of a palace erected between 1845 and 1856.

North of Zanzibar Town, Marahubi Palace, Mangapwani

There is far more of historic interest north of the town than south of it. On the way out past the old harbour, where dhows are often being careened and repaired, you pass Livingstone's house and the Bwawani Hotel. Six km further on, along the road to Bububu, stand the remains of Mtoni Palace, built early in the nineteenth century by an Arab merchant called Saleh bin Haramili. Alas for Haramili, the Sultan Seyyid Said accused him of dealing in slaves, and as a punishment confiscated the palace, together with its valuable clove estates. The Sultan thus became considerably richer, while Haramili died a beggar. Mtoni is believed to have accommodated a thousand people and today you can still see its courtyard, with a row of stone baths at one end, and the aqueduct that brought water to the house. Down on the beach, embedded in the coral sand, lie some of the old guns that were used as flagstaff stays in the garden, for what was the garden is now foreshore.

Mtoni Palace

Marahubi Palace

About a mile further on, to the left of the road, is another palace—the Marahubi Palace which housed the harem of Seyyid Bargash (Sultan 1870–88). You approach it down a treelined drive from the road. The gardens are thickly planted with mango grees and there are two ponds of blue lilies. The remains of the Palace itself are a series of pillars which used to support balconies, walls now covered in creepers and a domed Persian bathhouse. Looking at these ruins you might well think them many centuries old. In fact the Marahubi Palace was burnt down accidentally in 1899. But its traditional style, and the speed with which the African climate weathers any structure, makes it appear much older than it is. Further on towards Bububu is the last Sultan's summer palace at Kibweni, a glamorous white building in striking contrast to the ruined palaces so near it.

Bububu itself had one of the world's shortest railways. It ran simply from the outskirts of Zanzibar Town to Bububu, less than nine miles, and was opened in 1906 by an enterprising American who had persuaded the Sultan that to be thoroughly up to date he must have a railway. It closed in 1927 and the track has long been taken up, but the stations and platforms are still there.

Not far beyond Bububu a track leads off to the right through a coconut plantation and a mile or so up a slope to the Persian Baths at Kidichi. This remarkably preserved series of domed bathhouses, with deep stone baths and massive seats set in the walls around them, were built by the Sultan Seyyid Said for his second wife.

Finally this road north divides, the right-hand fork going on to Mkotoni, off which lies Tumbatu Island. The left fork takes you to Mangapwani, and one of Zanzibar's notorious slave holes. This is not easy to find. Usually there is a man selling coconuts near a large house where the road ends past Mangapwani village, and one of the children around will show you the way to the slave hole. Otherwise take the footpath past the large house towards the sea, which is only a few hundred yards away. The path comes out on a low coral cliff overlooking a delightful small bay. The slave pit is to the right, covered over by stone slabs. The slaving dhows used to anchor in the bay at night and take the slaves off secretly.

PEMBA

There are no hotels in Pemba and as the island is only very seldom open to visitors you should not set off for it without first consulting the Tanzania Friendship Tourist Bureau or the Tanzania Tourist Corporation, if you are in Dar es Salaam. The airstrip is at Chake Chake, near the centre of the island, but it could be difficult to obtain transport when you get there. Probably the best way to go would be by taking a round trip from Zanzibar on one of the steamers, which enables you to know precisely where your next meal is going to be served, viz. in the ship's dining saloon.

Pemba is almost certainly much older than its neighbour, although geographically similar. Both were once covered by primeval forest, of which the Ngezi forest in the north of Pemba is a remnant. The island has its own species of grey monkey, antelope and flying fox. The beaches are superb, both for swimning and goggling, though less accessible than those of Zanzibar.

The Pemba Channel, between the island and the mainland, is up to 400 fathoms deep, and in consequence is magnificent for game fishing, though the well known Pemba Channel Fishing Club is based on the Kenya Coast. By comparison, the channel between Zanzibar and the mainland is only 25 fathoms.

The towns are Wete, the port, and Chake Chake, both situated at the head of long creeks, which give them their importance, since warships could never penetrate to them. Both have populations of between 7,000 and 8,000. There are remains of a Portuguese fort at Chake Chake, while the most outstanding ruin in the island is at Pujini, some seven miles north of the town. This is thought to have been the palace of a ruler of Pemba and consists of a citadel, the massive ramparts of which are still standing, a mosque, a few graves, a lily pond and the foundations of numerous houses.

Other relics in the island are "Harun's Tomb" in the north-east at Chwaka, a traditional pillar tomb 15 feet high, believed to be the memorial to a former Shirazi Prince; and the "Lonely Tomb" close to the village of Vitongoje, standing between the beach and the jungle, traditionally said to be the burial place of the leader of a new settlement, who died suddenly and whose followers then took to their ships and sailed away, no-one knows whither.

Bull Fighting

Finally Pemba has an unexpected tradition of bullfighting, derived from the Portuguese occupation of the sixteenth and seventeenth centuries. The fights are held in the hot months of December—February, when the ground is hard, and are more games than fights. As in Southern France, the bull is not killed.

Useful Facts—TANZANIA

Banks

Banking hours are 8.30 am to 12.00 Monday to Friday and 8.30 am to 11.00 am on Saturday. Banking facilities are provided by the National Bank of Commerce.

Currency

The Tanzania shilling is divided into ten 10 cent pieces. There are strict currency regulations and you may only take a maximum of Shs. 40/- out of the country.

Diplomatic Representation

There are Tanzanian diplomatic missions in Addis Ababa, Bonn, Cairo, The Hague, Kinshasa, London, Moscow, New Delhi, Ottawa, Paris, Peking, Rome, Stockholm, Tokyo, United Nations and Washington. Visas and visitors' passes are obtainable from them.

The following countries maintain Embassies or Consulates in Dar es Salaam—Algeria, Angola, Australia, Austria, Belgium, Burundi, Canada, Communist China, Cuba, Czechoslovakia, Denmark, Ethiopia, Finland, France, German Federal Republic, Great Britain, Guinea, Hungary, India, Indonesia, Israel, Italy, Ivory Coast, Japan (resident Nairobi), Korean Republic, Morocco, Netherlands, Nigeria, Pakistan, Romania, Rwanda, Somali Republic, Sweden, Switzerland, Turkey, UAR, USA, USSR, Yugoslavia, Zaire, Zambia.

Licensing Hours

Bars can serve alcohol from 12.00 to 2.00 pm and 5.00 pm to midnight

Frontiers

At the time of writing the border with Kenya was closed.

Public Holidays

Official public holidays, when Government offices, banks and shops close, are Christmas Day, Zanzibar Revolution Day (January 12), CCM Day (February 5) Good Friday, Easter Monday, International Workers Day (May 1), Union Day (April 26), Maulid Day (mid-June), Independence and Republic Day (December 9), Idd-ul-Fitr, Idd-ul-Haj. These last two are Moslem religious festivals and the actual dates vary from year to year.

Shopping Hours

7.30 am to 6.00 pm (1800) on weekdays, usually with a lunch break from 12.30 to 2.00 pm (1400).

Baganda women in a market

Uganda

The Country

Ugandans are understandably proud of their country. Though not as large as Tanzania or Kenya, its fertile valleys are well farmed, producing coffee, tea, sugar and cotton for export. Its mountains and lakes are magnificent (over 13,000 of Uganda's 91,000 sq miles are water). Being mostly 3,000 ft or more above sea level it has an agreeable climate. Both the fabled Mountains of the Moon (the Ruwenzori) and the source of the Nile lie within its borders. Nor need Ugandansconcede any advantage to their neighbours in the matter of wildlife, for the National Parks teem with game.

History

Moreover the country is founded on one of Africa's oldest established cultures, of which the outside world was ignorant, knowing East Africa mainly through trade and settlement along the coastline. There was plenty of legend about great potentates, inland seas and King Solomon's Mines—but not much genuine knowledge. However, when the first white men to enter the country, Grant and Speke, footslogged their way up the shores of Lake Victoria in 1862, they walked straight into an organised civilisation. They were received at the court of the Kabaka (the King) of Buganda and it was from there that Speke made his famous journey to the source of the Nile, at the spot near Jinja where it leaves Lake Victoria to start its long journey through the Sudan and Egypt to the Mediterranean. The acceptance of Christianity in Uganda led to the opening up of East Africa.

People

The population is 10 million, mostly Christians or Moslems. The largest single group are the Baganda (the people of Buganda, whose language is called Luganda) but there are many others, from the pygmies of the Ituri Forest in Western Uganda to the superb Karamojong tribe of the north-east who are cattlemen and warriors, or the Acholi, famous for their Bwola dancing. Because under British rule, conceded by the Kabakas, the country became a Protectorate, no European settlement was permitted.

Government

Uganda used to comprise a number of districts, plus four kingdoms—Buganda, from which Uganda has derived its name, Ankole, Bunyoro and Toro—and a special territory, Busoga. However, these kingdoms no longer exist, and today the country is divided into 18 districts for administrative purposes. It became an independent state within the British Commonwealth on October 8, 1962, and a Republic a year later. The National Assembly sits in Kampala.

Tourists

Shortly before this was written (mid-1979) President Amin was overthrown, ending a period of seven years in which tourism was discouraged. However all the infrastructure of hotels and lodges remains and the new Government announced that visitors would again be welcome.

Climate

The Equator runs through Uganda, but the altitude keeps the temperature pleasant and the humidity low. In the day it seldom rises above 80°F (26°C), and at night falls to around 60°F (15°C). Obviously it becomes cooler as you climb towards the mountains, and at Kabale, for instance, log fires are welcome in the evenings. Rainfall is fairly evenly spread out, with slightly heavier falls in March–May and October–November, but it does not normally disrupt safaris. See also under General Information.

National Parks and Game Reserves

There are three National Parks. They are served by airstrips and roads, and it is possible to drive to all three in one circuit. There is a speed limit of 50 kph (30 mph) in the Parks. The entrance charge to each Park is Shs. 20/– per adult (Shs. 5/– for Uganda residents and children under 14). Ordinary cars are let in free. Note specially that blowing of horns is strictly forbidden, you should not drive off the Park tracks and not alight from vehicles within 100 metres of a dangerous animal, such as elephant or lion. Rules in the National Parks are mainly designed for visitors' own safety and are worth observing. The National Park Wardens are assisted in running the Parks by uniformed Rangers. As well as dealing with poachers—a permanent problem—they man the gates and Headquarters and can be hired to act as guides.

The National Parks are:

THE RUWENZORI NATIONAL PARK

767 sq miles in a fantastic area of extinct volcanoes on the shores of Lakes Edward and George in south-west Uganda. See page 131.

THE KABALEGA FALLS NATIONAL PARK

1,504 sq miles in north-west Uganda, named after the spectacular Falls on the Nile, formerly called Murchison. See page 137.

THE KIDEPO VALLEY NATIONAL PARK

500 sq miles on the borders of the Sudan in north-eastern Uganda. It is one of the wildest parts of the country, with magnificent scenery. For detailed description see page 140.

The Parks have excellent lodges run by Uganda Hotels Ltd and bookable through the Uganda Tourist Development Corporation (Box 7211, Kampala). There are also campsites which can be booked through the Park wardens' offices, or consult the National Parks Office (Box 3530, Kampala).

Professional photographers are charged according to a scale of fees for taking pictures in the National Parks. For further information write to the National Parks Office. Amateur photographers are not charged any fees.

Uganda has 14 Game Reserves, mostly without lodge accommodation. In the southern part of the country there are Kikagati on the

Tanzania border; Lake Mburo in Ankole; the Gorilla Reserve (home of the rare mountain gorilla) in the Gahinga Forest on the Rwanda border in the extreme south-west; Kigezi, Kyambura and Kibale, all of which adjoin the Ruwenzori National Park; Katonga in the south and the Toro Reserve adjoining the Semliki Flats Reserve at the southern end of Lake Albert (see page 137). In the north-west the Karuma and Aswa Lolim Reserves adjoin the Kabalega Falls National Park, while Ajai's Reserve in the West Nile District is the best place to see the rare white rhinoceros. In the north-east are the Matheniko, Pian-Upe and Bokora Reserves which between them provide year-round grazing for many varieties of plains game. For detailed information, contact the Game Department, Box 4, Entebbe.

Hunting and Fishing

Outside the National Parks there are controlled hunting areas, including some of the Game Reserves, where quotas are set for the number of animals which may be shot in each area in any year. Licences are then issued until the quota has been filled. For information write to the Uganda Tourist Development Corporation (Box 7211, Kampala). Safaris are organised by Uganda Wildlife Develpoment Ltd (Box 1764, Kampala). The best hunting season in northern and eastern Uganda is December–April, and in southern and western Uganda it is June–November, though the Toro Game Reserve, south of Lake Albert is accessible at all times of the year. In addition there is good bird shooting in certain areas, including duck, geese, snipe, bustard, guinea-fowl, francolin and quail. The bird-shooting season lasts from October 1 to March 31.

Fishing

The fishing is good, cheap and unspoilt, both big-game fishing for Nile perch in Lake Albert and the Nile (with catches up to 200 lb) and fishing for trout, black bass, and other fish in mountain streams or lakes. A licence is required for trout fishing only and can be got through the Fisheries Dept, Box 4, Entebbe, or the Fisheries Office, Box 524, Mbale.

Hotels and Lodges

During the 1970s Uganda Hotels Ltd embarked on a substantial development programme, designed to improve tourist amenities throughout the country, especially for people organising their own safaris to remoter parts.

The new government is expected to ensure that these hotels, numbering 31 in all, realise their potential. They are indicated in the text by the initials (UHL). Bookings can be made centrally through the Uganda Tourist Development Corporation, Metropole House, 8/10 Entebbe Road, Kampala (postal address Box 7211, Kampala).

Prices are not quoted but at the time of writing were around Shs. 290/– a night single without breakfast in a first class Kampala hotel. Game lodges normally provide full board at about the same cost.

Other organisations run good hotels, such as the Imperial in Kampala. Addresses of these are given.

Remember that away from the capital meal times are inflexible and travellers arriving outside the standard hours may not get a hot meal. These hours are 12.30 pm to 2.00 pm (1400) for lunch and 7.00 pm (1900) to 9.00 pm (2100) for dinner.

Licensing hours are from 8.00 am to midnight.

Internal Transport

Air

Uganda Airlines operate regional and internal flights, including ones to the National Parks. They also offer air charter facilities from the international airport at Entebbe.

Rail

The railway bring Uganda's imports up from Mombasa 700 miles away in Kenya and the 24-hour trip from Kampala to Nairobi is deservedly popular; it passes through magnificent scenery and the first-class fare is lower than the air fare. Although the journey is slower than going by road it is decidedly more comfortable. From Kampala one line cuts west to Kasese at the foot of the Ruwenzori Mountains, 200 miles away; another line makes a marathon run north from Tororo (near the Kenya border) to Mbale, Soroti, Lira, Gulu and Pakwach, where a new bridge has been built to carry both rail and road across the Nile into the West Nile District.

Road

There is a network of good bitumen roads radiating from Kampala, which are steadily being extended into the furthest parts of the country. The main directions they take are the areas into which we will divide Uganda for the sake of convenience, namely *south-west* to Masaka, Mbarara and Kabale; *west* to Fort Portal and Kasese, which can also be reached by going directly north from Kabale and making a circuit of one's return journey to Kampala; *north* to Masindi, Gulu, the Murchison Falls, and the West Nile District; *east* to Jinja, Mbale and Moroto. In places these roads cease to be tarmaced and are surfaced in murram but they are passable all the year, except perhaps after very heavy rain, although black murram patches on the roads are very slippery when wet and you should drive cautiously. *Driving* There is a 88 kph (55 mph) speed limit on all roads in Uganda. As elsewhere in East Africa you drive on the left-hand side of the road. Kilometres have officially replaced miles for the measurement of distance. On the whole the signposting is adequate, but a good map is useful. You should take great care when driving after dark, as there are numerous cyclists with no lights. It is often worth hiring a self-drive car, if available, though this is expensive. You can drive in Uganda for up to 90 days on a current licence issued in your home country. You will find a warning notice "Elephants have right of way" at the National Parks entrances. It is quite serious and the elephants themselves take their precedence for granted! Petrol is usually available in towns and large villages.

Buses

Finally there are bus services to most parts of the country at very cheap rates. Details and timetables can be had from the Uganda Transport Co, Box 7038, Kampala. There are also frequent taxi services between the main towns. Enquire for these at Kampala Taxi Park.

Entebbe and Port Bell

Entebbe, 3,730 feet up, is not merely the international airport. It is a most attractively laid-out town in a parklike setting by Lake Victoria and it's a real pity simply to pass though on the airline bus to Kampala and never stop to see more. Originally it was a fishing village called Ntebe, meaning throne. In 1893 the British Commissioner, Sir Gerald Portal, set up the headquarters of the British administration there. Today it is still the seat of several Government Ministries, though the majority are in Kampala. State House is the official residence of the President. Before Independence this rambling colonial-style building housed the Governor.

The Entebbe Club, which may re-open, has a pretty nine-hole golf course, tennis, squash, cricket and football, and there is a swimming club. (Do not swim in the lake, inviting though its waters may seem. There is a risk of catching bilharzia, which infests most freshwater lakes in tropical Africa.) The Sailing Club, which also has a campsite, is half a mile from Entebbe on the Kampala road. The lake itself has risen several feet in recent years, almost submerging a memorial at Hippo Bay to the first missionaries, who came by boat across the lake from near Mwanza in 1877. There used to be pleasure cruises on the lake, which one hopes will be re-started.

Along the lake shore lie 70 acres of botanical gardens, which have a fine collection of vividly flowering tropical trees and plants and splendid sweeps of lawn. Lastly Entebbe has a zoo. You may well ask why anyone should start a zoo in a country so full of wildlife at liberty. The answer is that the Game Department started it as an orphanage for young animals found abandoned and it has now blossomed into a full-scale collection. Some of the "safe" animals and birds are housed in open enclosures, into which visitors may walk.

The Lake Victoria Hotel (UHL) set on a slope overlooking the water, is one of the best known in Uganda. Its lawns are a popular place to take tea in the afternoons and there are occasional Saturday night dances. The address is Box 15, Entebbe telephone 2644. Facilities for golf, tennis and other sports can be arranged. There are shops in the hotel, and a large swimming pool. Other shops are in the main street, half a mile away, while bus and taxi services start from near the market. There is a hospital. Finally of course there is the country's international airport, scene of the Israeli commandos' dramatic rescue of hostages held captive by pro-Palestinian guerillas after the hijacking of an airliner in 1976.

Port Bell

Port Bell, 11 km (7 miles) from Kampala is a boarding point for steamer services to other ports on Lake Victoria. Built as a port for Kampala, it was named after Sir Hesketh Bell, first Governor of Uganda, in 1907. The port consists of a single pier, but the township contains a group of new industries.

Kampala

From Entebbe to Kampala is a 34 km (21 miles) drive, through lush green countryside, mainly devoted to coffee, banana and cotton growing. It becomes hillier as you approach Kampala, and indeed the name means "the hill of the antelope". Kampala was always Uganda's commercial centre and on Independence, in 1962, it replaced Entebbe as official capital. Much of its history revolves around Buganda and the Kabakas, whose kingdom used to have its own government buildings at Mengo. The city is dotted with churches and mosques, while on Old Kampala Hill stand the remains of the Old Fort where the flag of the imperial British East Africa Company was first flown by Captain Lugard in 1890. There is a small museum, and the fort has a nostalgic interest, as well as a fine view. Indeed most of the city's important buildings are on the tops of hills, while houses and shops fill in the valleys. The Parliament Building stands on Nakasero Hill, above central Kampala. It is a distinguished example of modern architecture and has an entrance hall dominated by a carved wooden mural illustrating the range of Uganda's countryside and people. If you want to look around Parliament contact the Serjeant-at-arms.

Shopping

Kampala's main street has two names—it's called Jinja Road at the eastern end and Kampala Road at the western end—and most of the shops a visitor needs are along it. For curios we recommend the Government-sponsored National Handicraft Emporium on Kampala Road, with a branch in the Kampala International Hotel, whose stock is of strictly genuine Uganda craftsmanship and reasonably priced as are the carvings at the Crafts Market by the Imperial Hotel. The Tusitukirewamu Handcraft Co-operative shop in Kampala Road specialises in Buganda crafts, including dolls. You will find itinerant curio-sellers around the town as well. Bracelets, skin-covered drums, wooden carvings and basketware are among the best buys. It's worth demanding genuine Ugandan work, as distinct from mass-produced "African" souvenirs. The markets of African cities are always fascinating and Kampala's are no exception. The Nakivubo Market is good for pottery, barkcloth, charms and craftwork, while the Nakasero Market deals in farm produce. You may also find it interesting to visit the Namanve Pottery, 11 km from Kampala on the road to Jinja, where you can buy handthrown pots.

Hotels

The leading hotel is the centrally situated Kampala International (UHL, Box 7041) on Gun Hill. It has 300 bedrooms with private bath and telephone, several restaurants and bars, a nightclub (see below), shops and a swimming pool. Allied to it and not far away is the luxurious Nile Hotel and International Conference Centre (UHL)

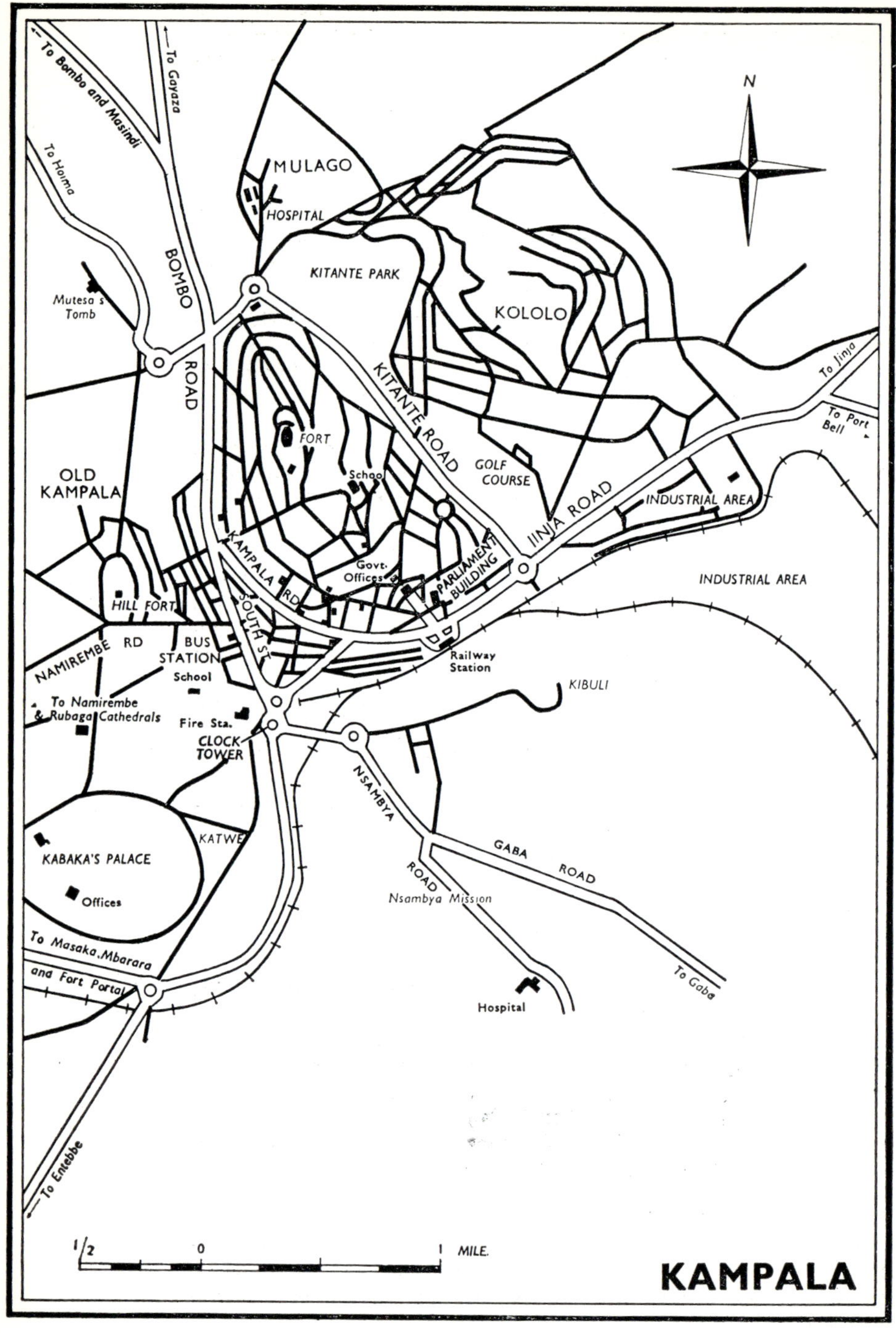
To Bombo and Masindi
To Gayaza
To Hoima
N
MULAGO
HOSPITAL
KITANTE PARK
KOLOLO
BOMBO
ROAD
Mutesa's Tomb
FORT
KITANTE ROAD
To Jinja
To Port Bell
GOLF COURSE
OLD KAMPALA
School
JINJA ROAD
INDUSTRIAL AREA
KAMPALA RD
Govt. Offices
PARLIAMENT BUILDING
INDUSTRIAL AREA
HILL FORT
SOUTH ST
NAMIREMBE RD
BUS STATION
Railway Station
School
KIBULI
To Namirembe & Rubaga Cathedrals
Fire Sta.
CLOCK TOWER
NSAMBYA ROAD
GABA ROAD
KATWE
KABAKA'S PALACE
Nsambya Mission
Offices
To Masaka, Mbarara and Fort Portal
To Gaba
Hospital
To Entebbe
1/2
0
1
MILE.
KAMPALA

with 95 double rooms and conference facilities for 2,000 people. The Imperial Hotel (Box 7088) also is an acknowledged social rendezvous. It has been completely modernised and all its rooms have private bath and telephone (Kampala, like the other cities of East Africa, is short of public telephones). A stone's throw away is the smaller Speke Hotel (Box 7036). All the above hotels are only a mile from the golf course, which welcomes visitors. Less expensive are the Antler's Inn in Bombo Road, where all rooms have a private bathroom, the Fairway and the Equatoria. Eight km from the centre on the Port Bell road is the rebuilt Silver Springs Hotel (Box 734, Kampala) which is good value for money; however, a car is necessary if you stay here. It has its own swimming pool and an attractive garden. Finally there is cheaper accommodation at the Lodge Paradise in Salisbury Road and the Amber Hotel in Portal Avenue. At most hotels laundry handed over in the morning is returned the same day. The electricity supply is 240 volts.

Restaurants

Kampala has always had a fairly wide range of restaurants, including those in the main hotels and others with Chinese and Lebanese specialities. The semi-open air restaurant in the Speke Hotel long enjoyed a good reputation. However at the time of writing it was not possible to make recommendations.

Drinks

All the main restaurants have bars. The two main types of local lager-type beer are called "Nile" and "Bell" and are served cold unless you ask for them "warm". They are much cheaper than imported beers. Wines from Europe, when obtainable, are fairly expensive. So are spirits. The local equivalent to gin, called *waragi*, is cheap and deservedly popular. It makes a good substitute for a gin and tonic and is now exported to Europe.

Nightclubs

The best known nightclub in the city is in the Kampala International Hotel. On the outskirts of town there are many African nightclubs, which in normal times fairly hum with life, particularly on Saturday and Sunday nights. These include the Susana Club at Nakulabye (5 km out) and the Arizona at Kibuye (3 km). They charge standard bar prices and there is a small entrance fee.

National Theatre

You can also see a cross-section of the community at the strikingly fine National Theatre and Cultural Centre, in the centre of the city, where a variety of professional and amateur companies perform; music festivals are also held there. For these and for cinema performance times consult the local press.

Tourist Association

A number of both local and East Africa-wide tours are organised from Kampala. For general information go to the Uganda Tourist Development Corporation on Entebbe Road.

Golf

The Uganda Golf Club, which runs the good 18-hole course we mentioned above, charges a green fee of Shs. 10/– a day on weekdays, Shs. 20/– a day at weekends or Shs. 40/– a week. You pay caddies Shs. 4/50 for the 18 holes.

Hospitals

Should you become ill it is worth knowing that the Mulago Hospital is a magnificent new one, with 800 beds, and fully qualified doctors. The Nsambya Hospital and the Mengo Hospital, both run by missionaries, are also good.

Makerere University

Art Gallery

Out along the Bombo road, where incidentally the fruit bats gather in incredible swarms in the trees and there are also millions of butterflies, is a hill completely devoted to Makerere University, founded in 1922. It's a beehive of activity and visitors are particularly welcome at the School of Fine Art, which has trained most of East Africa's leading artists. Indeed a large proportion of East Africa's top men in most other spheres graduated from Makerere too. If you want to know what tomorrow's leaders think now, go and chat to the students or attend one of the public lectures. The Makerere Art Gallery, near the School of Fine Art, was built as the result of a grant from the Calouste Gulbenkian Foundation and houses a permanent collection of contemporary East African paintings, sculpture, prints and ceramics. It is open every day except Tuesdays.

Museums

The Uganda Museum, a short bus ride (Kira Road Service) from the city centre, also exhibits paintings from time to time, though its fame rests on its collection of African musical instruments, which the attendants will play for you on request. Its varied range of historical exhibits tell the story of the cultures that have influenced Uganda, while the models of scenes from royal ceremonies are especially fascinating. There is no entrance fee. The museum is also the headquarters of the Uganda Society, which arranges lectures on African subjects.

Mosques

Cathedrals

In the past Uganda was the focal point of a great missionary effort, especially in the late nineteenth century. Despite the mosques and temples that strike the eye in Kampala—and "strike" is the word because some are so highly coloured they look as though they are carved out of Neapolitan ice-cream—the Christian churches have counted more in Uganda's history. This is not to decry the interest in seeing the minareted Kibuli Mosque, or the Bahai Temple, both fine buildings. Nor should one forget the importance today of the country's many devout Muslims, but it was the Church Missionary Society that insisted on the building of the Uganda railway after the conversion of the Kabaka and so began modern development. Namirembe Hill bears the rambling red brick Protestant cathedral, to which the congregation is called for services not by bells but by the beating of drums. The cathedral has a foundation of rails from Uganda's first single line railway, which ran six miles from the foot of Nakasero Hill to Port Bell.

There are remarkable views over the city both from Namirembe and from Rubaga Cathedral (Catholic), whose two towers rise from the site where the Kabaka Mutesa I originally had his palace. The Kabaka donated the ground to the first Roman Catholic missionaries, the White Fathers, and between 1912 and 1921 African worshippers carried two million bricks up the hill to build the cathedral. Africa's first African Archbishop, the late Dr Joseph Kiwanuka, lies in a glass-topped coffin here—an object of great veneration.

It was from Rubaga that the explorer Stanley, continuing the travels of David Livingstone, wrote his historic letter to the *DailyTelegraph* newspaper in London urging that missionaries should be sent to the Kabaka's court. The first Church Missionary Society missionaries arrived in 1877, and the first White Fathers two years later. However, during the reign of Mutesa's successor, Mwanga, hostility to the changes that the missions were making came to a head and resulted in the tragic martyrdom of 25 young Africans in 1885 and 1886. In Namugongo village, ten miles east of Kampala, there is a Catholic church built in memory of 22 of the martyrs and a shrine dedicated by Pope Paul when he visited the country in July 1969, while there is a stone cross at Natete, six miles out, on the spot where the three others were burnt to death. The martyrs were recently canonised by His Holiness the Pope.

Kabakas

Dead Kabakas themselves, Mutesa I, Mwanga, Sir Daudi Chwa and the last Kabaka, Sir Edward Mutesa II are buried on Kasubi Hill, just to the west of Makerere. Their tombs lie within a huge reeded hut erected on the death of Mutesa I in 1884. It is one of the finest examples of traditional Buganda thatched buildings. There is a small entry fee, your shoes must be left outside and photography is not allowed. The tombs are guarded by the King's "widows", who expect a small donation from visitors.

Buganda

The former Kingdom of Buganda, within which both Kampala and Entebbe lay, had a special constitutional status and was ruled from Mengo, a hill only a mile south-west of central Kampala. The Buganda Parliament, the Lukiko, used to meet in an imposing green-roofed administrative building, topped with a spire, called the Bulange. From the Bulange a broad ceremonial avenue a mile long sweeps across to the site of the ancestral Palace of the Kabakas. The Palace itself was surrounded by an intricate reed fence of a design reserved exclusively for Royalty. The area is used by the Uganda army and is not open to the public.

In area Buganda totals a quarter of Uganda, including the towns of Masaka, Bombo, Mubende and Njeru (a new town on the west bank of the Nile opposite Jinja). Large quantities of cotton and coffee are grown in the area, while everywhere you will see the banana trees that provide the staple food of all southern Uganda.

National Dress

Buganda women wear a colourful traditional dress with puffed sleeves and a long wrap-around skirt with a slight bustle at the back, known as the *busuti*. The women illustrated at the start of this chapter are wearing them. The *busuti* has effectively become a national dress, though other regions do have different traditions. Quite often its made up from a gay printed cloth called *kitenge*, a name that refers to the style of print (as *Paisley* does) not the style of dress. *Kitenge* is very popular and has been used for evening dresses specially designed for Uganda Hotels' hostesses.

The male traditional dress is the long white *khanzu*. Simple and dignified it is highly regarded by Ugandan men and also originated in Buganda, where the former royal *khanzus* had purple trimmings.

South-west to Mbarara, Kabale, the Gorilla Reserve and the Ruwenzori National Park

One of the most rewarding circuits you make in Uganda is that taking in the magnificent hill country around Kabale and the great Ruwenzori National Park, formerly known as the Queen Elizabeth National Park. Virtually the whole Kampala—Mbarara—Kabale—Ruwenzori Park—Fort Portal—Kampala circuit can be made on tarmac. Nonetheless we do not advise attempting it in less than three days, with two night stops, and four or five days would be much better if your sightseeing and game viewing is going to be more than perfunctory. Distances look deceptively small on maps and in the south-west the roads wind up and down among the hills. Even driving fast the 426 km (265 miles) from Kampala to Kabale needs a good five hours, while from Kabale to Mweya takes an afternoon or morning. Incidentally although Mweya has a good airstrip, Kabale has not got one. Leaving Kampala you branch right from the Entebbe road one mile out of town and then drive parallel to the shore of Lake Victoria, though out of sight of it. This is a good tarmac road with easy gradients and curves, running through lush cultivation, especially of bananas, and occasional areas of swamp. You will notice that most of the Buganda countryside is occupied by small farms, each farmer living on his own land. In consequence there are few villages. At Budo, 16 km (10 miles) from Kampala, and off the main road to the left is the hill on which by tradition the Kabakas used to be installed when they inherited the throne.

You cross the Equator 80 km (50 miles) from Kampala, an easy spot to recognise from the broad white band across the tarmac and a circular sign by the road. Masaka is 130 km (81 miles) from Kampala, and 21 km (13 miles) before you reach it a road turns off to the delightful Lake Nabugabo. The lake is safe for swimming, being free from bilharzia, boats can be hired, and you may see hippo round here, too.

Lake Nabugabo

Masaka

Masaka itself is a busy market town, 4,300 feet up and the centre of a rich coffee growing district. The Tropic Inn (UHL, Box 565, Masaka), is modern and comfortable. It is set in a pleasant garden where there are regular displays of African dancing. All the rooms have private baths and there is a golf course nearby. There are two banks in the town. Thirty-eight km (24 miles) away is the small lake port of Bukakata, from which it is possible to get by boat to the Sese Islands and the Nkosi Island Sitatunga Sanctuary. This must be arranged through the Game Department (Box 4, Entebbe) well in advance. The sitatunga is a medium-sized antelope which inhabits swamps and is remarkable for having greatly elongated hooves, which spread out to assist it on soft ground. When frightened it

Sitatunga Sanctuary

submerges until only its face is above water. Sitatunga also live round Lake Nabugabo and in the Ruwenzori National Park.

Directly south from Masaka you come to the Tanzania frontier and after that can cross the Kagera River by ferry, and so reach the lake port of Bukoba. The main tarmac road goes south-west to Mbarara, 148 km (92 miles) from Masaka, through rolling open country being developed for cattle ranching, and past the Lake Mburo Game Reserve, where there are bushbuck, oribi, impala, buffalo, lion and leopard, among others.

Lake Mburo

Mbarara

Mbarara is a small town, 3,600 feet up, that is nonetheless the capital of Ankole District. The palace of the former bishop of Ankole stands on a hill just outside the town and both Anglican and Roman Catholic bishops have their seats here and so there are, necesarily, two cathedrals. The Agip Motel (UHL) is small but good while the Uganda Coffee Shop, in the main street, is a useful spot to break a long journey. There is also the Parkway Hotel. A tarmac road, going west from Mbarara to the Kabale–Fort Portal road, facilitates the journey direct to the Ruwenzori National Park.

Ankole

Ankole is really famous for its cattle, whose long curving horns reach a length of four feet. You will often see them being herded along the roadsides, or grazing near the villages. They are tended by the tall Bahima tribesmen. In this district the agriculturalists are a short, sturdier people called the Bairu. There are strong similarities between these tribes and the Tutsi and Hutu tribesmen of the Republic of Rwanda, not far away.

Onwards to Kabale, a further 148 km (92 miles), you climb up through the Kinoni hills into Kigezi District.

Kigezi

You are now coming close to both Rwanda and Zaire (the Congo), one of the most remote and fascinating parts of Africa, boasting one of the few active volcanoes in the world, glorious mountain lakes, and some of the densest forest, yet very productively farmed where there is cultivation. Being high up the district is cold at night and there is heavy rainfall, but when clear, its magnificent. Driving in the early morning along this road we saw the twin volcanoes Muhavura and Gahinga towering above the surrounding hills to our south, Muhavura a pure cone reminiscent of Fujiyama, while the snow-capped Ruwenzoris were visible 100 miles to the north.

Kikagati Game Reserve

Lying right on the Rwanda border is the Kikagati Game Reserve. Close to it is an attractive guest house situated on an island in the middle of the Kagera River. Rare orchids can be seen. Check with the Tourist Development Corporation as to whether the guest house is open. Forty-four km (28 miles) from Kabale a turn to the left leads to Lake Mulehe where there is good fishing.

Being scenically so spectacular, with steep hillsides that are terraced for growing tea and other crops, this south-western corner of Uganda is sometimes called the Switzerland of Africa and indeed the placid lakes with mountains rearing behind do remind one of Alpine landscapes. But comparisons with Europe start to collapse when you climb up into the Birunga mountains. Like the Ruwenzori, or Mount Kenya, they have the fantastic lichens, ferns and other giant tropical vegetation that we have described in the Kenya chapter.

Kabale

Kabale itself is Uganda's highest town, being 6,136 feet up, and the obvious centre for a holiday in this region. The White Horse Inn (UHL, Box 11, telephone 20, Kabale), was rebuilt in 1971/72, though keeping the old bar and lounge with its roaring log fire, round which mining prospectors from Rwanda, hunters, wildlife experts and other visitors gather in the evenings. All the hotel's rooms have private baths. Golf and tennis are available free of charge, there is a 9-hole golf course in the town. Incidentally, the Mutolere Catholic Mission near here makes locally famous cheroots, a slight variation on monasteries distilling liqueurs, though a more common drink is the local beer, called *Mulamba*.

Lake Bunyonyi

Only ten km (6 miles) from Kabale is the superbly beautiful Lake Bunyoni, long, narrow and deep, its shores alive with water lilies, which lies among the green hills on the Rwanda border. The setting is spectacular and sounds carry across the water with uncanny clarity—you can hear people on the other side talking. Hiring a dugout canoe costs a few shillings if you are feeling adventurous, and the water is safe for swimming, though cold. Meals and motorboats are available at the Lake View Lodge, Kyabahinga (P.O. Box 249, Kabale) which has a few rooms at reasonable prices. The Manager also arranges duck shooting and fishing for carp. There are camping sites at the Lake Bunyonyi Christian Centre, address Box 33, Kabale. It is possible to drive right round the lake. On the western side there is a former mining camp at Lushayu and there are elephant in the bamboo forest.

Kisoro

About one and a half hour's drive from Kabale is Kisoro, the acknowledged centre for visiting the mountains and seeing the shy and elusive mountain gorillas, not to mention the Impenetrable Forest. On the way, 44 km (28 miles) from Kabale a turn-off to the right leads to Lake Mulehe, one of seven lakes in the vicinity that offer fishing and duck shooting. At Kisoro itself the Travellers Rest Hotel (UHL, Box 1015, Kisoro via Kabale) has simple but comfortable accommodation and can provide an experienced mountain guide for Shs. 30/– a day. There are plans to enlarge the hotel.

Volcanoes

It's a 2–3 hour climb up the slopes of Mts Muhavura (13,540 ft) and Gahinga (11,400 ft) to the camp owned by the Travellers Rest on the saddle between the two, and at least three hours' climb to the lesser summit. Mt Muhavura steep and cone shaped, is still active and last erupted in the 1960s. The upper slopes of the mountains are covered in thick tussocky savannah grass. Below this grows a belt of thick bamboo forest where the mountain gorilla live, eating wild celery and bamboo shoots and keeping away from strangers. It had been feared they were dying out, but recently they have been breeding again both here and in the Impenetrable Forest. The Gorilla Reserve is in fact a 15 sq mile Forest Reserve on Gahinga. If you seriously intend looking for gorilla you must be accompanied by a game guard, which can be arranged by the Travellers Rest. From the Kanaba Gap, 59 km (37 miles) from Kabale there are magnificent views over the mountains and the Kisoro Plain.

Gorilla Reserve

To reach the Ruwenzori Park from Kisoro you can either return to Kabale and follow the tarmac, or take the more exciting dirt road through the Impenetrable Forest to Ishasha and Mweya, a drive of at least 5 hours. In spite of having a road through it, the Impenetrable Forest is aptly named. From the air the forest looks like a solid carpet. On the ground lianas and tree creepers twining among the tall trees make progress extremely slow. Reputedly gorillas are to be found at two places in the forest, near Luhizha and Rwanzu—and its difficult enough to find them! We will return to Ishasha, at the southern tip of the Ruwenzori Park in a moment.

Impenetrable Forest

It is an easy drive north on the tarmac from Kabale to Lakes Edward and George, named after British Sovereigns and re-named by President Amin, but not we suspect with any durability, so we stick to the old ones. The road twists and turns through the mountains before dropping down to the flats alongside the Kazinga Channel joining the two lakes, which can claim to be the ultimate source of the Nile because they supply water to Lake Albert through the Semliki river, though Lake Victoria of course is a far more important source. There is a breathtaking view of the Park from Kichwamba on the edge of the escarpment.

Ruwenzori National Park

The Ruwenzori Park lies along the shores of the lakes, with the Kigezi Game Reserve adjoining its southern end, while to the north rise the massive Ruwenzori Mountains. Founded as a Game Reserve in 1934, the area had been largely cleared of human occupation by sleeping sickness in the early years of this century—hence its vast wildlife population—though a few fishing villages remain. The total area of the Park is 1,994 sq km (767 sq miles) covering savannah grassland, scrub and forest, and it's open all the year round. North of the Kazinga Channel is the "explosion area" where some 87 volcanoes, now extinct, once burst through the earth's surface. Some of them now form crater lakes. These geological upsets apparently killed all the crocodiles in the region and none have been able to pass the natural barriers between Lake Albert and here since. The Park is renowned for its herds of elephant and buffalo estimated to total 4,000 and 18,000 respectively, while the two main lakes and the Kazinga Channel linking them are thought to contain the largest concentration of hippo anywhere in Africa—anything up to 14,000. The channel which teems with fish, mostly tilapia, attracts a wonderful variety of waterbirds. Curiously enough the bridge across the channel is a 1939–45 war Bailey Bridge that once spanned the Thames in England and was later re-erected here. On the open plains there are large herds of Uganda kob, waterbuck and topi, and you can expect to see lion, leopard, giant forest hog, warthog, sitatunga antelope and chimpanzees in the Maramagambo Forest.

The air-conditioned Mweya Safari Lodge (UHL) is beautifully sited on the shore of Lake Edward with its own swimming pool and airstrip, and is in daily contact with Kampala by radio-telephone for bookings. Through the Park Information Office you can book launch trips to see the wildlife in the Kazinga Channel, a "must" for any visitor. Land Rovers can be hired, and Ranger guides and maps are available. Mweya is 382 km (239 miles) from Kampala. Near the lodge is the old fishing village of Katwe, where salt is now processed.

Ishasha

Right down in the southernmost tip of the Park is Ishasha, the best area in Uganda to view lion. Its also one of the few places in Africa where the King of Beasts likes to take his siesta lying along the branch of a tree, here usually a fig or acacia. There is a rest camp, for which you should book in advance with the Chief Warden, Box 22, Lake Katwe. The Park also has several campsites.

If you leave the Park to the north it's worth looking out for the charming little Royal Pavilion at Kikorongo some 24 km (15 miles) north to Mweya on the route to Kasese. It stands on a rise among the crater lakes, only a few yards from the road. An inscription records that it was built for the official opening of the Park on April 30th 1954 by Queen Elizabeth II and the Duke of Edinburgh, while an engraved copper map shows the royal route through the park that day. There is a good view from the pavilion and we saw elephant, kob and other game, since the salt licks and water in the craters attract much wildlife.

Kasese

An alternative place to base oneself is Kasese, which has both air services from Entebbe and train services from Kampala. The Hotel Margherita (UHL, Box 90, Kilembe), named after the highest peak of the Ruwenzori, adjoins the Kilembe golf course where hotel residents can play free of charge, and is only 13 km (8 miles) from the Ruwenzori Park entrance. It is also a similar distance from the starting point for Ruwenzori climbs.

Fort Portal, Pygmies, Semliki and the Mountains of the Moon

Kilembe

Despite all the legends about King Solomon's Mines being in the Mountains of the Moon, the only mineral extracted from the Ruwenzori is copper, at Kilembe. This mining town, cradled in a valley, boasts the golf course mentioned above. Today the mountains' selling points are their giant vegetation, the eerie weirdness of their slopes and the opportunities for mountaineering.

Fort Portal, 319 km (217 miles) from Kampala by the direct tarmac

Opposite top: Rhino and egrets. EAA photo
Bottom: Diani beach, Kenya. Photo Richard Cox

road through Mubende, is, like Kasese, a base for mountaineering in the Ruwenzori and for touring western Uganda. The Omukama (King) of Toro had a palace here. The last monarch's daughter, Princess Elizabeth of Toro, is now one of the leading fashion models in America. It is a green and pleasant town, 5,000 ft above sea level, with lawns and gardens, a fair range of shops, three banks and good hotels. The Mountains of the Moon Hotel (UHL, Box 36, Fort Portal) is in the town, while the Ruwenzori Tea Hotel (UHL, Box 53, Fort Portal) is 8 km (5 miles) out along the Kampala road, and slightly higher up with splendid views of the mountains. In both hotels all rooms have private bathrooms.

Semliki Reserve

The safaris possible around here are numerous. You can drive round the north side of the Ruwenzoris to the Bwamba Pass, with its wonderful landscape, and to the Hot Springs of Bundibugyo. Not far from Bundibugyo you can go to Ntandi in the Ituri Forest to have a look at the pygmies—they are, we should warn you, a trifle blasé about tourists nowadays and expect to be paid large sums for being photographed. Or you can make rather longer trips up to the southern end of Lake Albert where the Semliki River debouches into the lake through one of the country's best game areas, the grasslands of the Semliki Flats and the Toro Game Reserve. Uganda Hotels Ltd have built a completely new Semliki Safari Lodge in discreet traditional style on the banks of the Wassa River, close to the old tented camp. It has an airstrip, all rooms have baths, and the atmosphere is relaxed and comfortable, while salt licks bring game to within sight of the lodge verandah. Not that you'll have any difficulty seeing hundreds of animals here. Fishing is available in Lake Albert, and it may be possible to arrange for hunting. For arrangements contact the Tourist Development Corporation in Kampala. The Reserve supports large herds of Uganda kob—about 10,000 of them all told—as well as buffalo, "pygmy" elephant of the small Congo Forest breed, leopard, hippo, Jackson's hartebeest, waterbuck and giant forest hog. It is also one of the best lion-viewing areas in Uganda.

Lake Albert

Lake Albert itself offers fishing for Nile perch, which come up to 200 lb, and for tiger fish—for their size, one of the best fighting fish in Africa. Alternatively, if you have a mind to see how Uganda is being developed, call on the new fishing industry at Ntoroko. Or you could take a trip on the steamboat *The Murchison*, which occasionally comes down Lake Albert to Semliki from Paraa.

Mountains of the Moon

These excursions, however, are all merely sideshows to our way of thinking. The Ruwenzoris, the Mountains of the Moon, legendary home of Rider Haggard's *She*, are the Big Show. Some classic books have been written about them, and with reason, for they are at the heart of the mysterious, tempting and frightening Africa which so

Opposite top left: Luo elder in tribal dress. Photo Peter Hill
Top right: boy at Bagamoyo, Tanzania. Photo George Baker
Bottom: Uganda kob

captures the soul of all explorers. This is a big continent. It may be God's back garden, but it's no-one else's. You feel it in the Ruwenzoris. The forest, inhabited by elephant and buffalo, is the thick Equatorial forest that once covered much of Uganda before man and fire cleared it. Above the forest you come out where the crater lakes and the giant vegetation create a completely unearthly landscape, behind which the mist occasionally breaks to reveal the glaciers and snowy peaks above. The Bakonjo tribe, whose short, sturdy men can be hired as porters, know the legends of the mountains, and the paths—which are about equally eerie. But do not be put off by this, the way is fairly well charted right up to three peaks, Mt Speke (16,080 ft), Mt Stanley (16,794 ft) and Mt Baker (15,988 ft). Depending how far you go a trip could take ten days, while a keen walker can do a circuit of the crater lakes up to 14,000 ft in seven days. The best months for climbing expeditions are January, February and July. The Mountain Club of Uganda (Box 2927, Kampala) owns three huts on the route and used to provide equipment: but check the availability for yourself.

North to Lake Albert, Kabalega Falls, Paraa and West Nile District

The direct road to the Kabalega Falls from Kampala passes through Masindi, 219 km (136 miles) north of the capital, a small township with an airstrip that is a good stepping-off point for visits to the Park. The Masindi Hotel (UHL, Box 11, Masindi) is comfortable. There are tennis and squash courts at the Masindi Club and a golf course. There is also a small resthouse, the Rafiki, which provides cheap accommodation.

Lake Albert

From Masindi it's only a short drive to various interesting spots. At Butiaba on Lake Albert you can go fishing for Nile perch and take launch trips up to the Kabalega Falls. It was round Lake Albert that the late Humphrey Bogart acted out the film story of C. S. Forester's novel *The African Queen*. To the south-west is Hoima, centre of a tobacco-growing district. The Budongo Forest near here is considered the finest stretch of equatorial forest remaining in Uganda. Like the rainforests of West Africa it is characterised by enormous buttressed mahogany trees, orchids, ferns and lianas, or monkey ropes. If you are lucky you may see chimpanzee, colobus monkey, many butterflies and a wonderful variety of birdlife. Further south, on top of the steep eastern side of Lake Albert, is a point called "Baker's View" where the famous explorer Sir Samuel Baker first saw Lake Albert (see below).

The Nile

At the extreme north of Lake Albert the Victoria Nile flows in from the east, while the Albert Nile goes north, forming the boundary of the Kabalega Falls National Park. Along here a new game lodge, the Pakuba Safari Lodge (UHL), with 100 beds and a swimming pool, has greatly increased the accommodation available in the Park. It overlooks Kateer Bay. Further up the Albert Nile is the town of Pakwach, the gateway to the West Nile District (see below). Here again there is a new lodge run by UHL, close to the Pakwach bridge and 19 km from Paraa. Normally the steamboat *The Murchison* makes trips from Pakwach to Paraa and 5 hour excursions on the lake, but at the time of writing was moored at Paraa.

Kabalega Falls National Park

The Kabalega National Park is 1,504 square miles of grass and bush, divided by the Victoria Nile flowing down from Lake Victoria to Lake Albert. On the way the river is forced through a rock gap only 20 ft wide and plunges 127 ft down into a gigantic pool. This is the famous fall, which now has a second set of falls not far away, made when the heavy rains from 1961–5 overflowed along another route. Originally called after the explorer, Murchison, the falls have been renamed after King Kabalega of the Bunyoro, a leader of legendary bravery.

There is a pathway up the cliff to the top of the falls, while the stretch of the Nile below is heavily populated with crocodiles, which you can often see basking on the bank in the sun with their mouths wide open. There are schools of hippo in the water too, and elephant cooling themselves in the shallows. It is estimated that there are 14,000 elephant, 30,000 buffalo, 13,000 hippo and 600 crocodile in the Park. A special attraction is the small herd of white rhino—one of the rarest animals in the world. Until recently, this animal (both larger and more docile than the more numerous black rhino) was found only in a small area on the west bank of the Albert Nile, where its future was threatened by poaching. To preserve the herd, it was captured and transported to the Kabalega Falls National Park in 1964, and the white rhinos have settled down well in their new surroundings. They are thriving, and now safe from the danger of extinction.

Paraa

Paraa Safari Lodge (UHL, P.O. Kabalega Falls, via Masindi) is situated on the bank of the Nile 11 km (7 miles) downstream from the falls. It's nothing unusual to find elephant grazing outside your bedroom window when you wake up in the morning. Each room has its own bath and airconditioning is available. Fishing for Nile perch can be arranged. Launch trips are run daily from Paraa to the falls; they offer a unique opportunity to see a wide variety of animals and birds, and we strongly recommend them. The approach to the roaring falls is unfailingly dramatic and we had close up views of hippo, crocodile, buffalo, kob, waterbuck, sacred ibis, weaver birds and many other species. Tickets may be obtained from the Parks' Information Office at the lodge. The Park has airstrips at Paraa, Chobe and Pakuba, and Uganda Airlines run regular flights from Entebbe to Paraa; book well in advance, as the flights are very popular. To reach the lodge by road from the south you have to cross the Nile on the Paraa ferry, which only operates between 8 am and 6.30 pm (1830).

The north bank of the Nile near Paraa Lodge is worth going to, where there used to be a tented camp. One evening at sunset we counted more than 130 hippo in the hippo pool below.

Chobe

About 16 km (10 miles) from the Masindi–Gulu road, and near the Chobe Gate to the Park is the Chobe Safari Lodge (UHL) overlooking the Goragung rapids. From it you get a superb view of the Nile, which at this point is narrow, rocky and dotted with jungly islands—quite different from the wide, lazy body of water below the falls. Salt licks within sight of the lodge attract buffalo, elephant, waterbuck and giraffe. There is swimming, a tennis court and an airstrip, while fishing is excellent, especially for the huge Nile perch. Indeed a noticeboard announces blandly "Please return all fish under 25 lbs to the river"—which gives an idea of the catches you can expect. In fact Nile Perch were only introduced to Lake Kyoga and the Victoria Nile above Kabalega Falls in 1955/6, so they've become established very well. Heavy fishing tackle can be hired at the lodge. If you have an admission ticket for the Paraa Gate you are let through the Chobe Gate free of charge.

Acholi

You can reach Gulu, administrative centre of the Acholi District, either through the Kabalega Park taking the Paraa ferry, or by going east and crossing the Nile at the Karuma Falls Bridge. There is also a train service. The road from Kampala is now tarmac all the way to Gulu.

The people of Acholi are dark-skinned Nilotics (which means their language originated in the Nile Valley) and are quite different from the southerners. They are famed as hunters and fighters. As well as being a fine game area, with part of the Kabalega Falls National Park and controlled hunting areas bordering the east and north banks of the Albert Nile, Acholi has strong historical associations. It was here that the early explorers entered Uganda, including Sir Samuel Baker, who was the first European to see Lake Albert in 1864 and the remains of whose fort still can be seen at Patiko, 27 km (17 miles) from Gulu, Patiko was a bastion against the slave trade in the Nile Basin and it is now an historical monument. Baker's descendants were invited out from Britain in his centenary year, a nice gesture by the Uganda Government. The Acholi Inn at Gulu (UHL, Box 239) is comfortable.

West Nile

From Gulu one road strikes north to the Sudan; another east to Kitgum, where UHL have built the new Hilltop Hotel, and to Karamoja (see below); while the third road, which is being tarmaced, goes west to Pakwach, with its bridge across the Nile, and on to Arua. The West Nile District on the other side produces large quantities of cotton, coffee and tobacco. It also has two sanctuaries of the rare white rhino, Ajai's Game Reserve, and another in the extreme north round Mt Kei, from which part of the herd in the Kabalega Falls

Arua

Park was rescued. The town of Arua has two UHL hotels, the West Nile and the newer Rhine Hotel. There are shops, a bank, golf and tennis and an airstrip.

East to Mbale, Mt Elgon, Karamoja and the Kidepo National Park

Jinja

Jinja 80 km (50 miles) east of Kampala, is an important commercial and industrial centre, with the biggest textile plant in East Africa. It stands by the source of the Nile, though now that the Owen Falls power station has been built this is not as impressive as it was when Speke first found it. Indeed the original plaque commemorating his discovery was submerged until it was moved higher up on the shore. However, the water is still vital to Egypt, though so far away, and the Egyptian Government has a representative here all the time to check that the Nile Waters Agreement is being observed, and the right volume of water let through the dam. Jinja has two hotels, the Ripon Falls Hotel (Box 30) and the Crested Crane (Box 444). Both are run by UHL and are conveniently situated but we recommend the latter. On the lakeshore there is a delightful yacht club, while the golf course is distinguished by the unique rule that if your ball lands in a hippo's footprint you are allowed to pick it out. Five km (3 miles) east of Jinja is Bugembe, headquarters of Busoga District.

Tororo

Both road and railway run, by different routes, from Jinja to Tororo and on to Kenya. But if you strike north you come up against the straggling swampy length of Lake Kyoga. The best route to Mbale, now tarmaced throughout, is through Tororo, which is fast becoming an industrial centre. The town is dominated by Tororo Rock, an outcrop jutting 500 ft above the flat surrounding countryside. It's easy to climb and provides a panoramic view. The Rock Hotel (UHL, Box 293), is on the outskirts of the town on the main road and is a good stopping place on a long journey. There is a golf course. The nearby Sukulu Hills, which contain large phosphate deposits, are scenically spectacular.

Mount Elgon

Forty-five km (28 miles) to the north in an area known for its arabica coffee is Mbale, nestling under Mount Elgon. This is one of Uganda's most pleasant towns, as well as its third largest, and the gardens of the modern and well-run Mount Elgon Hotel (UHL, Box 670, Mbale) are full of flowering shrubs. The hotel is the normal base for climbing the mountain (see below). Mbale is a good shopping centre and has golf and tennis. Mountain scenery and forest drives are within easy reach of the town, which is also the starting point for the interesting road that runs round the north of the mountain to Kitale, 192 km (120 miles) away in Kenya. The road has steep gradients and sharp bends but offers glorious views in return for one's efforts. This is not an all-weather road and you should check its condition with the DC's office at Mbale before setting off. If you want to climb Mount Elgon, which is a vast extinct volcano rising to 14,178 feet, the best way is from Mbale along a route where the Mountain Club (Box 2927, Kampala) have a hut about three hours' walk from the road. From there, three days of stiff walking will take you to the summit and back, and you will find much of the same giant vegetation that grows in the Ruwenzoris. There is sometimes snow on the summit.

North-west from Mbale the railway and the roads lead to the Lango

Soroti

District and eventually to Gulu, passing near interesting late Stone Age rock paintings at Nyiro. Soroti, in the Teso District, has the Soroti Hotel (UHL, Box 397, telephone 269) while the main town of the Lango District is Lira, also with a hotel, the Lira (UHL, Box 350, telephone 24). The road from Mbale is tarmaced as far as Soroti. The Lango people are very similar to the Acholi. But the most interesting way to go from Mbale is up north into Karamoja, through the Sebei Controlled Hunting Area, past Mount Debasien (10,074 ft) and the Pian Upe Game Reserve west of Kapachorwa.

Karamoja

In many ways Karamoja is one of the most fascinating parts of Uganda. It's backward, hot, dusty, dry, but it has the grandeur of the great open plains and it's thick with game—zebra, ostrich, eland, giraffe, gazelle, elephant and all the others who thrive in this kind of country. It was here that one of the most famous elephant hunters of all time earned his name—"Karamoja Bell". His book, *Wanderings of an Elephant Hunter*, still makes fascinating reading more than half a century after its publication. Today Karamoja is divided into two Game Reserves, Matheniko and Bokora, and two Controlled Hunting Areas, North and South, with the Kidepo Valley National Park in the extreme north of the district.

The Karamojong tribe fits this background. They are of the same tall, slim athletic build as the Turkana, across the frontier. Their cattle are their pride, and much of the Government administrators' time is occupied with stopping their traditional sport of cattle raiding. The men are fiercely handsome and carry spears, while their women deck themselves out superbly in beads, necklaces and bangles. They do not particularly like being photographed, though the arrival of a stranger always attracts their interest. If you stop your car in an area where the population is only four people to the square mile you can be certain that all four will materialise within a few minutes.

Moroto

A small but expanding town in Karamoja is Moroto, though there are several Mission stations. Moroto is basically a line of small *dukas* (shops) and an administrative area, all dominated by the 10,116 ft of Mount Moroto, a glorious red mountain, its slopes clustered with thorn trees. The 42 bed Moroto Hotel is run by Uganda Hotels. But the most exciting developments in this remote part of Uganda are at Kidepo further north.

Kidepo Valley National Park

The Kidepo Valley National Park of 1,365 sq km (525 sq miles) was established in 1962. It covers magnificent, rugged country on the Sudan border, most easily reached by flying into one of its two airstrips, though the roads have been improved so that it can be reached easily by road via Moroto. From Kampala to Kidepo is 768 km (480 miles). However it is still unwise to take the murram road west to Kitgum and the Kabalega Falls Park unless you have four-wheel drive.

Kidepo is actually a large kidney shaped valley, through which two rivers run, the Kidepo and the Narus. The valley floor is 3–4,000 feet above sea level, while the surrounding mountains reach 9,000 feet. The Park Headquarters, the old Kidepo Lodge, and the magnificently sited new Katurum Safari Lodge, are all near the Narus river. Herds of waterbuck, gazelle and hartebeest are so unafraid here that in the dry season they graze right in the camp. Landing on our last visit we had to wait for an elephant to move off the airstrip. Overall, Kidepo supports some 600 elephant, 2,000 buffalo, 50 lion and 3,000 hartebeest, as well as such rarities as greater kudu, Bright's gazelle (a variant of Grant's gazelle), roan antelope, and Chandler's reedbuck. Whilst the Narus river side is mainly savanna grass with some woodland, around the Kidepo river there are extensive groves of impressive borasus palms. The best time to visit Kidepo is December to March, you are less likely to see a lot of game in the April to September wet season, when the roads cannot be used for at least four hours after rain.

The Katurum Lodge, run by UHL, provides full service and is one of the most imaginatively designed lodges in East Africa. Bookings through the Tourist Development Corporation, Box 7211, Kampala. The old Kidepo Lodge, now called Apoka rest camp, is much cheaper. It has 16 double bandas with bathrooms, a central lounge, dining-room and kitchen, laundry service, and servants who will cook simple meals. You provide your own food, but a camp shop sells non-perishable goods and there is a bar. Guides and transport are available. For bookings contact the Warden, Kidepo Valley National Park, Private Bag Kitgum, radiocall Kampala 8646. There is also a campsite.

Useful Facts—UGANDA

Banks

Banking hours are 8.30 am to 12.30 pm Monday to Friday and 8.00 am to 11.00 am on Saturdays. The principal banks are the Bank of Baroda Barclays Bank Uganda Ltd, National and Grindlay's Bank, the Standard Bank and the Uganda Commercial Bank.

Currency

The Uganda shilling is divided into ten 10 cent pieces. Only hotels and banks are allowed to exchange foreign currency, which must be declared on entering the country.

Diplomatic Representation

There are Ugandan diplomatic missions in Accra, Addis Ababa, Bonn, Cairo, Kinshasa, London, Moscow, New Delhi, New York, Paris and Washington. Visas and Visitors' Passes are obtainable from them.

The following countries maintain Embassies or Consulates in Kampala—Belgium, Burundi, Communist China, Zaire, Cyprus, Czechoslovakia, Denmark, France, German Federal Republic, Ghana, Great Britain, Greece, India, Israel, Italy, Korean Republic, Netherlands, Nigeria, Norway, Poland, Rwanda, Sudan, Sweden, UAR, USA, USSR, and Yugoslavia.

Golf Courses

There are golf courses at Fort Portal, Entebbe, Gulu, Jinja, Kampala, Kabale, Kilembe Mines, Masaka, Masindi, Mbale, Mbarara.

Public Holidays

Official public holidays, when Government offices, banks and shops close, are New Year's Day, Good Friday, Easter Monday, Independence Day (October 9), Christmas Day, Boxing Day.

Shopping and Business Hours

Shops are open 7.30 am to 6.00 pm (1800) on weekdays, usually with a lunch break from 12.30 to 2.00 pm (1400). Businesses usually start later and close by 5.00 pm (1700).

Zambia Airways Corporation, 163 Piccadilly, London W1V 9DE. Telephone: 01-491 7521. Telex: 27127. **For Reservations Telephone 01-492 0568.**

Elephant crossing the Luangwa river

Zambia

This chapter does not attempt a complete coverage of a large and varied country. It is a summary of the principal attractions in areas which can be easily reached from the neighbouring States of East Africa, and in which the wildlife, birds and climate are similar.

The Country

The unspoilt nature of Zambia is its greatest asset to the visitor, even though copper mining provides much of the nation's wealth. This apparent paradox is possible because Zambia's 750,000 sq km (289,575 sq miles) cover an area as large as Austria, Hungary, France and Switzerland combined. From the tumultuous Victoria Falls on the Zambesi river to the great elephant herds of the Luangwa valley and lakes in the north, the country offers a constantly changing spectacle.

Roughly kidney shaped, Zambia lies in the tropics between ten and eighteen degrees south of the Equator. Its northern border is with Tanzania and Zaire, its southern with Mozambique and Rhodesia. Basically the country is a plateau some 3,000 ft above sea level, which creates a pleasant climate. There are three seasons. It is cool and dry from May to August, hot and dry from September to November and warm and wet from December to April, when the rains come. May to November is the period for a visit, though October is the hottest month.

Climate

Human habitation goes back thousands of years to the original small bushmen whose rock paintings can still be seen. They were displaced by Bantu tribes from the north, who established a number of kingdoms, notably of the Lozi in the south arround the Zambesi and the Kazembe in the north near Lake Banguelu. Mercilessly exploited by Arab and Portuguese slave traders from the eighteenth century onwards, all the kingdoms save that of the Bemba declined and in the late nineteenth century the Ngoni, a breakaway group of the Zulus, moved in from the south.

The area first became known to the western world through the travels of the great Scots missionary, Dr Livingstone, in the 1860s, who is still deeply honoured here.

British rule began through the British South Africa Company towards the end of the nineteenth century. The two territories it comprised then were amalgamated into Northern Rhodesia when the Colonial Office assumed direct rule in 1921. In 1953 it was incorporated in the ill-fated Federation of Rhodesia and Nyasaland, which broke up a decade later. The independent Republic of Zambia was born on October 24, 1964.

Today Zambia's population totals 5 million, of whom some are Europeans. The country is the world's fifth largest producer of copper and the second largest of cobalt, while its other great natural resource, its game parks, are among the least spoilt in Africa.

The National Parks, Wildlife and Hunting

Zambia has eighteen National Parks, covering 59,420 sq km (22,872 sq miles) and constituting the largest conservation area in Africa. The best known are the South Luangwa (National Park No 11), the Kafue (National Park No 11) and the Mosi oa Tunya, or Victoria Falls,

(National Park No 17). These three are described below. Of the others only the Blue Lagoon, Lochinvar, Luambe, Nyika and Sumbu also have accommodation. The first two are described in the Lusaka section. Luambe is a very small park of only 254 sq km on the east bank of the Luangwa river, consisting almost entirely of woodland. It shelters most of the species seen in the South Luangwa. The Nyika, only 80 sq km, scenically magnificent, lies on the Malawi border and is primarily of botanical interest, with montane grassland and relict forest, flowers and butterflies. Sumbu is in the extreme north on the shore of Lake Tanganyika. It protects many mammals, including elephant, buffalo and puku. The well known Kasaba Bay lodge is on the lake.

Generally speaking Zambia's parks are inhabited by the large east and central African mammals, which are here much less overrun by the demands of tourism than in east Africa itself. In a word, Zambia remains unspoilt. An excellent book on them is *A Guide to the National Parks of Zambia* by John Clarke and Ian Loe, published by the Anglo American Corporation, price Kw 4.50

The parks are managed by the Department of National Parks and Wildlife, whose full-time game rangers and wildlife guards have been supplemented since 1975 by a remarkable corps of unpaid, volunteer, honorary game rangers. The Wildlife Conservation Society of Zambia has also done much to raise funds for game conservation, with the help of such well-known supporters as the painter David Sheppard.

Hunting

Hunting is permitted in the game management areas, often adjacent to the parks. The season is from May to November. A national licence costing Kw 225 permits you to shoot one buffalo, three bushpig, and one each of duiker, oribi, impala, puku and warthog. Other game require individual licences (eg Kw 360 for a male elephant). The official policy is that controlled hunting deters far worse destruction by poachers, who might otherwise be undisturbed. Two of the best safari companies are Zambia Safaris (Box 2955, Lusaka) and Big Game Safaris (Box 2784, Lusaka). They can provide the full back-up needed at around US $500 per person per day. Only members of the Professional Hunters Association of Zambia are allowed to lead hunting parties.

Walking Safaris

A major innovation, now being copied in Kenya, are walking photographic safaris, originated by Norman Carr Safaris (Box 3876, Lusaka) in the Luangwa valley. These are described below. Other companies now operate them too.

Transport and Hotels

Air

Zambia Airways operate both international and domestic services, including daily flights to Livingstone and the Copperbelt. There are several flights a week to Mfuwe for the Luangwa and to the Kafue. The internal airport tax is Kw 2.00, for international flights it is

Kw 4.00. At the time of writing no private flying was allowed. A taxi from Lusaka airport to the city should cost Kw 8.00, or more if shared. There are no airport buses at Lusaka.

Train

The line of rail traversing the country from Livingstone through Lusaka to Kitwe offers cheap but slow trains. It passes through Kapiri mposhi, where the Tazara railway to Dar es Salaam in Tanzania starts.

Road

There are many local bus services and taxis in the towns. Always negotiate a taxi fare in advance. Car hire can be difficult, though a good travel agent should be able to secure a self drive vehicle. If you come to a police road block – STOP. Main roads are of a good standard.

Hotels

The Zambia National Tourist Board (ZNTB) classifies hotels from "five star" down to "ungraded". Five star establishments charge about Kw 25.00 a night single with bed and breakfast, or Kw 31.00 double; four star charge Kw 17.40 and 21.75 respectively; and three star Kw 11.70 and Kw 14.62. In addition there are a 10% sales tax and 10% service charge. Book in advance as accommodation is limited.

Information

The Zambia National Tourist Board's head office is on Cairo Road, Lusaka (P.O. Box 17, telephone 72891/5) with subsidiary offices in Livingstone and Ndola. In the United Kingdom it is at ZIMCO House, 129/139 Finsbury Pavement, London EC2 1NA, telephone (01) 638 8333. The New York address is 150 East 58th Street, New York, NY 10022, telephone (212) 758 9450.

Lusaka

Hotels

Zambia's capital is a spaciously laid out city, 4,270 ft above sea level The spine of its commercial area is Cairo Road, a mile long avenue where you will find the ZNTB, airline offices, banks and shops, also the Lusaka Hotel (3 star, Box 44). However the best hotels are up in the diplomatic quarter on the Ridgeway, a ten minute taxi ride from Cairo Road. The Intercontinental (5 star, Box 2201), the pleasantly rambling Ridgeway (4 star, Box 666) and the new Pamodzi (5 star) all have swimming pools and shops. Apart from these hotels, one of the better places to eat is the Andrews Motel, about 6 km from the city centre. Bowls, golf, tennis and sailing are available at clubs which offer temporary membership.

Excursions from Lusaka

Near the city are the famous Munda Wanga botanical gardens, to which the ZNTB arranges tours, while it is quite feasible to make a day trip to either of the two nearest National Parks, the Blue Lagoon and Lochinvar, both to the west.

Blue Lagoon National Park

The Blue Lagoon Park is 420 sq km (162 sq miles) of flood plain north of the Kafue river which shelters large herds of lechwe, an antelope unique to Zambia with three sub-species: red, black and Kafue. Roan and sable antelope, zebra and buffalo also inhabit the area, as well as many waterbirds. An elevated causeway facilitates game viewing. The park is two hours' drive from Lusaka.

Lochinvar National Park

Lochinvar is reached via the Great North Road, turning off at Monze, and is three hours from Lusaka. Its 410 sq km (158 sq miles) are also flood plain, the peak inundation being in May. Its many animals include 35,000 lechwe, while there are close on 400 species of birds recorded. There is a non-catering lodge at the park gate. One distinction of Lochinvar is that visitors are encouraged to leave their vehicles and explore on foot.

The Luangwa Valley

There is such an abundance of wildlife along the Luangwa river, which flows down from Tanzania to join the Zambesi, that three National Parks have been created along it: the South Luangwa, the North Luangwa and the Luambe (already mentioned). The valley as a whole has been christened the "Kingdom of the Elephant", the estimated population being 100,000, the largest concentration in the world.

The South Luangwa Park covers 9,050 sq km (3,494 sq miles) bounded to the east by the river, which has many oxbow lakes and lagoons: the spectacle of elephant crossing the river is famous locally. The park is mainly miombo woodland, with a few areas of open grassland in the north. Its fauna include buffalo, hippo, black rhino, impala, puku, zebra, waterbuck – and near the river – greater kudu.

Walking Safaris

It is here that Norman Carr, a well known former game warden, pioneered the walking safari. Usually these last five days, stopping each night at a different camp, and taking a leisurely look at anything you want to see under the guidance of an armed trail leader. The season for these is June to November. As the smaller rivers dry towards October, tremendous concentrations of game come down to the Luangwa, while marabou storks and pelicans fish in the lagoons. Norman Carr Safaris (Box 3876, Lusaka) maintain two luxury tented camps in the area, one open all the year at Chinzombo, not far from the Mfue airfield, the other (seasonal) at Chibembe. Two permanent lodges, both bookable through ZNTB or through Country Hotels Ltd (Box 3200, Lusaka) are Mfuwe and the more luxurious Chichele, the latter beautifully set on a hill with a view of the river.

North Luangwa

The North Luangwa Park is smaller, being 4,636 sq km (1,790 sq miles) and is deliberately kept as wilderness area, with no lodges, which means it can only be visited on an organised safari. The wildlife is similar to that in the southern park. Lying between the two is the tiny Luambe Park, already mentioned.

The Kafue National Park

The largest and oldest of Zambia's parks, the Kafue is half the size of Switzerland, a vast 22,400 sq km (8,690 sq miles) of undulating plateau, cut through by several rivers. All the "big five" are here, with the buffalo in herds of up to 2,000. The many antelope include the handsome sable antelope, while red lechwe inhabit the Busanga plains, as do sitatunga in the swamp areas. Lion, leopard and hippo are common and there are 600 varieties of birds.

During the wet season (November to May) much of the park is inaccessible to motor vehicles, especially in the north. However in the dry months it is revealed as one of the great animal sanctuaries of Africa. The airfield at Ngoma is served by scheduled flights from Livingstone and Lusaka, while there are two good lodges near: the Ngoma Lodge (Country Hotels Ltd, Box 3200, Lusaka) and the Musungwa Safari Lodge (T G Travel Ltd, Box 2591, Lusaka). There are self catering camps and lodges in many parts of the park, for details consult ZNTB. Just outside the park is the Itezhitezhi hydro electric scheme on the Kafue river, which has created a new lake along the park boundary.

The Copperbelt, Kitwe, Ndola

Zambia is the world's fifth largest producer of copper and the second largest of cobalt. The "anticline" in which the rich mineral deposits lie runs through thousand million year old granite rocks in a twenty mile wide belt continuing into south-eastern Zaire. The mines themselves range from 6,000 ft deep shafts to the enormous, three km long, Nchanga open pit, the largest in the world. Although they are security areas, the mines and their associated smelting plants can be seen by organised groups. Apply to the Public Relations departments of either of the two corporations, Roan Consolidated Mines (Box 851, Lusaka) and Nchanga Consolidated Copper Mines (Box 1986, Lusaka). Though not a conventional tourist attraction, they are fascinating to visit.

Two major towns have grown from the copper industry, Kitwe and Ndola. Some fifty miles apart, both are well laid out with modern shops and daily flights from Lusaka. Kitwe boasts the better hotel, the four star Edinburgh (Box 1800), while Ndola has an excellent golf course. The memorial to the late UN Secretary General, Dag Hammarskjold, killed in an aircrash in 1961, lies off the Kitwe road a few miles out of Ndola.

Livingstone and the Victoria Falls

Named after the explorer, Livingstone was formerly the capital and is a pleasant, relaxed town of 75,000 inhabitants. Its main attraction today is the National Museum, the four galleries of which include dioramas of wildlife with many well mounted specimens. The history galleries are a must for anyone interested in Zambia's development, while there are many mementoes of Dr Livingstone.

Livingstone's broad main street has banks, shops and the ZNTB's tourist office, while the old colonial style North Western Hotel (2 star, Box 69) is a comfortable place to stay or to stop for a drink on the verandah. Flights are met at the airport by ZNTB buses which charge Kw 3 to the town or Kw 4–6 to the falls.

The famous Victoria Falls are 5 km away on a good road. The local name for them is Mosi oa Tunya, "the smoke that thunders", and you soon see why. The spray rising hundreds of feet above this great natural wonder can be seen from twenty miles away. The falls are at the point where the Zambesi river, flowing wide from its flood plains, suddenly reaches a 1,600 metre wide chasm. Plunging down 300 feet, it creates this magnificent spectacle. At the height of the flood season 120 million gallons a minute cascade over the edge. By walking across the Knife Edge bridge you can get excellent close up views, and also pass into the rain forest created by the spray. But beware the wet. An umbrella is some protection. To walk in a bathing suit is best! Well worth while is the river trip on a launch. Right by the Falls the Mosi oa Tunya Inter-Continental Hotel (5 star) is well designed and run. There are several other places to stay, notably the Rainbow Hotel, aptly named since there are rainbows everywhere in the spray.

Near the falls is the ancient baobab tree which Dr Livingstone used as look-out post. He actually stayed at the village of Chief Mukuni, still in existence, after finding the falls on 16 November 1855.

Opposite top left: Thorneycroft's giraffe, unique to Zambia, ZNTB photo
Top right: Crested cranes
Bottom: Hippo family

Malaria risk?

One tiny Paludrine at breakfast and the danger's gone!

PROGUANIL TRADE MARK

One tiny Paludrine tablet each day gives you the best protection you could possibly have. So when business or pleasure takes you to malarious areas, don't forget to pack the Paludrine. Even for babies and expectant mothers, Paludrine is safe; so you can take it with complete confidence. Twenty four hours before reaching your destination, take your first tablet. Then continue daily until one month after leaving the malarious area. Detailed dosage instructions for this simple precaution against malaria are carried on every Paludrine pack. Obtainable from chemists and drug stores everywhere.

Paludrine - the safe, reliable antimalarial from ICI.

IM-135-644

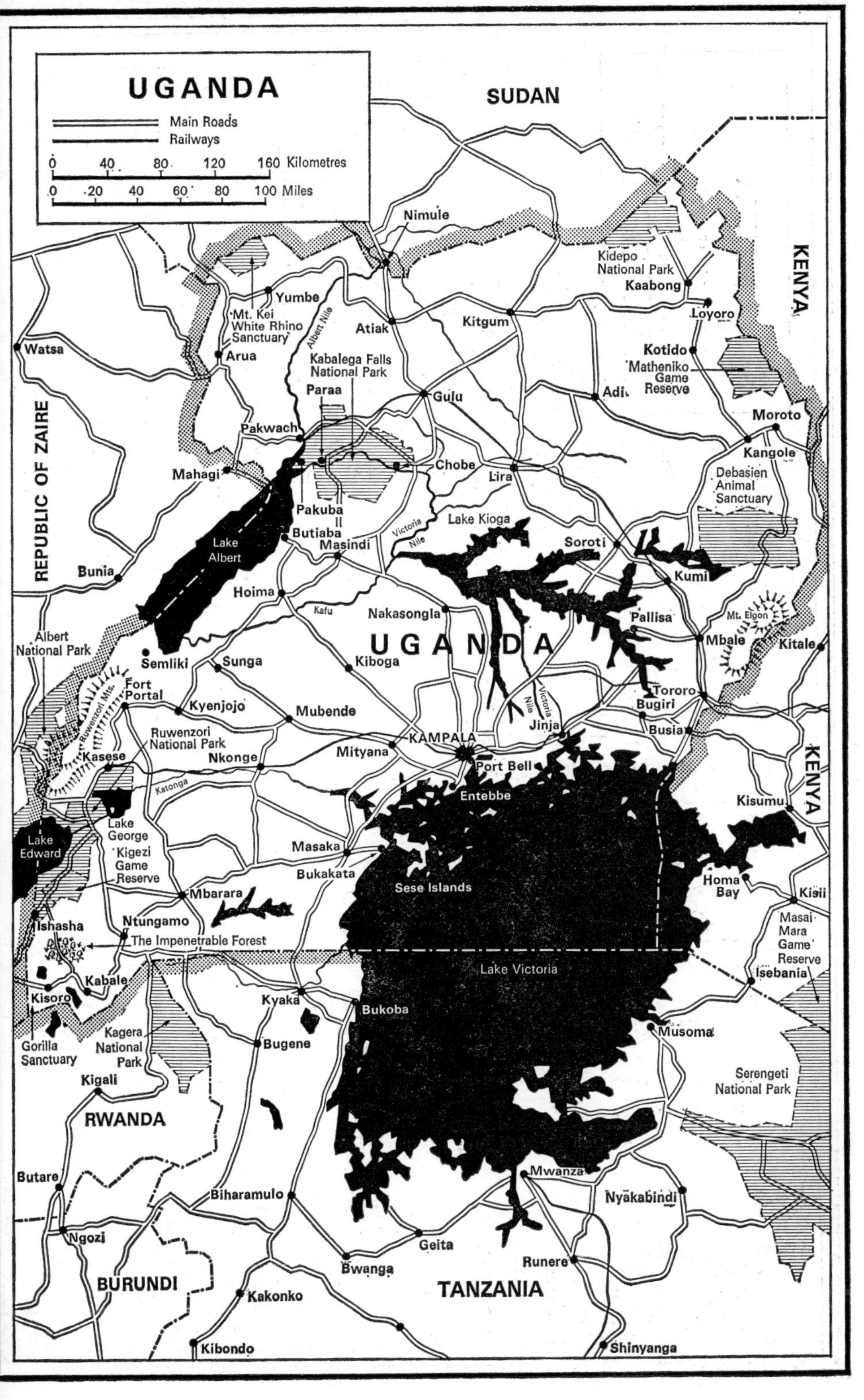

UGANDA
Main Roads
Railways
0 40 80 120 160 Kilometres
0 20 40 60 80 100 Miles
SUDAN
KENYA
REPUBLIC OF ZAIRE
RWANDA
BURUNDI
TANZANIA
UGANDA
Nimule
Kidepo National Park
Kaabong
Loyoro
Yumbe
Mt. Kei White Rhino Sanctuary
Albert Nile
Atiak
Kitgum
Watsa
Arua
Kabalega Falls National Park
Kotido
Matheniko Game Reserve
Paraa
Gulu
Adi
Moroto
Pakwach
Kangole
Mahagi
Chobe
Lira
Debasien Animal Sanctuary
Pakuba
Lake Kioga
Lake Albert
Butiaba
Masindi
Victoria Nile
Soroti
Bunia
Kumi
Hoima
Kafu
Nakasongla
Pallisa
Mt. Elgon
Albert National Park
Semliki
Sunga
Kiboga
Mbale
Kitale
Fort Portal
Ruwenzori Mts.
Tororo
Kyenjojo
Mubende
Bugiri
Jinja
Ruwenzori National Park
KAMPALA
Busia
Kasese
Nkonge
Mityana
Port Bell
Katonga
Entebbe
Kisumu
Lake George
Lake Edward
Kigezi Game Reserve
Masaka
Bukakata
Sese Islands
Homa Bay
Mbarara
Kisii
Ishasha
Ntungamo
Masai Mara Game Reserve
The Impenetrable Forest
Lake Victoria
Kabale
Isebania
Kisoro
Kyaka
Bukoba
Gorilla Sanctuary
Kagera National Park
Bugene
Musoma
Kigali
Serengeti National Park
Butare
Mwanza
Biharamulo
Nyakabindi
Ngozi
Geita
Runere
Bwanga
Kakonko
Kibondo
Shinyanga

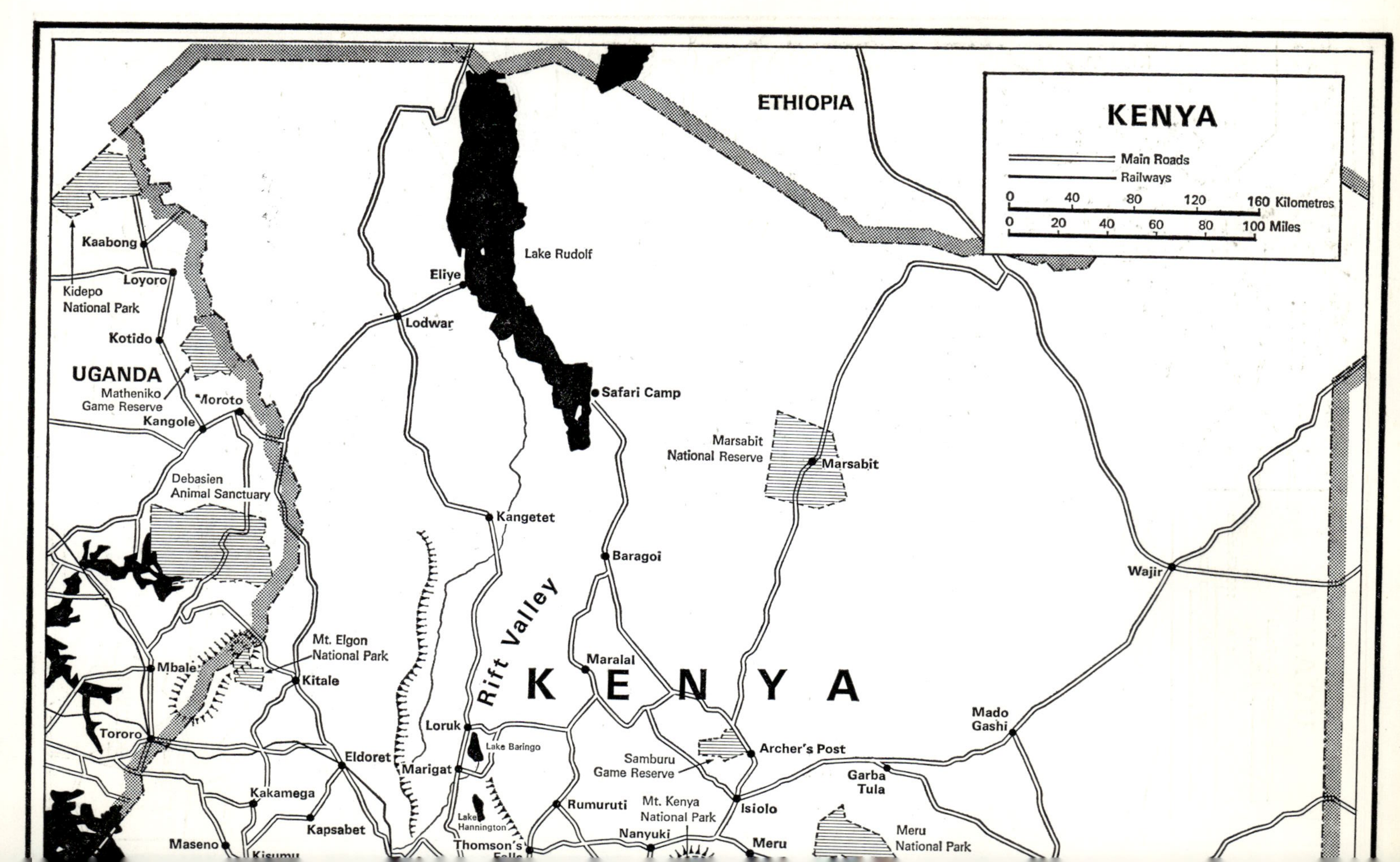
KENYA
Main Roads
Railways
0 40 80 120 160 Kilometres
0 20 40 60 80 100 Miles
ETHIOPIA
Lake Rudolf
Eliye
Lodwar
Safari Camp
Kaabong
Loyoro
Kidepo National Park
Kotido
UGANDA
Matheniko Game Reserve
Moroto
Kangole
Debasien Animal Sanctuary
Marsabit National Reserve
Marsabit
Kangetet
Baragoi
Wajir
Rift Valley
Maralal
K E N Y A
Mt. Elgon National Park
Mbale
Kitale
Mado Gashi
Loruk
Lake Baringo
Tororo
Eldoret
Marigat
Samburu Game Reserve
Archer's Post
Garba Tula
Kakamega
Rumuruti
Mt. Kenya National Park
Isiolo
Lake Hannington
Kapsabet
Nanyuki
Meru National Park
Maseno
Thomson's
Meru

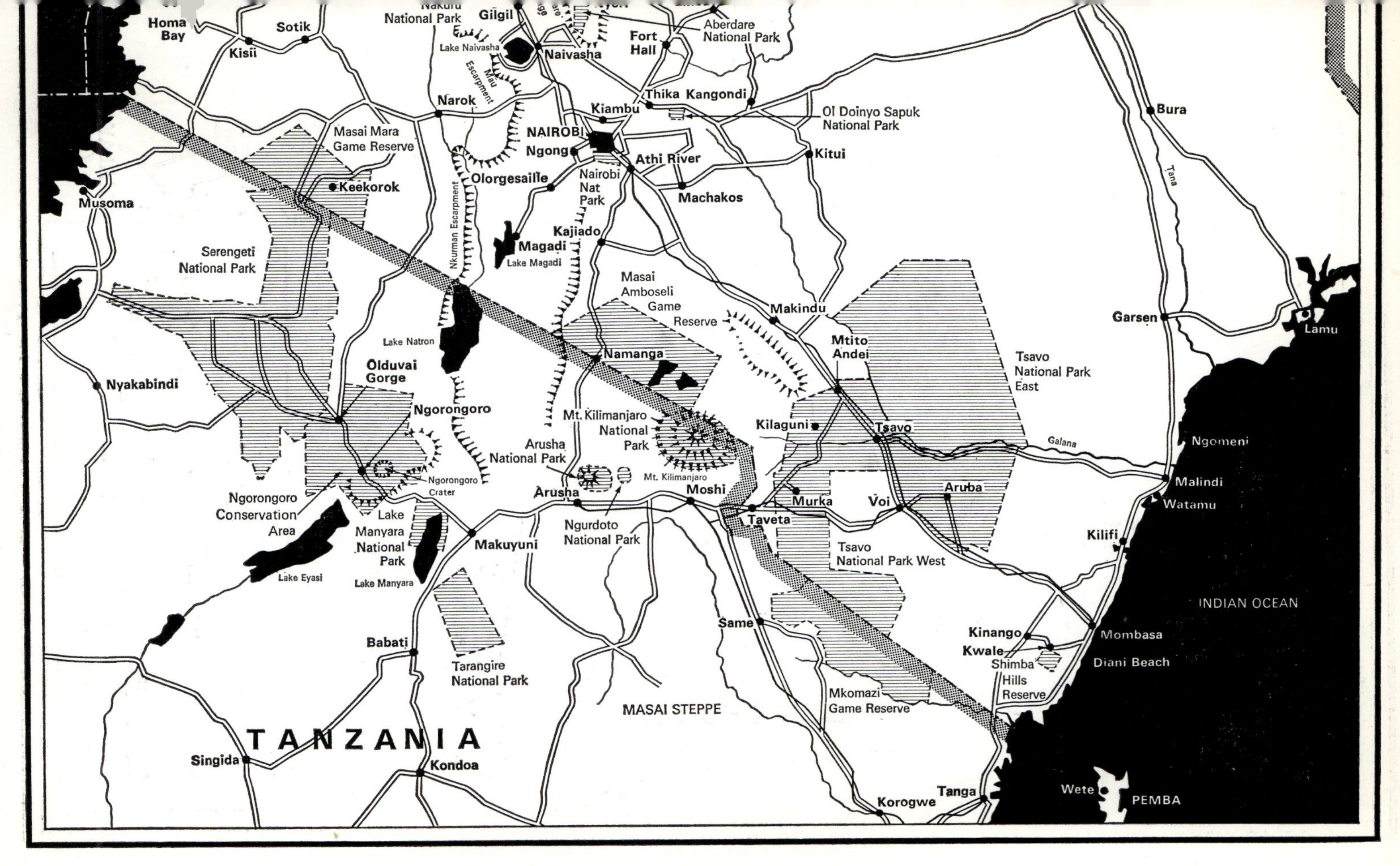
Homa Bay
Sotik
Kisii
National Park
Gilgil
Lake Naivasha
Naivasha
Fort Hall
Aberdare National Park
Mau Escarpment
Narok
Thika
Kangondi
Kiambu
Ol Doinyo Sapuk National Park
Bura
Masai Mara Game Reserve
NAIROBI
Ngong
Athi River
Kitui
Tana
Musoma
Keekorok
Olorgesailie
Nairobi Nat Park
Machakos
Kajiado
Magadi
Lake Magadi
Nkurman Escarpment
Serengeti National Park
Masai Amboseli Game Reserve
Makindu
Garsen
Lamu
Lake Natron
Namanga
Mtito Andei
Tsavo National Park East
Olduvai Gorge
Nyakabindi
Ngorongoro
Mt. Kilimanjaro National Park
Kilaguni
Tsavo
Galana
Ngomeni
Arusha National Park
Ngorongoro Crater
Mt. Kilimanjaro
Arusha
Moshi
Murka
Voi
Aruba
Malindi
Watamu
Ngorongoro Conservation Area
Lake Manyara National Park
Taveta
Ngurdoto National Park
Makuyuni
Tsavo National Park West
Kilifi
Lake Eyasi
Lake Manyara
INDIAN OCEAN
Same
Kinango
Mombasa
Babati
Kwale
Shimba Hills Reserve
Diani Beach
Tarangire National Park
Mkomazi Game Reserve
MASAI STEPPE
TANZANIA
Singida
Kondoa
Wete
PEMBA
Tanga
Korogwe

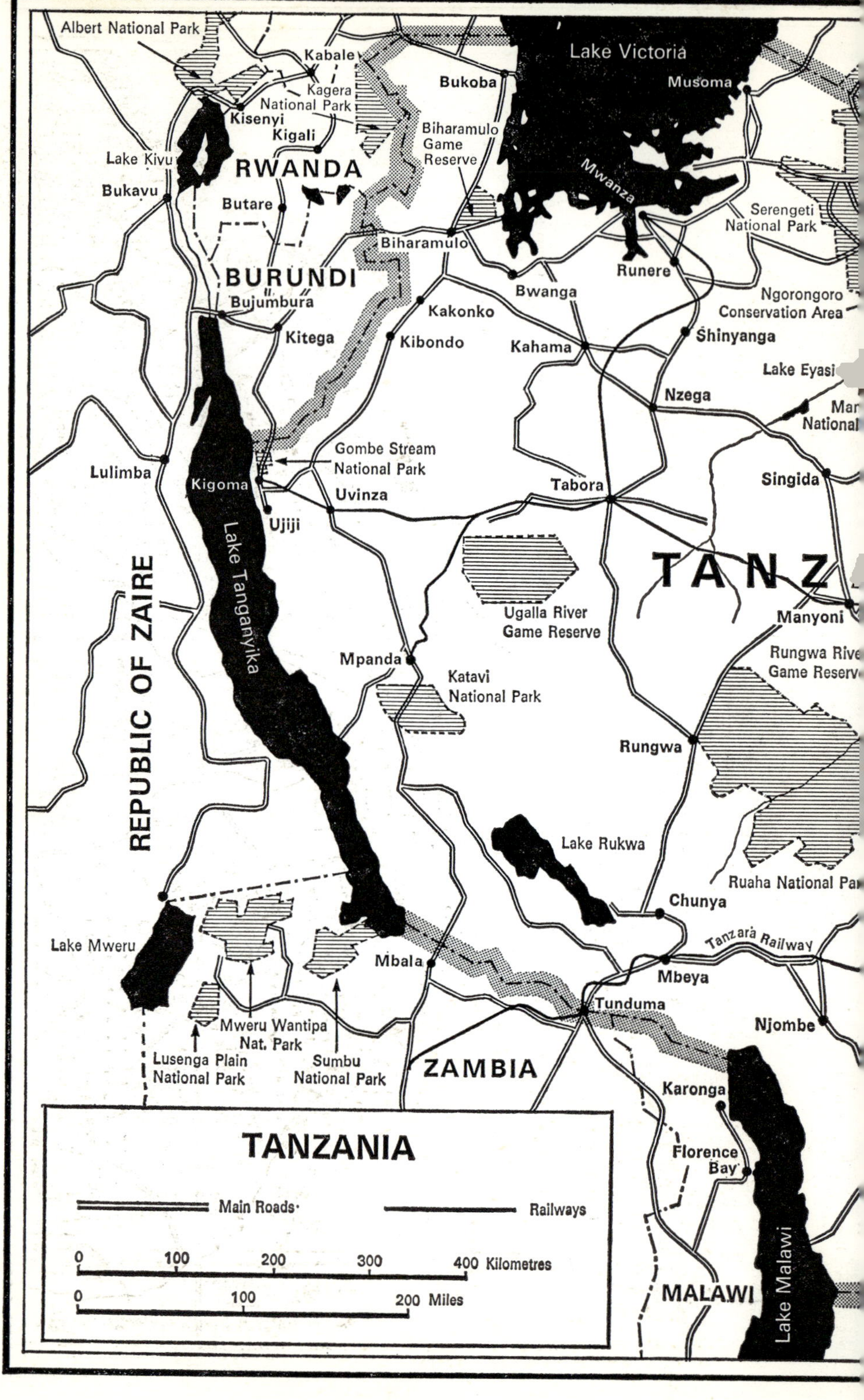
Albert National Park
Kabale
Kagera National Park
Kisenyi
Kigali
Lake Kivu
RWANDA
Bukavu
Butare
BURUNDI
Bujumbura
Kitega
Lake Victoria
Bukoba
Musoma
Biharamulo Game Reserve
Mwanza
Serengeti National Park
Biharamulo
Runere
Bwanga
Ngorongoro Conservation Area
Kakonko
Kibondo
Kahama
Shinyanga
Lake Eyasi
Nzega
Gombe Stream National Park
Lulimba
Kigoma
Uvinza
Ujiji
Tabora
Singida
Lake Tanganyika
REPUBLIC OF ZAIRE
TANZ
Ugalla River Game Reserve
Manyoni
Mpanda
Katavi National Park
Rungwa
Lake Rukwa
Ruaha National Pa
Chunya
Lake Mweru
Mbala
Tanzara Railway
Mbeya
Tunduma
Njombe
Mweru Wantipa Nat. Park
Lusenga Plain National Park
Sumbu National Park
ZAMBIA
Karonga
Florence Bay
MALAWI
Lake Malawi
TANZANIA
Main Roads
Railways
0 100 200 300 400 Kilometres
0 100 200 Miles

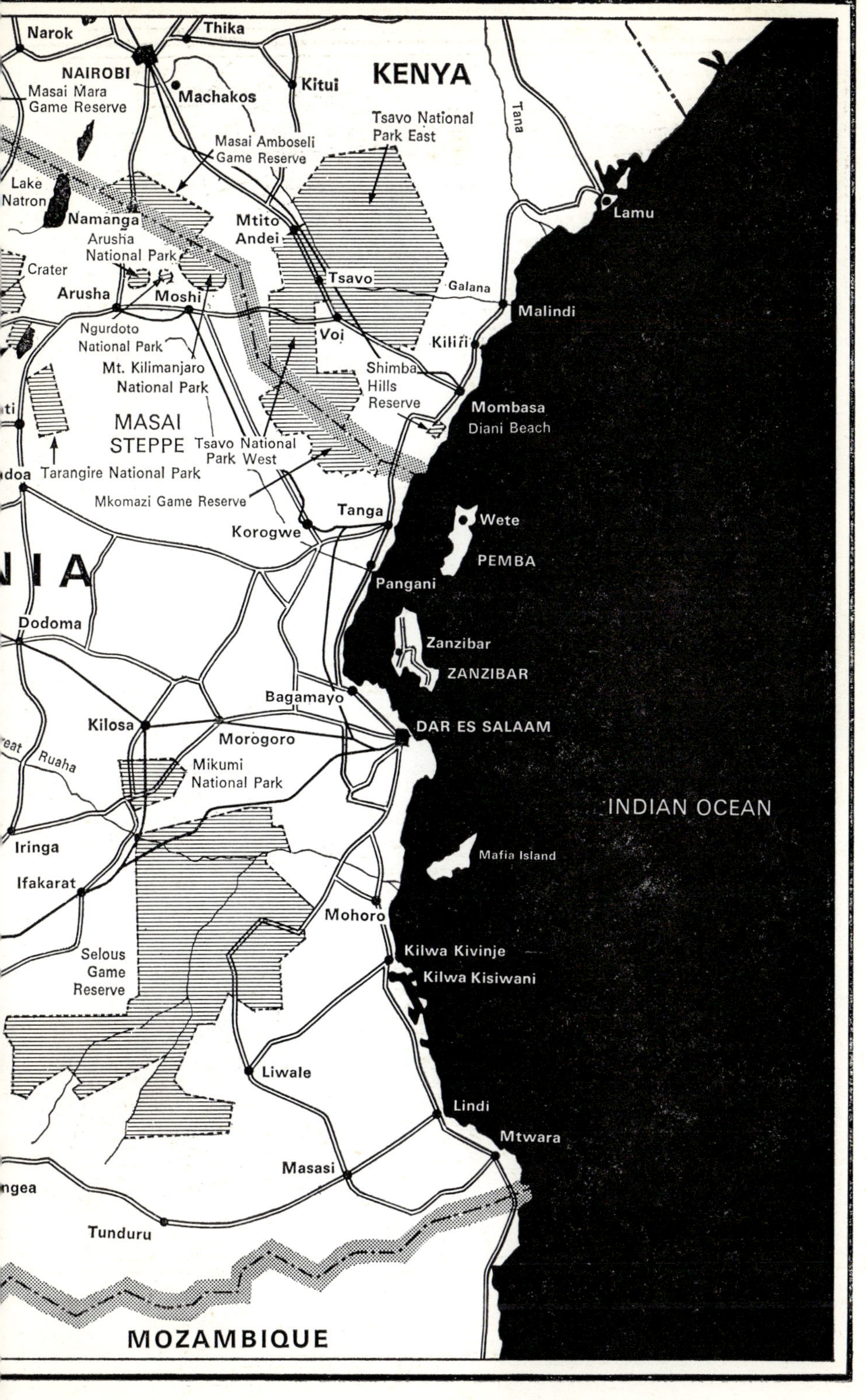

Narok
Thika
NAIROBI
Masai Mara
Game Reserve
Machakos
Kitui
KENYA
Tana
Tsavo National
Park East
Masai Amboseli
Game Reserve
Lake
Natron
Namanga
Mtito
Andei
Lamu
Arusha
National Park
Crater
Tsavo
Galana
Arusha
Moshi
Malindi
Ngurdoto
National Park
Voi
Kilifi
Mt. Kilimanjaro
National Park
Shimba
Hills
Reserve
Mombasa
Diani Beach
MASAI
STEPPE
Tsavo National
Park West
Tarangire National Park
Mkomazi Game Reserve
Tanga
Wete
Korogwe
PEMBA
Pangani
Dodoma
Zanzibar
ZANZIBAR
Bagamayo
Kilosa
DAR ES SALAAM
Morogoro
Ruaha
Mikumi
National Park
INDIAN OCEAN
Iringa
Mafia Island
Ifakarat
Mohoro
Selous
Game
Reserve
Kilwa Kivinje
Kilwa Kisiwani
Liwale
Lindi
Mtwara
Masasi
Tunduru
MOZAMBIQUE

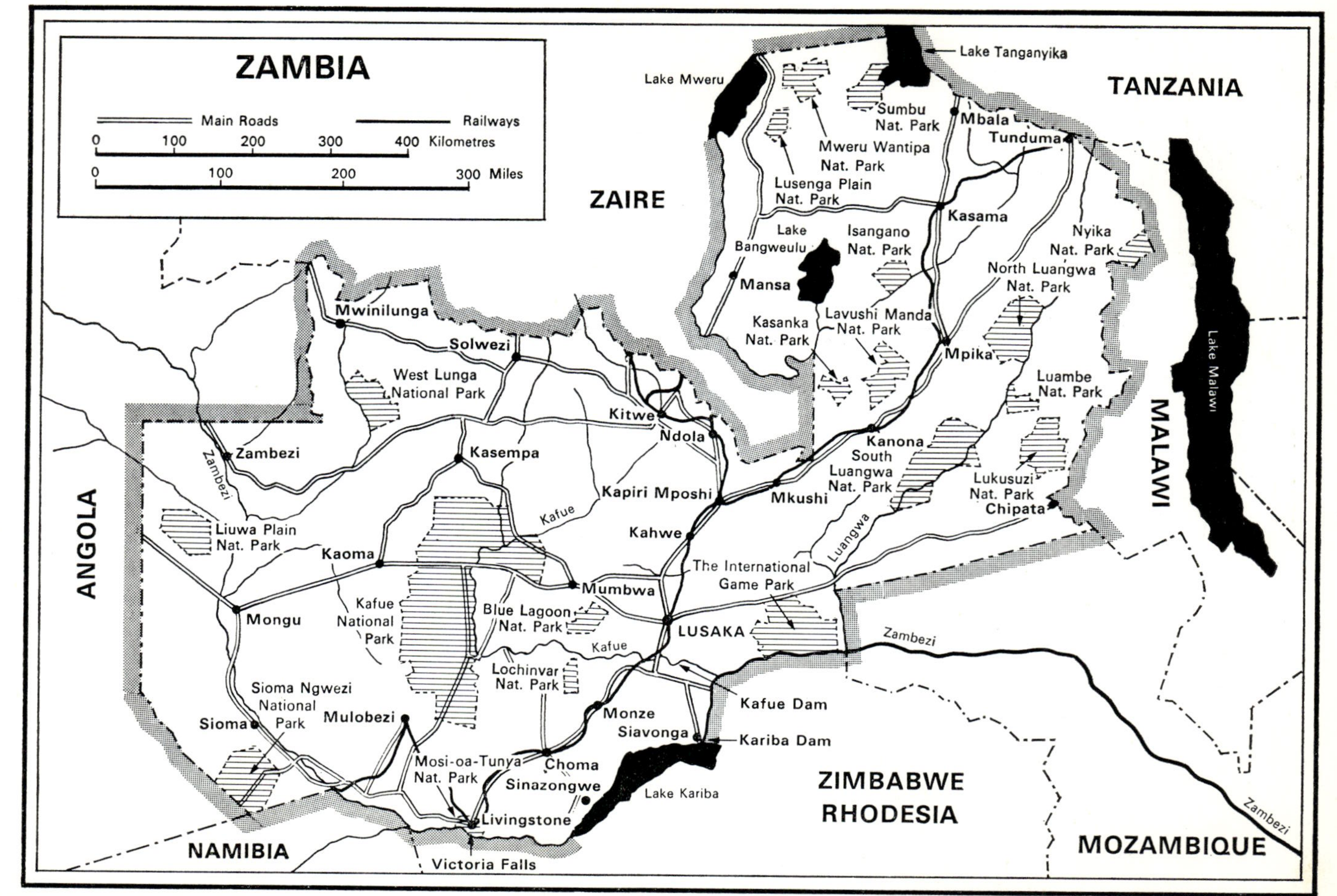
ZAMBIA
Main Roads
Railways
0
100
200
300
400 Kilometres
0
100
200
300 Miles
ZAIRE
TANZANIA
MALAWI
ANGOLA
NAMIBIA
ZIMBABWE
RHODESIA
MOZAMBIQUE
Lake Mweru
Lake Tanganyika
Lake Malawi
Lake Bangweulu
Lake Kariba
Sumbu Nat. Park
Mweru Wantipa Nat. Park
Lusenga Plain Nat. Park
Isangano Nat. Park
Nyika Nat. Park
North Luangwa Nat. Park
Kasanka Nat. Park
Lavushi Manda Nat. Park
Luambe Nat. Park
South Luangwa Nat. Park
Lukusuzi Nat. Park
West Lunga National Park
Liuwa Plain Nat. Park
Kafue National Park
Blue Lagoon Nat. Park
Lochinvar Nat. Park
Sioma Ngwezi National Park
Mosi-oa-Tunya Nat. Park
The International Game Park
Mbala
Tunduma
Kasama
Mansa
Mpika
Kanona
Mkushi
Chipata
Mwinilunga
Solwezi
Kitwe
Ndola
Kapiri Mposhi
Kahwe
Kasempa
Zambezi
Kaoma
Mumbwa
Mongu
LUSAKA
Kafue Dam
Kariba Dam
Monze
Siavonga
Choma
Sinazongwe
Sioma
Mulobezi
Livingstone
Victoria Falls
Zambezi
Kafue
Luangwa

Index

Index to Advertisers

We don't believe a long-haul holiday to Kenya should leave you short.

How many times have you ever thought of visiting Kenya but haven't because you thought it would cost too much.

Now Inghams, with flights by Kenya Airways, have brought this far-away place within reach of your pocket. For instance, 2 weeks full board for £429. Prices like that are usually a lot nearer home. Send the coupon now for our brochure.

Inghams Travel, 329 Putney Bridge Road, London SW15 2PL.

Please send me a copy of the Inghams Worldwide Holidays brochure.

Name

Address

TGEA

Inghams Holidays Worldwide

Notes

Tsavo

Hartebeest
Impala
Elephant (9 together)
Giraffe
Zebra
Maribou
Dikdik
Baboon
Hippos - (Mizuma Springs)
Waterbuck
Warthog
Ostrich (Jet Black)
Jackal (1)
Serval Cat (Mondo
On balcony of our room

Notes

Amboselli -

Cheetah - 1 (rare)
Zebra
Wildebeest (gnu)
Oryx - 3
Lion
Hippo
Elephant
Giraffe - R1 - 7
Gazelle (thompson's and Grant's)
Buffalo - about 10
Impala
Eland
Ostrich
Maribou
Eagles
Vultures
Heron
Jackels 3
Monkey

Tree Tops

White rhino
Colobus Monkey
Baboon
Mongoose
Black Buffalo
Bush Pig
Warthog
Elephant (1)
Maribou
Spotted hyena
Water Buck
Bushbuck
Sykes Monkey

Notes